DESIGN YOUR OWN GARDEN

By the same author:
OASIS OF THE NORTH *Hutchinson* 1963
A BOOK OF HERBS *Duckworth* 1968

DAWN MACLEOD

DESIGN YOUR OWN GARDEN

GERALD DUCKWORTH & Co. Ltd.
3 HENRIETTA STREET LONDON WC2

First published in 1969 by
Gerald Duckworth & Company Limited
3 Henrietta Street, London, W.C.2

© DAWN MACLEOD 1969
All Rights Reserved. No part of this publication may be reproduced, stored in a retrieval system, or transmitted, in any form or by any means, electronic, mechanical, photocopying, recording or otherwise, without the prior permission of the Copyright owner.

SBN 7156 0499 6

Printed at The Curwen Press
North Street, Plaistow, London, E.13

TO ENID

WHOSE GARDEN AT QUENINGTON
IS A JOY TO SEE AND AN INSPIRATION
TO FOLLOW

*Fair houses are more frequent than fine gardens;
the first effected by artificers only, the latter
requiring more skill in the owner.*
JOHN REA, *Gentleman*, 1681

CONTENTS

PART ONE

Chapter 1	Planning a new garden	3
Chapter 2	A new look for an old garden	21
Chapter 3	Designing in detail	39
Chapter 4	Personal tastes	52

PART TWO

Chapter 5	Trees and shrubs	67
Chapter 6	Climbers and wall-trained shrubs	83
Chapter 7	Specialized gardens	98
Chapter 8	Lawns, hedges and paths	115
Chapter 9	Etceteras	127

PART THREE

Chapter 10	Some famous gardens in England	141
	Hidcote	141
	Tintinhull	147
	Sissinghurst	155
Chapter 11	Inverewe	163
Chapter 12	Rowallane	175
Chapter 13	Smaller gardens in town and country	184
	East Lambrook Manor	184
	Moyles Cottage, Quenington	191
	Greyfriars	197
	A garden in Kensington	202
	Herbers	207

CONTENTS

Book list	213
Suppliers of trees, shrubs, climbers, etc.	214
Index	215

ILLUSTRATIONS

Plate *between pages 100–101*

    I The White Garden at Sissinghurst

   II (a) The Cupressus path at East Lambrook Manor
      (b) Artemisia 'Lambrook Silver'

  III (a) Buttress of Golden Privet at Greyfriars, Worcester
     (b) The author at Quenington, with *Clematis tangutica* on apple tree

  IV Natural pond garden at Inverewe

   V (a) Rose Mme. A. Carrière at Sissinghurst
     (b) Enid Money with her *Lilium auratum* at Quenington

  VI Chusan Palm at Inverewe

 VII (a) Herb garden, American Museum, Claverton Manor, Bath
     (b) Sunk garden by Nathaniel Lloyd, Great Dixter, Sussex

VIII Small pool, Tintinhull

  IX Shadows on the grass, Sissinghurst

   X (a) The George Washington garden at Claverton Manor, Bath
     (b) The large pool, Tintinhull

  XI Hidcote, Gloucestershire, the cedar

 XII The vestal virgin, Sissinghurst

XIII (a) Path beside Loch Ewe, Inverewe
     (b) Woodland planting, Inverewe

XIV (a) *Rhododendron falconeri* at Rowallane
     (b) The old wood, Rowallane

 XV (a) Angelica at East Lambrook Manor
     (b) Basin at Greyfriars, Worcester

XVI (a) Garden in Kensington made by Mrs. Cecily Mure
     (b) Garden in Kensington made by Mrs. Cecily Mure

PLANS

	page
1. Suburban back garden	6
2. Front garden of a modern house	12
3. Garden of Sussex bungalow	16
4. Plan of gardens, Sissinghurst Castle	25
5. Georgian walled garden	33
6. Garden of Moyles Cottage, Quenington	36
7. Two modern designs	41
8. Simple design for a narrow garden	45
9. Plotting the ground, Sussex bungalow (in Figure 3)	50
10. Alexander Pope's garden at Twickenham	133
11. Hidcote	143
12. Tintinhull	151
13. Plan of Inverewe gardens	165
14. Irish design—Rowallane	181

Plates: I, V a by J. E. Downward; II a, II b, X b, XIII a by permission of *The Field*; III a, XV b by Horniblow, Worcester; III b, V b by Peter Reason, Lechlade; IV, VI, XIII b by R. M. Adam; VII a, X a by permission of The American Museum in Britain; VII b by Quentin Lloyd; VIII, IX, XV a by permission of *Amateur Gardening*; XI, XII by Edwin Smith; XIV by M. E. I. McIlwaine; XVI by Harry Smith.

FOREWORD

This book summarizes the ideas that I have had in a lifetime with plants. Although not academically qualified in horticulture I received a full training in the art of design in two schools of art. I began to garden at the age of four, and designed my first full-sized garden when I was a student. In the 1950s I worked with the late Mairi Sawyer at the famous gardens of Inverewe in Wester Ross, Scotland, and in 1964 was engaged on a herb exhibit for the American Museum near Bath. I have of late made my own little garden of herbs in a Wiltshire town, described in The Royal Horticultural Society's *Journal* for September 1968.

This is not an instructional book in the detailed sense; directions for levelling, paving, terracing and constructing steps must be sought elsewhere—in the numerous technical manuals that are now available. It is rather, as the title suggests, about the all-important matter of design, and its aim is to help the inexperienced gardener to think about the possibilities of his ground, as influenced by his own personal tastes and needs, before embarking on the business of laying out and planting. As a successful garden must of necessity depend on the informed use of trees, shrubs and other living growth, my main theme is the employment of plant-lore in the composition of a harmonious whole, much as the painter uses his brush and paints to create a picture on canvas.

A number of gardens, some famous and others less well-known, are pictured and discussed, with a view to finding out what the maker of a humbler project may learn from purposeful visits to gardens open to the public. Nothing in the horticultural world is too great or too small to be of interest and service to the keen

FOREWORD

designer; but this book is addressed mainly to people with half an acre of ground or less—that is, to the majority of gardeners in Britain today.

Bradford on Avon D.M.
June 1969

PART ONE

PLANNING A NEW GARDEN

ASK ANY gardener what he thinks about the designing of gardens, and in nine cases out of ten he will gaze at you in astonishment and say that this is a matter for experts. If by 'experts' he means landscape architects, this is certainly true of large properties, whether public or private; but for millions of people with small plots of ground such engagement would prove far too costly. For them, it must be a do-it-yourself job. We are all becoming so clever at this *inside* the house that the abbreviation D.I.Y. is commonly used and understood, and the truth is that many of us are equally competent at the D.I.Y. cultivation of plants and trees; but the designing of our gardens is too often a hit-or-miss affair. The main trouble is that we are in such a hurry to clothe the naked ground that planting is undertaken without enough consideration for the over-all effect.

Inside our homes it is a different matter. People today are highly conscious of interior decoration, and choose furniture, carpets, wall-finishes and woodwork with careful regard to the type of setting they require. If similar study and imagination were devoted to garden design, the results would be quite as rewarding. The chief difficulty stems from the fact that so many books and articles on gardening deal with the choice of plants and their cultivation, while arrangement of the garden as a whole is—if touched upon at all—

given only a side-glance. There *are* splendid books about garden design; but those by eminent landscape architects tend to be grand, while the humbler sort have as a rule many pages devoted to standardized plans of gardens for specific sites, with little analysis of the problems, and few details of how and why the designer solved them in this particular way. It is rather from the angle of general principles that I propose to approach this complicated subject.

The first thing to do is to use our eyes and put our minds to work on the designs of gardens which we see already in being around us, and from this to reach an idea of what sort of garden we would like to have ourselves. After that, it is essential to take a serious look at the land and the means at our disposal. If either or both seem inadequate, we then have to decide how best to cut our coat to suit the cloth. At such a moment it is heartening to remember that the good and thoughtful gardener can, as a rule, make a pleasing garden on a small plot of ground and with limited means.

My own first realization of what planning a garden meant was unforgettable—although, to be sure, I could not have given it a name. It came at an early age—a time when each new flash of understanding makes a deep impression on the mind. Circumstances were not happy, for we had 'come down in the world' following World War One, and the loss of my father. That he would never return seemed unbelievable; but the resultant plunge from upper-town professional ease to lower-town semi-detached restriction was clear and disagreeable, even to a child.

Our old garden had been greatly loved. Although not the sort that people write articles about, or throw open to the public, it was large enough to contain a tennis lawn, rose beds, a swing and a trapeze, and a clump of tall trees inhabited by companionable rooks. There was also an immense white owl, which fascinated and sometimes scared me with sudden cries after dark. Against such memories the new garden made a depressing contrast. It was a long, narrow strip of poor ill-kept grass, with a shabby asphalt path down one side and a bed of Campanula, Montbretia and Japanese Anemone on the other, bordered by far too much London Pride—a plant that looks its best in delicate arrangements rather than in clotted mats. This garden had a wooden fence all round it, and at the bottom another asphalt path divided two patches of snail-ridden greens. Certainly no fairies there.

An enterprising member of my mother's family, daughter of a green-fingered MacLeod, decided to improve the scene. Even if her elder sister had to live in a nondescript house, the surroundings might be given a little distinction, she said. This end was achieved, not by installing expensive screened patio and exotic flowers in tubs, as is often done now, but by the addition of a few simple things and some re-arrangement of existing features.

The measurements were roughly 75 feet by 25: that is, three squares placed end to end, which gave it a lean and hungry look. The first change was made by shutting off the farthest square to form a separate vegetable plot. This was not done with any snobbish idea that the 'kitchen' garden was better hidden, but to divide up the awkward space, and, by making it impossible to see all the ground at one glance, to add a little mystery. Even a small mystery is better than none. For this job wattle hurdles were used and a small wicket gate. Such hurdles cost two or three shillings each in those days, and they are now ten times the price. With care they will last for at least seven years. Attractive in colour and texture, full of homespun character, and appropriate in almost any garden, they are still worth their money.

The remaining rectangle, now a double square, was a somewhat easier shape in which to plan a garden. In fact it had become a *shape*, and not a mere strip cut off a parcel of land. This was lesson number one for me: it isn't size that matters, but proportion. (Figure 1.)

Next, most of that hideous cracked asphalt was removed, leaving only the bottom section within the vegetable plot, now screened from view by hurdles, and a standing-place for dustbins by the back door. This had a trellis fixed round it to take a pleasing jumble of Honeysuckle and Everlasting Pea, which soon clothed the kitchen entrance.

The rest of the ground was carefully levelled and reseeded with

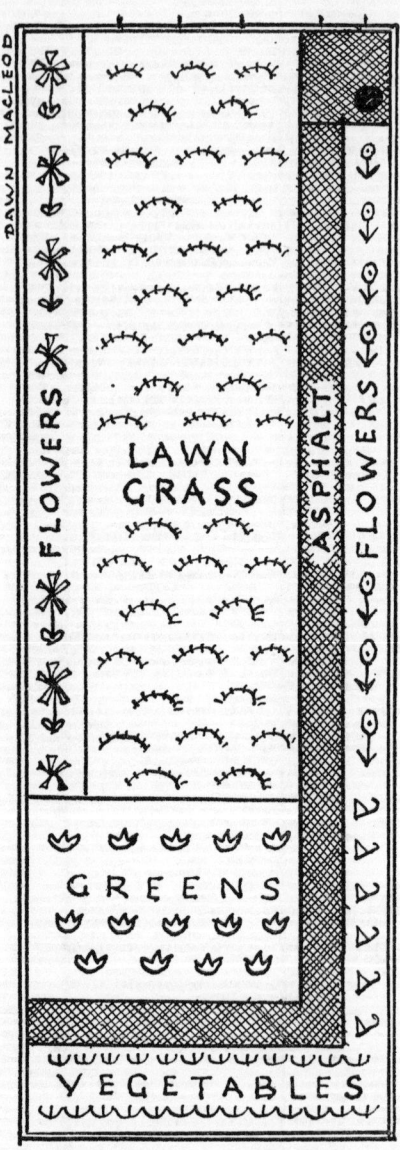 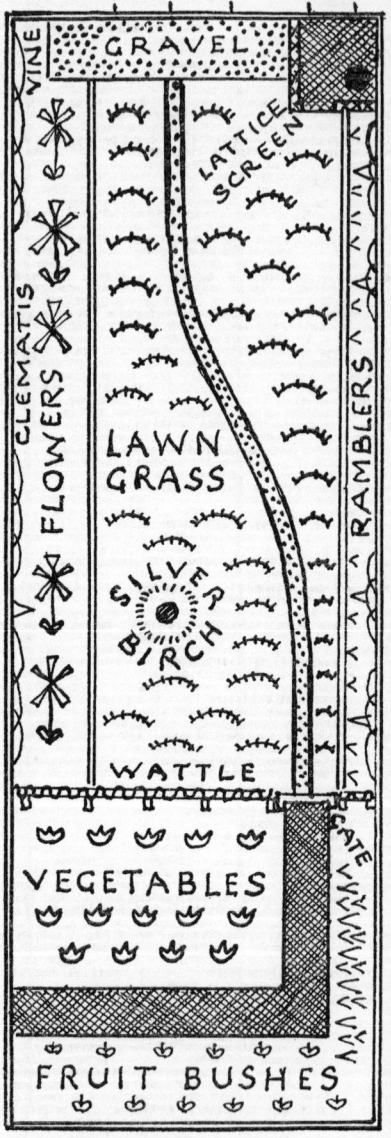

Original layout   As re-designed

1 Suburban back garden

PLANNING A NEW GARDEN

lawn grass, except for two borders and a new path, running in a subtle 'S' curve (laid out with rope) from the french windows at one side of the house to the gate in the wattle fence. This winding path, surfaced with fine gravel, looked right from the far end, for the back of the brick-built house was roughcast in similar grit of a sandy hue. How important—and how often overlooked—is the need to 'marry' paths or terraces to the buildings they complement and serve. A gravel strip was laid also along the back of the house, for sitting out, to save the new lawn, and for use when it was sodden. That superfluity of London Pride was divided up, and the best plantlets put in a thin row primly dividing gravel and lawn with a quaint nursery-rhyme effect.

Along the fence on the kitchen side a very narrow bed held climbing roses and Jasmines, with a footing of annuals and spring bulbs. The roses were all in gentle colours: pale pink, primrose yellow, peaches-and-cream (probably that old favourite 'Phyllis Bide', now coming back into favour). The annuals, including Flax, Clarkia, Love-in-a-Mist, Mignonette and Larkspur, were in pastel tints too. At the opposite side of the lawn a fairly wide bed held clumps of the original Campanula and Japanese Anemone. The fiery Montbretias were removed to the vegetable plot. On the fence behind the herbaceous border a vine (I think *Vitis vinifera purpurea*) was planted to give autumn colour, and a *Clematis montana* for early summer blossom. Canterbury Bells, Goat's Rue, Jacob's Ladder, Monkshood, Bleeding Heart, Solomon's Seal, and other old-fashioned plants filled up the pattern, with an edging to the grass of sweet-scented 'Mrs. Sinkins' Pinks. A line of greyish-yellow bricks, bought cheaply from a builder's yard, was laid along each side of the lawn, slightly below the grass level, so that a mowing machine pushed half on bricks and half on grass would cut right to the edges. Shears were required only for the winding path where grass met gravel, and the narrow ends.

Into that Watteau-like picture the principal character entered last of all. This was an elegant silver birch tree. Its placing in the design, a matter of supreme importance to my aunt, was not left to chance.

Someone had to stand holding the young tree while others ran hither and yon to survey and discuss the effect from every angle. Finally the precise spot on the lawn was fixed with a cane, and the ceremony of planting carried out. It was the first tree I had ever helped to put into the soil, and the excitement, mystery, and sense of achievement are with me still. I have been a tree-planter ever since. What matters it if one has to leave within a year or two? The thought of a tree flourishing where none did before, and mental pictures of other people enjoying the sight of it, not to mention the birds perching on leafy boughs in summer and frosty ones in winter, are surely enough reward? Would that our educational system gave every child at least one chance to take part in a tree-planting ceremony!

That little silver birch proved to be the perfect choice for our small garden. It looked 'right' at all seasons. At its base a ring of grass was left rough in the early part of the year, and here a delicate embroidery of small species crocus, winter aconite, scilla and snowdrop thrived and increased. Soon the glories of the past were forgotten. We had a great deal of pleasure from our remodelled strip of garden, and our visitors were astonished by its transformation. This was a triumph of good design, although the work of an untrained amateur.

It may be argued that it was not designing a new garden, but rather the re-planning of an old one. Yet only a single asphalt path, or a section of it, had to be removed, and many a purchaser today finds himself saddled with more than that in the way of cement paths and driveways and areas around his new house—and a great nuisance it can be. Not that there is anything wrong with cement as such; but, just as weeds have been described as 'plants in the wrong place', so the concrete imposed by builders without regard to the buyer's needs and taste often brings odium upon the material. As with weeds, the thing to do with paths in the wrong place is to remove them at once. Trying to force a garden plan around existing slabs of cement is frequently fatal. Only the drive is as a rule fixed by relationship between road and garage, and must be retained.

How, then, do you plan a garden from scratch? It all depends, as a certain famous radio character used to say, what you mean by

PLANNING A NEW GARDEN

'garden'. This provides us with a useful question: what *do* we mean by it? There are a great many possible answers. We had a neighbour once who liked nothing so much as an expanse of freshly dug, well-raked soil. That was his idea of gardening, and he constantly battled with his wife and daughters to get rid of their unwanted plants. Of course he was a freak; but 'grass and path' gardeners are much more common. So long as lawns are well kept and paths free from weeds, they scarcely trouble about the rest. Anything goes, so far as the flower borders are concerned, and 'anything' is often a scruffy collection of elderly unpruned shrubs with matted ground-cover of St. John's Wort and Periwinkle underneath, and a few worn-out bulbs struggling through in the spring.

Then there is the sergeant-major of the garden, who likes plants so long as they can be strictly regimented. The flowers he chooses are usually scarlet and gold, Salvias and Tagetes being prime favourites. I have walked a garden path between giant specimens of red and yellow Gladiolus, each one tied tightly to a 6-foot cane, and the rows so rigidly aligned that the effect was menacing. Flower-power indeed! Gardeners of the type just described know exactly what they like, and if we disagree with their tastes we can still admire their certainty.

Many of us know only vaguely what we want to find in our gardens. They should look attractive for most of the year, if not at every season; they should supply us with cut flowers for the house; if big enough, provide our requirements of fruit and vegetables as well. All this with the minimum expenditure of time and cash. But it is a far cry from ideas as general as that to the detailed planning of a garden. How do we set about it? This takes us back to the re-designed garden of my childhood. Although the expression 'labour-saving garden' had not then been coined, my relative had in fact produced one. It was very small and simple, but many of the ideas may be adapted to larger schemes. The edging of grass with bricks, paving stones, or slabs moulded from cement, saves the tiresome work of shearing; the mower runs on the stone, beyond the turf, and so cuts and trims in one operation.

Our old-fashioned border plants needed very little staking. It is the gigantic modern Delphiniums, Lupins, top-heavy Dahlias and Chrysanthemums that demand so much support, to withstand gales and rain. Hedges are often pleasant to look at, but most types give the gardener a lot of work. By using wattle hurdles for a screen to the vegetable plot, we were saved that task. Even the silver birch was trouble-free. The leaves were small, and came down more or less in one drop, so that a single sweep cleared the grass of their presence. There was a simple method of training climbers on the fences. Lengths of stout wire were run horizontally, threaded through staples, and the plants were tied to these with strips cut from outworn stockings. A material known as artificial silk was common then; the modern nylon works even better. It lasts a long time, is easy to unfasten when necessary, and being elastic it does not chafe the expanding stems.

Our fences were between 5 and 6 feet high, and there were three rows of wire. These are easy to fix on wood, less easy on stone walls, and where there is only chain-link fence or paling there is seldom enough height. A way out of these difficulties may be found by setting up a row of strong posts in front of an existing fence to hold the wires. Climbing roses and ramblers; the Clematis and the Vine; Ceanothus, Jasmine, Honeysuckle, and many other plants will provide a quick screen, and often these are more attractive than a solid hedge of Beech, Privet or Macrocarpa, or the row of *Cupressocyparis* × *leylandii* so commonly put in now to shelter gardens on new estates.

Suppose we now look at a piece of ground in front of a new house known to me on the outskirts of a medium-sized West country city. There are in being three adjacent residences of so-called 'executive type', built by the same firm for private customers. These detached four-bedroom houses have built-in garages. The front gardens retain their original mixed country-style hedges, with mature beech and elm trees at intervals beside the road. Each frontage is some 70 feet wide and 45 feet in depth. (The long strips behind the houses do not concern us.) The builder laid a 12-foot-wide drive, which runs slightly uphill to gateway and road, from each garage, and 4 feet of concrete across the front of the house as a path. Then, assuming that people would not bother to go along it and turn at right angles into the drive, he installed another path running diagonally from the front door to join the drive just inside the gate. (Figure 2 (a).) Two purchasers accepted this, and in an attempt to balance the triangular flower bed left between paths and drive, cut out another bed in the grass—for they all laid turf on the main section. The third owner, after a long look at the diagonal path, decided that he disliked the line of it, and so wisely had it picked up and started his plan with an uncluttered rectangular space. He laid some paving stones in front of the main door, and repeated this paved 'step' against the drive near the gate, also on the opposite side, where it served as a stand for a tub of hydrangeas in summer. Then he drew a curve between the three paved areas (Figure 2 (b)). The large semi-circle was grassed, and the plots in the angles to left and right of the house became rose beds. A good deal of treading went on between door and gate over the lawn, but many walkers passed along the front of the house and up the drive. As the sitting-room window was on the opposite side of the door, this traffic did not disturb anyone.

Had it been considered desirable to make a walk in a direct line from door to gate, 'stepping-stones' let into the grass, whether composed of stone or of cheaper blocks of moulded cement, would have looked much less obtrusive than the original raised path of solid concrete. So often the cement laid by builders projects several inches above the soil, and this makes the edges difficult to clothe. The best plan, if such paths have to be accepted, is to edge them with closely set rows of dwarf Lavender, Hyssop, Winter Savory, or even Box. All these plants can be clipped into neat miniature hedges, and severe concrete walks will take on a certain distinction when so bordered, not to mention the fragrance distilled to beguile the nose.

If any more is said on the subject of unwanted concrete, it may be thought that I am suffering from cementia. What about those new plots where no ready-made paths exist, and the owners flounder ankle-deep in uncharted seas of mud? In 1929 my first experience

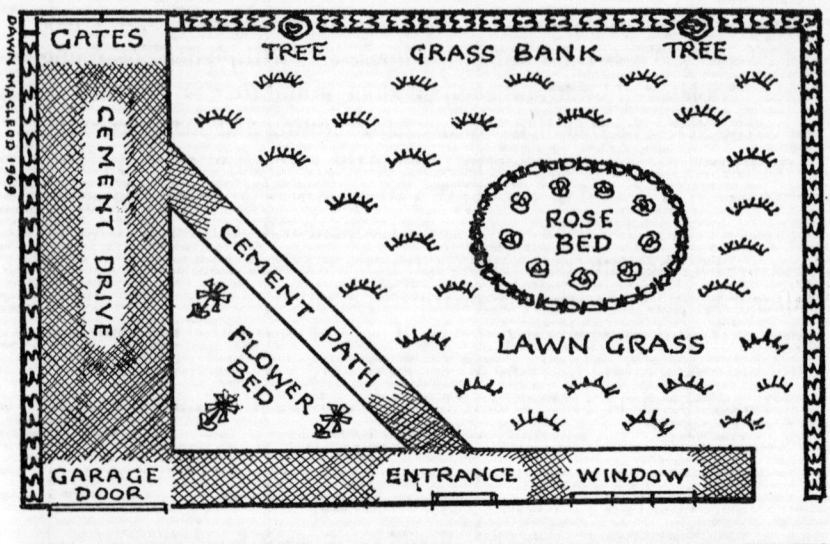
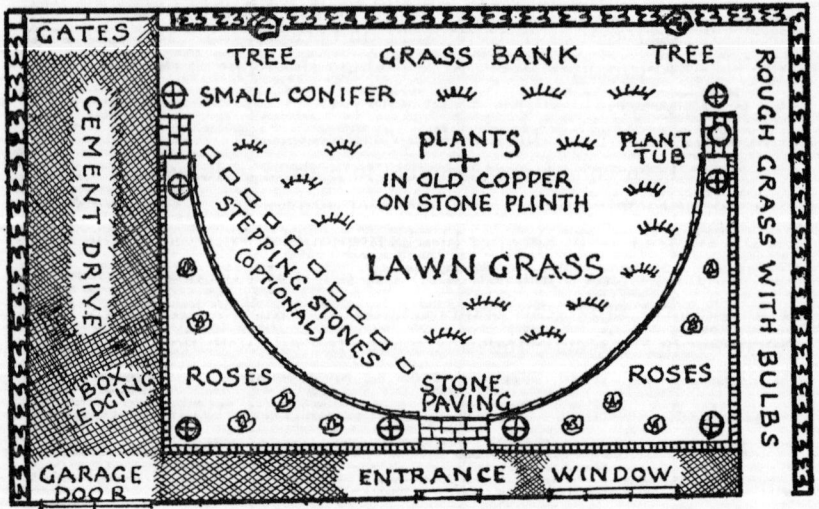

2 Front garden of a modern house
(a) original layout (top)
(b) as re-designed (below)

of garden-making began in circumstances of that sort. Situated on the levels, once beneath the sea, which surround the Ancient Town (appendage of the Cinque Ports) of Rye in Sussex, our ground was not exactly marsh, but near enough to Romney and sufficiently wet in that very rainy winter to warrant our nickname for it—'The Swamp'. When the first dry days came in February I went out, full of optimism, to turn a stretch of heavy clay into a flower bed. Soon it became depressingly obvious that a side-effect of my labour—the transfer of mud in large slabs from my boots and implements to places where it was unwelcome—made the construction of paths a prime necessity.

Having decided on the most convenient layout for these, and pegged down lines as markers, I had to consider the purchase of material, bearing in mind the low-lying nature of the ground, with its need for good drainage; the limited money available; the appearance of the finished work; and last, but not least, the sort of paving that could most easily be obtained in the district. No York paving stone for us! The great shingle bank of Dungeness lay a few miles to the east, and the coastline from Rye Harbour curved in even closer to us, so that the suck and spew of wave with pebble sounded constantly in our ears. Here then was the natural choice: our paths would have to be made from local shingle. A drainage bed of clinker and rubble was laid first, surmounted by a fairly thick layer of sea-worn stones. These raised walks were edged with home-made slabs of concrete, about an inch and a half thick, to which I gave an earthy tinge by mixing in cheap powder-colour when moulding. All this took time, and the glorious plants of which I dreamed seemed as far off as ever.

On the whole those novice attempts at path-making proved to be reasonably efficient. They did not become waterlogged or weedy, and if clay was inadvertently trampled into them the shingle managed to digest it without getting sticky. In effect the pebbles looked 'at home' in this coastal environment, and so far as my young feet were concerned they seemed agreeable to walk on. Older people were less pleased; tender corns and bunions were unhappy on the knobbly surface, and later I improved matters by adding sand to bind the stones, which enabled me to provide a smoother, rolled, surface. By that time the clay had been brought under some sort of control, and we did not again experience so much rainfall in consecutive months.

One or two other aspects of that first experiment in making a garden from scratch may be worth mentioning here. Some instinct (or may be a guardian angel) warned me that permanent planting should only be carried out after thought and experience had had time to dictate a scheme; but the impatience of youth, combined with the dreary look of wet clay and bedraggled remains of sheep pasture surrounding our new bungalow, made it imperative that some gaiety be achieved without delay. For our first season I managed to solve the problem by having a burst of extravagance with packets of annual seeds—not so extravagant after all, in terms of cash, for a large amount of the commoner subjects could be had for sixpence then. But the broadcasting of packet after packet of Shirley Poppy, Eschscholtzia, Godetia, Mignonette, Nasturtium, Clarkia, Night-scented Stock and Marigold gave me a feeling of opulence that I have never again experienced. And the rich virgin soil produced results to match my visions, or even to surpass them.

By midsummer the carpet of flowers was quite dazzling when the sun shone on it; passers-by leaned on the garden gate to admire the blaze of colour. Most of the ground-cover was in 'hot' hues, but on the chestnut spile fences I grew great clusters of the clear blue *Ipomoea caerulea*, 'Morning Glory', which flourished beyond all my expectations, and made a splendid foil to the fiery glow of the beds. This colour scheme was startling, almost savage; yet the total effect was balanced and subdued by the wide skies above and great green spread of marshland surrounding the demesne. Furnishing a new garden with annuals is cheap, even now, and it provides enormous scope for bold colour schemes, which gain in charm by their impermanence. Above all, it has the advantage of winning time for the gardener who requires this to work out a planting plan, and it is worth the consideration of everyone who has a bare piece of ground to clothe, as an initial performance designed for short-term enjoyment.

With paths made and main beds furnished for the summer, the next concern was the choice of trees and shrubs, to be ordered for autumn planting. Being on flat land and at a level slightly below that of the sea, we felt an intense desire for vertical growths to break the long, low horizon; yet there was a lovely vista of wooded escarpment and a glimpse of distant hills which must not be cut out. Luckily the view lay to the north-west of us, and prevailing winds blew from the south-west; so in that corner of the land I formed a mixed plantation of Rowan, Gean (or Bird Cherry), Golden Poplar, Goat Willow, Stag's Horn Sumach, Holly and Elder—fairly tough subjects which were likely to withstand winds and perhaps some salt spray, although we were about a mile from the sea. Farther in towards the bungalow there were smaller flowering trees and shrubs, diminishing in height as they approached the house walls on the seaward side.

The land was roughly a wedge, with a wide frontage and a 'tail' narrowing behind the building until it met the river bank. The front garden was to be for flowers, trees and grass, and the back mainly for vegetables and fruit. I left a good deal of the original grass there untouched at first, and in the lambing season many a young lamb thought it saw better pasture on our side of the fence and got itself wedged between the spiles, so that gardening and lamb rescue were continually alternating. In return for my first-aid I was allowed to take sheep manure, with which I layered my compost heap.

In spite of the tree planting, we still had a wish for verticals in the front garden. I therefore constructed a wooden pergola across the north-west corner, carefully sited and designed so that the precious vista, framed in climbing roses, could be seen from each of the west windows. Ever since that time I have felt that the rather maligned pergola can be extremely valuable in a garden, provided that it is in scale with the whole design, and placed where it is really needed—not just made somewhere or other for the sake of having one. In our rich clay soil, roses grew with terrific vigour; but, as a high pergola would have been disproportionate to house and garden, I kept it

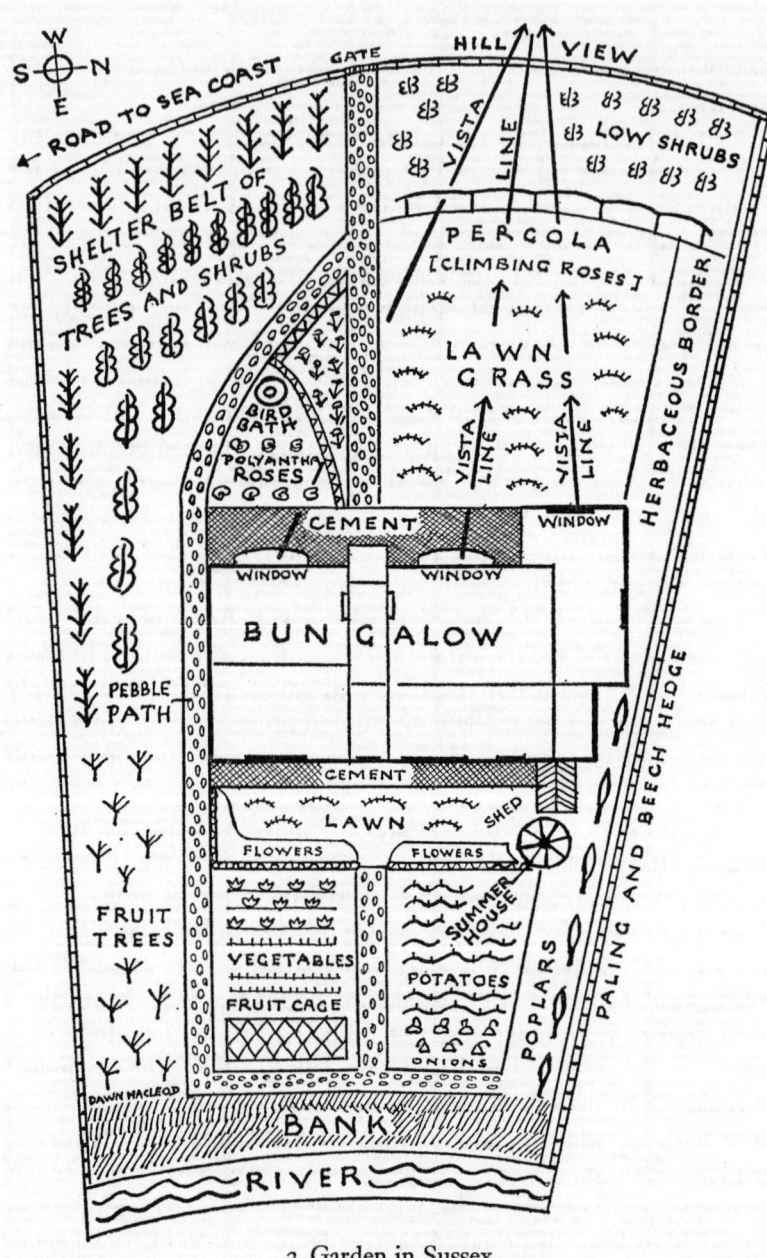

3 Garden in Sussex

low, and sternly disciplined the climbers to avoid an unwieldy tangle. On that windy level it would not have been practicable to allow heavy top-hamper, in any case. (Figure 3.)

Apart from trees and pergolas, the monotony of flat land may be broken in a very different way—by the construction of a sunk garden. If a pool is wanted, this feature will take its place most naturally within such an artificial valley. But on land as low-lying as that of my first garden-making experiment it would have been foolish to excavate, as the resultant hollow might have turned into one large pond in wet seasons. On level sites at slightly higher altitudes, the sunk garden is a practical proposition. In addition to the charm of surprise, it makes an excellent home for smaller and perhaps less hardy alpine plants, set apart from the shrubby and herbaceous subjects.

The most effective rockeries known to me are all to some extent sunk below, not raised above, the level of the main garden; although some are sited on single slopes leading down to a lower part of the ground, and not wholly sunk. Another good use for a sunk garden is to plant it with herbs. These aromatic plants mostly enjoy warmth and shelter, and they provide the greatest pleasure when their fragrances are contained and concentrated within banks, walls, hedges, or in a hollow.

Another way to diversify a level garden—a very old device which I should like to see back in fashion—is the artificial mount or mound beloved by the first Elizabethans. According to the late Eleanour Sinclair Rohde, these were descendants of the 'holy hills' of Druidic times, when they symbolized the dry land appearing above the waters. The very name of our capital city, London, is said to be a corruption of *Llandin*, or sacred eminence. History apart, the mound can make a very interesting feature of a garden, and in its construction builders' spoil may be put to good use. I often pass what was once the terminal section of a large garden surrounding an eighteenth-century house. About a hundred years ago this piece of land was sliced off from the main garden by a branch railway, and the remains are forlorn and overgrown. One striking feature is still to be seen: a

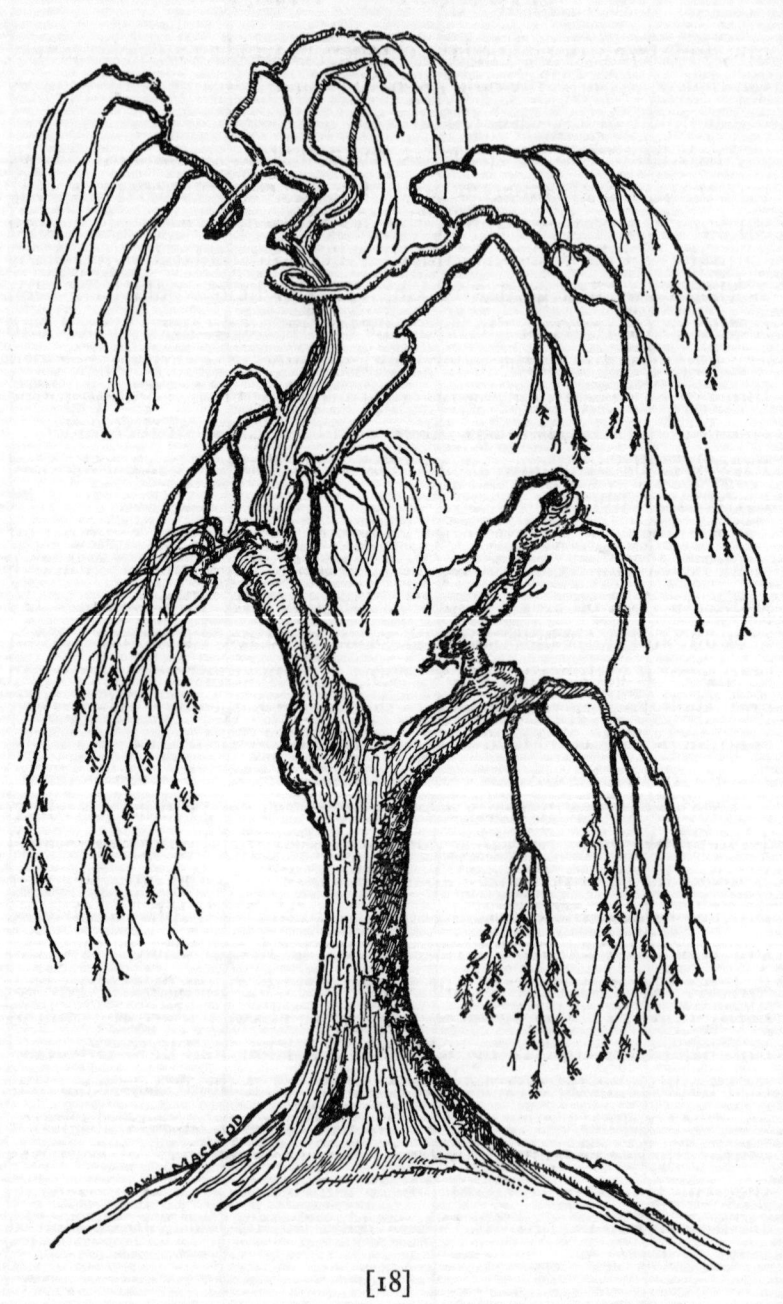

substantial mound, obviously artificial, on which a fine Weeping Ash tree is enthroned. The gnarled roots writhe in fantastic designs down the sides of the hillock, and the whole forms a delightful picture.

I do not know of any small modern garden in which such a mound has been constructed, but according to the *Bristol Evening Post* a park being made for public use by the Sodbury Rural Council at Yate in Gloucestershire is to have an artificial hill made from spoil. Few of us in the twentieth century would essay the grand project described by Francis Bacon: 'A fair mount with three ascents, and alleys enough for four to walk abreast; which I would have to be a perfect circle, without any bulwarks or embossments: and the whole mount to be 30 feet high, surmounted by a fine banqueting hall with some chimneys neatly cast'; but a modest mound, perhaps some 6 or 7 feet high, with a specimen tree upon it, might become popular if an enterprising gardener took the plunge and brought it into fashion.

I end this chapter where most books on garden design begin: with the soil itself. For a start, it is necessary to find out whether the builder has left any topsoil, for the horrid practice of removing it seems to be on the increase. If that has occurred, fresh topsoil will have to be imported, at a cost of 20 or 30 shillings a ton. It is important to spread a generous layer on beds for flower, vegetable or shrub culture, but where lawns are required the topsoil may be thinner. Before the subsoil is buried it should be broken up. If the builder has left the original topsoil *in situ*, it will only be necessary to dig it thoroughly before planting can begin. It is often possible to have it rotavated by a garden contractor, to save manual labour. Of course it is useless to possess topsoil unless it is carefully left *on top* after the subsoil is broken up.

While most people realize that soil may be acid or alkaline, it is less well known that this can vary within quite a small compass. It is not invariably safe to assume that, because lime-hating plants such as Rhododendron and other *Ericaceae* flourish down the road, they will be sure to do so with you.

The pH scale used in measuring the acid-alkaline content has the figure pH 7 for neutral, pH 7·5 or pH 8 being alkaline and the figures from pH 6·5 down to pH 5 denoting greater and greater acidity. Above pH 6·5 few of the ericaceous subjects are happy. There are methods of rendering the soil less alkaline, but most of these are temporary in effect, and, unless raised beds are constructed from peat blocks to take the smaller species of lime-haters, it is generally wiser to accept what soil you have and make use of it to the best advantage, without trying to force alien growths upon it. Inexpensive do-it-yourself soil-testing outfits are obtainable from garden shops and some nurseries, or the local Horticultural Advisers and Instructors will supply information on this matter. Every county has its own Adviser; their addresses may be obtained from Education Departments and Schools of Agriculture or Horticulture.

A NEW LOOK FOR AN OLD GARDEN

By 'an old garden' we may mean anything from a formal period piece (often very costly to maintain) to a neglected villa jungle with Victorian laurels, monkey-puzzles and quantities of leprous-looking tufa rock. Usually it falls to people of modest means to tackle the modernization of the latter sort, and very hard work it can be. For my part, I have always wanted to operate in the reverse direction—that is, to re-design a section of garden at some stately home of the sixteenth or seventeenth century, where accretions of the naturalistic Victorian and later periods might with advantage be removed in favour of a return to earlier formality. Surely we now overdo those endless beds of floribunda roses! What fun it would be to install a pattern of scrolls or Elizabethan strap-work, using the very wide range of plant form and colour now at our disposal. It could be a delight to the eye on a terrace near some such building as Lord Bath's Longleat, or the National Trust property Montacute.

At the royal gardens in Hanover there is a whole series of these confections, each designed as a self-contained unit, but leading through from one to another. Designs include a chequer-board parterre with orange trees in tubs standing on the 'black' squares in alternate rows and at the outer corners, twenty of them in all; and a French baroque pattern made from coloured sand and gravel, outlined with box borders. Seen from the air, the whole layout is reminiscent of an old-fashioned book of wallpaper samples or tiling; but at ground level each section comes alive as an entity, and they undoubtedly possess character and charm. I should prefer fewer on one site, and would choose to make at the most three of these little formal gardens, strung out like jewels along a terrace, as surprise items in a larger and less artificial setting.

Topiary work could easily be given a chapter to itself, or even a whole book. The sculptural use of evergreens is of ancient origin—the Romans in Pliny's day had fleets of ships and hunting scenes made in this craft—but it is commonly considered to be too slow a process to be worth much thought in these hurried times, although I have come across an Irish gardener (a Roman Catholic) who, outwith his employer's orders, fashioned a cross and a crown of thorns on either side of her entrance gates. The Protestant lady had no objection to his use of religious symbols, and was rewarded for her compliance by the gradual appearance of a spirited topiary horse beneath her bedroom window, she being an ardent horsewoman. In Scandinavian countries, where evergreens are highly prized, topiary work is carried out in the winter-hardy and fairly fast-growing spruce, in place of the yew and box usual in this country.

In her well-known Somerset manor of East Lambrook, the late Mrs. Margery Fish in the 1930s remodelled a run-down garden in what she referred to as the 'cottage' style. It is now really a set of simple little gardens leading from one to another—simple in their informality and lack of 'show', but crammed full of treasures, many of them rescued and propagated by the owner when they were almost extinct. Even here a certain amount of formal topiary of a quiet kind has been found essential to give strength to the rambling design of pathway and bed, and bind them into a whole. A double row of the formidably named *Chamaecyparis lawsoniana fletcheri* has been kept down to about 5 feet in height, and constant clipping has made them into solid little grey-green cones. Combined with a cross-strapping of low Lonicera hedging, they provide rest for the eye and stability to the whole conception. The more 'naturally' you allow plants to entwine and sprawl where they choose, the more rigidity is needed in some contrasting growth, if the effect is not to degenerate into a sort of horticultural rag-bag. (Plate II a.)

Vita Sackville-West understood this principle well when she rehabilitated Sissinghurst Castle and remade the garden. She wrote of it as 'a Sleeping Beauty's Castle running away into sordidness and squalor, a garden crying out for rescue. It was easy to see even then what a struggle we should have to redeem it.' This famous garden, now a National Trust property, is visited by thousands each year; but few of those who see it know that the place was such a rubbish heap forty years ago as to keep an old man and his son busy for three years carting away the refuse.

Clearing the site was, however, a routine job. Planning the new layout was not. Miss Sackville-West said that she could never have done it by herself. Fortunately her husband, Harold Nicolson, had a flair for garden design, and Sissinghurst became at once his great challenge and his splendid opportunity. There was little existing growth to aid the newcomers—no majestic timber trees or fine old hedges. Underneath the mountain of scrap-iron and a mass of weeds a few smaller treasures were found, including a plantation of Kent cobnuts and filberts, which was retained and improved, and is now known as the 'Nut Plat'. There was also a charming old rose, a *gallica*, named 'Tour de Maures', which they propagated. There were three valuable features of inanimate kind: the aged walls of mellow rosy brick, a central tower of similar construction, and the remains of a moat.

In a description written by his wife, Harold Nicolson, 'the worried designer', is shown bent over his immense sheets of squared paper and his measuring tapes and his indiarubbers, 'pushing his fingers through his rumpled hair, trying to get the puzzle worked out'. Problems were many. 'The walls were not all at right angles to one another; the courtyard was not rectangular but coffin-shaped; the tower was not opposite the main entrance; the moat-walk, with its supporting wall, ran away on so queer a bias that the statue we placed on the bank behind the moat stood opposite both to the tower and to the seat at the upper end of the moat-walk. All this was disconcerting, and there were also minor crudenesses which had somehow to be camouflaged.'

Although Vita confessed that she could never have done it herself, the couple were in complete agreement about the main principle to be established in their garden: a very simple one in theory, however hard to implement. It must have two long axial walks running more or less from north to south and from east to west right across the demesne, crossing at right angles in the centre of the lawn by the tower. (Figure 4.) Once they had arrived at this strong framework and its exact placing, shorter vistas were contrived at various angles, cut off by intervening walls or hedges (many walls and all the hedging being new), to the space of one 'room' or section of the garden—or at most two. These small self-contained units were arranged to open off the principal walks, rather as rooms in a great house open out of a main corridor. Provided with a strictly formal basic plan, Vita Sackville-West then planted it with the 'profusion, even extravagance and exuberance' which she loved. This marriage of the severe and classical with the wildly romantic attitude has produced one of the loveliest gardens in England.

What practical ideas can be gleaned from such grandeur as this, for use in humbler spheres? I believe they are legion. First, the importance of a good 'bone structure' for any garden, and the value of measuring and sketching it out on paper before doing the practical work. Then the separate 'rooms' at Sissinghurst, together with those in other gardens of similar style, such as Hidcote in Gloucestershire, may well be studied as individual designs for gardens. I should be content to have as my entire demesne the white garden at Sissinghurst (Plate I), or the three small sections between the west front of Tintinhull House and the pool (Plate VIII), or Mrs. Winthrop's garden and pool at Hidcote, or the charming sunk garden at Great Dixter (Plate VII b)—and many others. Although planned as parts of larger schemes, these are all satisfying in themselves. The plants used, and the way they are combined, will give fresh inspiration however many times these gardens are seen. They

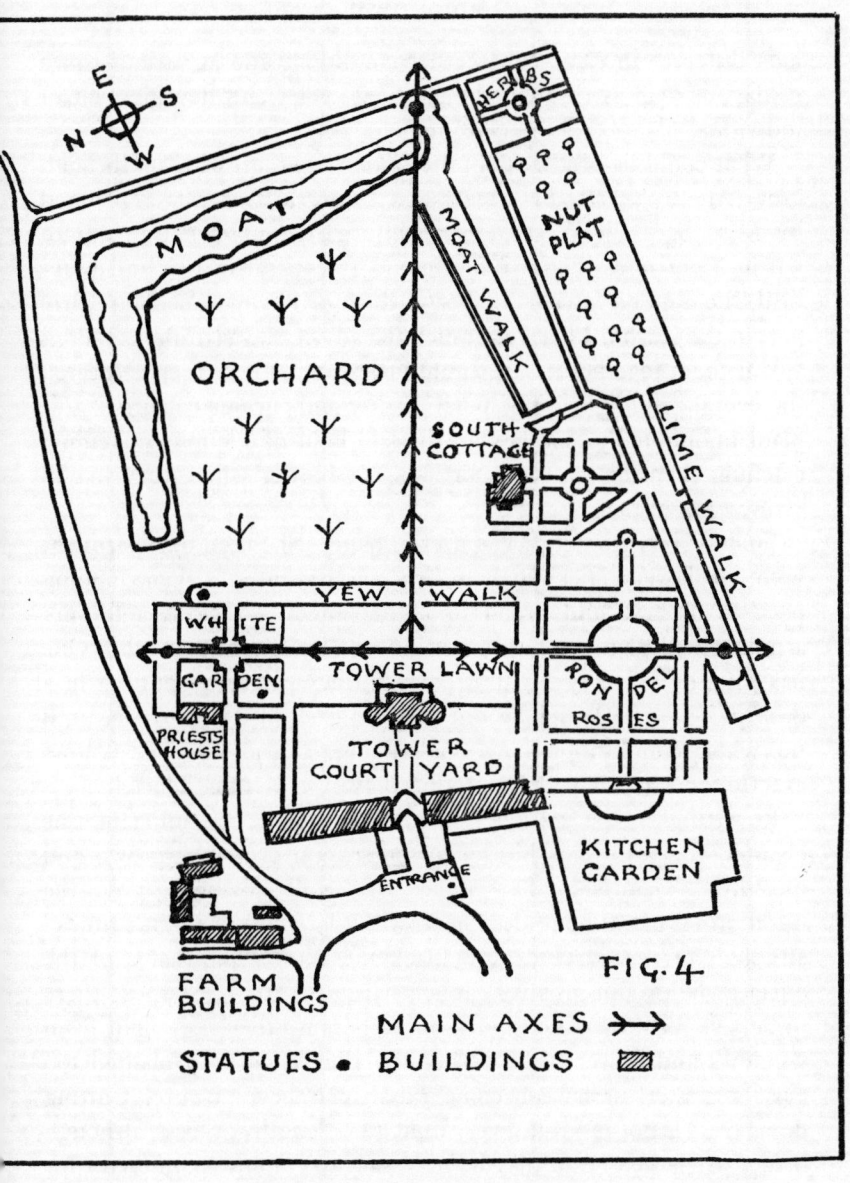

4 Plan of gardens, Sissinghurst Castle

look different in changing weather conditions and at various times of day, as well as through the seasonal cycles and development of individual plants that are continually taking place.

What could be prettier than the *Lilium regale* growing up through grey Artemisias, *Stachys lanata* and *Cineraria maritima* as planned by Miss Sackville-West in her white garden? Then the idea of letting *Rosa filipes* climb into almond trees is attractive and practical, the almond having so short a flush of bloom at such an early part of the season. I like very much the advice she gave about Phlox: 'plant them together in a separate little patch where they will catch the evening sunlight'. The petal quality and curious colours of this plant undoubtedly look best in the late light of a summer evening, catching them in the cool, north-aspect border where they like to grow.

Such secrets are not picked up by chance. She used to experiment with cut flowers, sticking them into the ground and then standing back to observe and brood upon the effect, rather as a flower-arranger will plan a composition indoors. In her own words, 'One has the illusion of being an artist painting a picture—putting in a dash of colour here, taking out another dash of colour there, until the whole composition is to one's liking, and at least one knows exactly what effect will be produced twelve months hence.'

Reverting to the gardener mentioned at the beginning of this chapter—he who finds himself in possession of an overgrown and unsightly Victorian villa jungle—that will obviously pose the question 'What, if he re-designs it, will it look like in a year's time?' although in this instance Vita Sackville-West's knowledge of the effect to be produced is very much harder to attain. Suppose there to be a superfluity of trees, unwanted because they keep light from windows and flower beds, or because they have been planted too close together, or have become misshapen beyond cure. Cutting down trees is not as a rule a very difficult or lengthy process, although if they are large ones it may be necessary to employ a contractor for the job. But getting rid of stumps and roots out of heavy, consolidated soil is a far tougher task, and naked stumps are not pleasing to the eye. There is available here a fairly satisfactory compromise, that of retaining some stumps and clothing them with climbers, such as Clematis—the golden-belled *C. tangutica* or *C. orientalis* will soon cover a tall stump (Plate III b)—while the lesser ones serve as hosts for variegated Ivy.

But, before anything is cut down, it is essential to study the doomed tree or shrub and the landscape or buildings which it screens from sight of your own windows. Cover that takes only an hour, or a day, to remove will probably require years to replace, and many an energetic tree-feller has been unpopular with his wife because the neighbours now have an uninterrupted view of her at the kitchen sink. It is surprising how much shelter and privacy even one medium-sized tree will provide, and how little most of us realize this until it has been removed. Before dispensing with trees it is well to face the fact that in the gap they leave there will be a wide-open vista to whatever lies beyond; and that when you are able to see out, so may your neighbours look in—or, if not neighbours, then south-westerly gales may have unimpeded access to your property.

Probably the best (though not the quickest) way to start on the rehabilitation of an overgrown old garden is to draw a sketch plan, showing more or less to scale your own house and any neighbouring buildings, with indications of principal trees and shrubs, together with paths, terraces and lawns. Also the arbour, grotto, and collection of tufa rock if you possess these things. The spread of any large tree may be estimated, and drawn as a compass circle centred on the dot which indicates its trunk. It is then a simple matter to lay a ruler over house and tree, thereby assessing how much your windows will be open to view from next door if the tree goes. Or you may be fortunate enough to want to open up a vista across parkland or fields, and the same method will help to determine which trees stand most in the way of it. Always mark the points of the compass on a plan, with a thought of the amount of sunlight to be let in, or perhaps the greater force of prevailing winds when the cover has been removed. Such matters are easily overlooked when working on drawings indoors.

If you decide that all the existing growth is too decayed and poor to be worth keeping, and think that a clean sweep must be made of all the top-hamper, remember that the soil in this case is almost certainly poor and impoverished also. I have met many novices who assumed that by buying a collection of young trees and shrubs they could revivify an old garden, without adding any fresh topsoil, or compost, or farmyard manure. Scattering an all-purpose fertilizer is insufficient. In gardens, as in cellars, the new wine seldom does well in old bottles. If I were given a choice, I would prefer to take a chance on reviving old trees and tatty shrubs, with good material added at the bottom, to attempting new plantings in poor, starved ground.

A lot can be done with old shrubs, given feeding and drastic pruning, provided that the gardener knows what he is doing. If he is unsure, it is worth while inviting a more knowledgeable friend to identify the plants, or making contact with the local Horticultural Adviser, or sending specimens by post to Wisley. When you know exactly what is there, it is usually a simple matter to find out the correct method of pruning, and the best time to do it.

The trouble about all this is that it takes time. If a wilderness is taken over in late autumn, it is very tempting to start felling and pruning at once, in the dormant season—yet this is the most difficult time for identification of plants. The best principle in these circumstances is 'when in doubt, do nowt'. A friend of mine, who recently bought a Georgian house in a city, looked at the 'bedded-out' strip of garden and wondered what a little evergreen bush was doing in a flower border. Luckily she left it in peace, and the previous owner later told her that this was an uncommon dwarf species of Myrtle (*Myrtus tarentina*)—not fully hardy, like all the Myrtles; but an elegant and aromatic little bush which she had nursed for several years until it was well established. It would have been easy for a newcomer to drag it out as a bit of unwanted 'privet'. Another friend wrote of her newly acquired garden in the Isle of Wight: 'A funny little tree of grey twigs is growing just inside the gate. The jobbing gardener wants to cut it down. What would you do?' That funny little tree was a Chinese Wych Hazel (*Hamamelis mollis*) and in a few weeks, when the shaggy yellow flowers burst out of those grey twigs, the owner sniffed their fragrance and was glad that my peremptory instructions—to sack the gardener rather than let him mutilate the Wych Hazel—had been attended to.

There are all sorts of pitfalls like this for owners of an old-established garden—or even a new one, for that matter. A year or two ago I was almost fooled by a Lemon Verbena. This most lovely of fragrant herb plants—really a small shrub—remained absolutely dormant until the second week in May, although we live in the West of England, have a walled garden, and in that year had had a long spell of warm, sunny weather with doses of gentle rain, making everything else burst into leaf. Was my precious Verbena dead? I left it alone, and on 12 May it developed a rash of little green knobs. Within days these had clothed the bush in fresh and fragrant leaves. Haste is nearly always a mistake where gardens are concerned.

This precept of course may be abused, as an excuse for needless procrastination or even downright laziness. One cannot but sympathize with the wife who has to live in sight of a wilderness, while her husband—absent for most of the week at his office—tells her at week-ends that he must wait and see what develops in the jungle before he does anything to improve it. Nothing is more exasperating than the companionship of a strong, muscular being who lolls in a chair while so much hard work is left undone. Patience, however, really is a virtue in the circumstances, and the aggrieved wife can always pave the way for action by getting advice from local experts, and having things in the garden identified. She might also make a plan, and mark on it the trees and shrubs she would like to see eliminated. After all, it is the woman of the house who has to live all the time with whatever growths may occur in view of her windows.

When the time comes to plant new trees and shrubs, she could also concern herself with their exact positioning. Tall canes stuck into the soil are useful as markers; but, unless one is accustomed to visualizing plant growth, something more solid is to be preferred as a stand-in. Old umbrellas or parasols tied to the canes are helpful, or the discarded Christmas-tree, or bundles of bracken. I have even seen floor-mops and shrimp-nets pressed into this service. Such exercises are never wasted, for the placing of long-term growths in a garden is quite as important as arrangement of furniture in a room; and plants, unlike furniture, are not fitted with castors.

I am now going to re-design (on paper) a garden known to me which is not by any means unkempt or unsuited to its owners, except that the lady of the house experiences a mild form of claustrophobia there. The garden consists of almost level ground, measuring about 128 ft. by 48 ft., with a 'bite' taken out by the two-storey kitchen wing of the Georgian house which forms the western boundary. On the other three sides there are high walls of mellow old brick—lovely in themselves, but giving their owner the feeling of being 'inside a red shoe-box'.

My first idea was to clothe those walls and put them to practical use by training fruit trees on them, giving welcome supplies to this vegetarian ménage and the constant pleasure to the eye which beautifully spaced branches in ordered pattern can provide. But the owners consider that later middle-age is not the time to embark on large-scale planting of fruit, because it would take too long to come into bearing; they also think that the job of training and pruning requires more skill and experience than they possess. Then there are fears that complete coverage of the walls, with necessary fixing of wires for training the trees, would be harmful to the old bricks. This ban meant that the problem had to be solved in a less obvious way.

In the plan (b) given in Figure 5, the aim is geared less to covering the brickwork than to distracting the eye from it. The present layout (Figure 5 (a)) is based entirely on lines running the whole length of the ground, which serves to accentuate the narrowness and boxed-in nature of the garden. Certain features must be retained, such as the vegetable plots, the espalier fruit on either side of the grass walk between those plots, the summerhouse against the north wall, the coal and wood store by the back door, and the terrace under the bay window with a door opening to it from the entrance hall.

There are also some trees: an old apple on the lawn is picturesque, even if its productive days are done. It would make a good host for a climber, such as the pink Jasmine (*J. stephanense*) whose pink and gold foliage in spring must be seen against sunlight and not trained on a solid fence or wall. Two elderly and rather misshapen trees near the fuel store—a yew and a tall Laburnum—should come down, for they obstruct light needed in the upper storey of the kitchen wing, and are not attractive in the general picture. A trellis screen round the fuel would soon be well covered with a plant or two of *Clematis montana*, and if some baffle against upper windows of next door is required, one of the quick-growing conifers such as *Cupressus leylandii* could be planted in place of the two over-crowded trees, and if carefully sited it would take less light from the house.

The major alteration would consist of removing some rather poor beds of roses near the summerhouse, and a little rockery, to make way for a large piece of formal paving in the shape of a cross, the longer arms of which would bisect the garden from summerhouse to the opposite wall. A circular centre bed, containing a specimen tree, preferably the greenish-yellow Japanese cherry 'Ukon', with Lavender and Rosemary around the roots, would in itself tend to draw the eye away from the walls; but this centre would be greatly emphasized by little hedges of Box in the angles, the 'arms' to extend about 4 feet in both directions, each angle housing a conifer. These accents could be of dark Irish Yew, or of *Chamaecyparis lawsoniana ellwoodii*, or the slow-growing Irish Juniper. Twenty spaces left in the paving would be used for shrubs, such as Hypericum, Potentilla, Elaeagnus (*E. argentea* and *E. pungens maculata*), *Skimmia foremanii*, Butcher's Broom (*Ruscus aculeatus*), *Choisya ternata*, Jerusalem Sage, *Senecio laxifolius*, or *S. monroi*, *Berberis thunbergii atropurpurea*, Caryopteris, *Kolkwitzia amabilis*, Daphne and Hebe.

In good rose-growing country it would be tempting to use nothing but standard roses on this paved centrepiece; but, apart from the fact that roses are not a success on this gravel, it is probably better not to put all the eggs in one basket. With a variety of shrubs it is possible to obtain interest of foliage, flower and berry all the year round.

The existing stepping-stones up the lawn would be retained as far as the new paving; interruption of this long walk by the centre bed and tree is important, but the walk continues beyond that in the shape of a grass path between the vegetable plots. Across the western end of those plots I would plant a hedge of golden Beech, to be kept low, forming an additional break in the long box shape, and providing winter colour. Island beds, at present cut in the grass on the south side, would be replaced by a narrow bed against the wall, to be planted with such shade-tolerant plants as Hostas, Hellebores, Bergenias, Lungwort, *Anaphalis triplinervis*, Astrantias, Sedums, perennial Candytuft, and one or two Hydrangea 'Blue Wave'. To break up the walls, in addition to the existing Kerria, *Garrya elliptica*, *Viburnum Bodnantense* 'Dawn', and wall-trained plum, I would plant golden Privet at 18 ft. intervals and clip and train these into 'buttresses'. This has been done with success in the garden of Greyfriars at Worcester (see page 201 and Plate III a). The golden Privet, the Beech, the *Elaeagnus pungens maculata* and the Ukon cherry (which has gold-bronze leaves in spring) would echo each other pleasantly.

Then I would install some fairly high poles, with lattice attached, at the outer angles of the vegetable plots at the far end, and plant them with Winter Jasmine. These permanent frames could be used for training scarlet runner beans in summer; the Jasmine will survive this competition, and provide a gleam of yellow in the winter months. The existing apple-tree in the northern plot might be given a new companion tree on the south side. I should also like to see the beautiful grey-leaved pear, *Pyrus salicifolia pendula*, planted against the south wall opposite the summerhouse; its foliage would be particularly beautiful against the mellow Georgian brickwork.

This garden would benefit from several loads of fresh soil, for the amount of compost being made cannot compensate for years of starvation and the depredations of large trees on the other side of the wall, whose roots must tap a large area of garden. As there is a

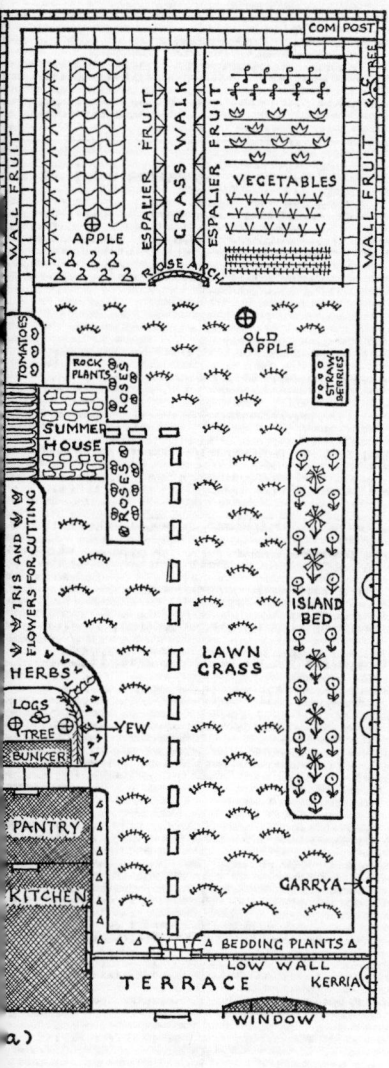
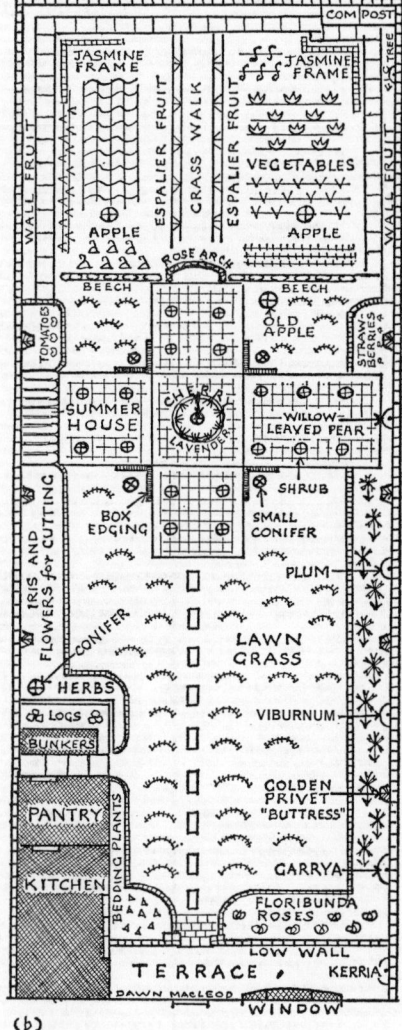

5 Georgian walled garden
a) original layout
b) as re-designed

side entrance from the street, the importation of soil would not be the messy business so often experienced in town houses where everything must be conveyed through the building. Given such a fillip, it would be worth while trying some floribunda roses against the terrace below the bay window. Here I would place also the only bedding plants: a few Nicotianas, preferably the lime green variety; with Heliotrope, Petunias of cream or Persian pink, and a selection of zonal Pelargoniums.

At this point it is useful to study the diagrams in Figure 5. Having completed the re-designed plan for this garden, Figure 5 (b), I thought it looked broader in relation to its length, and momentarily feared some error in measurement. It was soon clear that no mistake had occurred. It is simply an optical illusion, due to the placing of the introduced paving, the centrepiece, and emphasis given to the angles. If anyone doubts the influence that layout can have on the appearance of a garden, here is something that may help to convince him of the importance of design. Although the entire garden is not seen directly from above, the effect (in this example) of the transverse arms of the cross-shaped paving will be to make the occupant less conscious of being in a narrow box. The asymmetrical cross, with its longer arm thrown over the lawn, is designed to emphasize width.

A friend who needs no convincing has herself re-designed an old Cotswold cottage and its acre of garden with conspicuous success. I saw her present home at Quenington, now named Moyles Cottage, before she bought it: a little square box of a place, smothered in creeper, with some pig and hen slum tenements close beside the windows, pieces of decaying stone wall half buried in rank nettles, and a neglected orchard with some twenty good trees in it—mostly apples, among many other, less acceptable, elderly fruit trees and some intruders from the surrounding country.

The prospective purchaser, who had already made gardens in many parts of the world, looked at the orchard trees with the eye of a connoisseur—less for their potentialities as fruit-bearers than as a valuable mature background to the new garden she wanted to create in their shelter. Her design was planned from the start as part of the unspoilt countryside outside the walls, which were seldom above 4 feet in height and so did not act as barriers between the demesne and the village. The established orchard trees formed a suitable link between the pleasure-garden and the practical agricultural scene beyond.

This was not intended to be one of those secret, withdrawn, private oases which some people require. The Georgian retreat just discussed could not possibly be concerned with its surroundings, walled in by 8 feet of solid brickwork. Moyles Cottage was entirely different, and the owner wished to keep it as a sociable place, much of it visible from the road. Mrs. Fish at Lambrook had similar ideas. She looked upon her house and garden as part of the village, and liked to be integrated. In a small community this is probably the best outlook, particularly for someone who lives alone. It is another matter for those who are perpetually in crowds and want to escape into a private solitude at home, however small that may be.

The ground at Quenington sloped gradually upward from the rear of the cottage, which has more or less a north aspect at the back. A considerable amount of soil had to be removed to make way for the enlarged kitchen, cloakroom and a new drawing-room, which were built on in Cotswold stone with the traditional casement windows and stone mullions. Had the excavating and levelling been restricted to the amount of ground needed by the builder, a retaining wall and raised bed must have been constructed close to the house. But this did not please the owner, who had a much wider strip of ground levelled than was required for the work on the house. This area, about 7 feet wide by the back door, curving out to double that width in the centre opposite the French windows of her new room, was laid with large rectangular concrete slabs of the type used on sidewalks in towns. The cost of stone would have been prohibitive for so large an area. Wisely, I think, the designer chose a wide space surfaced with concrete material, rather than a pinched-up terrace paved with local stone. (Figure 6.)

This broad expanse of level paving is an essential element in the

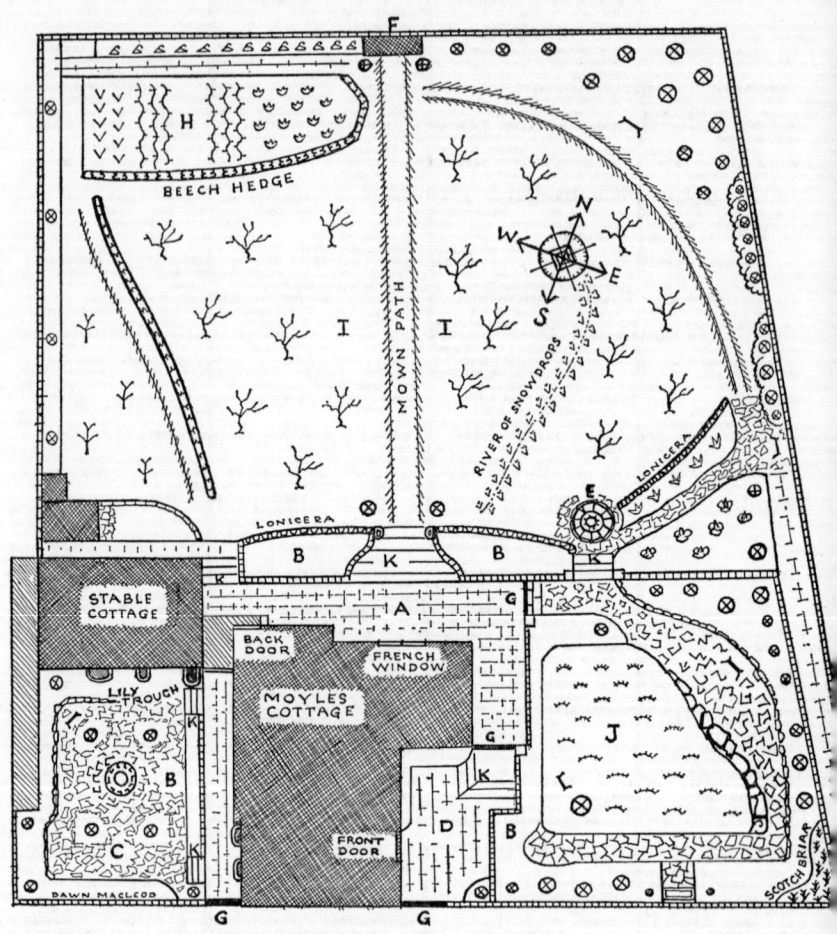

6 Garden at Quenington

A Terrace
B Raised beds
C Well court
D Sunk entrance court
E Sundial
F Summerhouse
G Wrought-iron gates
H Kitchen garden
I Orchard
J Lawn
K Steps

whole conception, contrasting with massed plantings of shrubs interspersed with foliage plants and bulbs, and with the overarching boughs of the orchard beyond. It is of practical value for sitting out, and it has resulted in the higher and rising ground being removed to a satisfactory distance from the house. Land that slopes uphill from a point near the ground floor windows is not easy to plant, or to live with, and often induces a feeling of constraint in the occupants of the house. The point is not always appreciated by purchasers of property who have not before met this problem, and then they are apt to leave the removal of the enclosing banks until too late. It is of course a much more expensive task to excavate soil after the house is finished and the garden made.

From the Quenington terrace a generously wide flight of stone steps leads up to the orchard level, with a dry wall on either hand to retain the raised beds. At each side of the top step are Irish yews, which have to be kept regularly shortened, thinned, and tied in so that their slim, dark accents are maintained in the correct size and shape. Beyond these, a broad and perfectly straight walk of mown grass takes the eye right through the orchard to a stone summerhouse built against the far wall. Spring bulbs are naturalized in the rougher grass beneath the trees, and in summertime Cow Parsley foams above the dwindling traces of narcissus and grape hyacinth. Once I remarked that a little stream would give life to this part of the garden, and pointed out a winding gulley which looked as though it had been carved out by water running between the trees. But no trace of a spring had appeared there within living memory.

For lack of water, we planted a counterfeit stream of snowdrops, hundreds of discarded bulbs which had multiplied too fast in another place. Early the next year, directly some light powder snow melted, there was our artificial river, looking at first like a drift of extra solid flakes left in the gulley. This idea might be carried out in many a small depression that bisects the orchard, copse, or rock garden. A stream of water could be simulated by Forget-me-nots, or Scillas. I wanted to prolong our floral rivulet by planting the native green-flowered Hellebore, which does well in the Cotswold country, and likes some shade. But it was feared that an old man who came to scythe the orchard grass in July would take off their heads. By that time of year he did little harm to the snowdrops. They were left alone to multiply and form a shining river, which rose in the New Year and ran dry before March winds awoke.

3

DESIGNING IN DETAIL

WHEN PLANNING a new garden, the four main considerations are (or should be) personal taste, practical requirements, size and type of ground, and financial resources. Provided that the tastes are not too grand—no antique statues, sculptures by Henry Moore, marble columns or rare plants being on your list—the fourth consideration is not quite as important as some people think. If one is short of cash, that disadvantage may be to a great extent overcome with time and patience. Small plants grow into a tall hedge in time, and these are not only cheaper to buy but usually do far better in the end. Many a shrub and climber may be propagated by the novice from a cutting, and this is really far more satisfying to own than a bought one raised by someone in a nursery. As for ground cover, one plant of Aubretia, Campanula or Pink will soon be induced to multiply, while others—such as Lady's Mantle, Anaphalis, Borage, Lamium and Bugle—invariably promote a population explosion without any encouragement.

Paths, especially paved ones, are inclined to be costly; but it is worth while to explore the dumps of local builders, or the town refuse tip, in search of material for these. Interesting patterns can be made from several different types in association: pebbles, with brick, surrounding a centre line of stone flag or cement block paving, is one way of using up an assortment of left-overs. Then there are the fabricated pavings, such as 'Noelite', which are cheaper than stone and obtainable in various tints; these may, in suitable places, be laid in chequer or other patterns. Or, given time for the job, the gardener may make his own hand-moulded slabs from a concrete mix. The Cement and Concrete Association, 52 Grosvenor Gardens, London S.W.1, issues a booklet called *Concrete in Garden-making* which supplies technical details.

Personal tastes, if these are inclined to waver, are best formed by visiting as many existing gardens as possible, small or large, then analysing both the gardens themselves and their effect on the beholder. Do they seem restful? If so, another question may be asked: Do we *want* our garden to be restful? There are many modern designers who set out to make everything they touch, whether it be a wall painting, a piece of sculpture, a dress fashion or a tea-set, what is commonly called 'exciting'. This approach is at present less often seen in garden planning, especially in this country, but it is beginning and will probably spread. Many 'Sunday painters' are practising modern techniques at home or in part-time art classes, while housewives of my acquaintance hand-print dress and furnishing materials based on very 'advanced' ideas. It is but a step to carry over such trends into the more conservative field of the garden plan.

In Scandinavia a school of garden design developed after World War II in which 'exciting' patterns composed of interpenetrating shapes of various paving materials and foliage became paramount. In Switzerland the rigid classical style was also superseded by much freer conceptions. In America all kinds of substances, including wood, metal, glass and concrete were used to form abstract patterns in association with plant forms and water. In Brazil the most completely fluid shapes of mosaic paving, water, and plant groupings have been designed exactly like abstract paintings by Burle Marx. (Figure 7 (a).)

That similar ideas will appear in Britain is fairly certain; in some larger schemes for factories and schools it has already been tried to some extent; but it should be remembered that climate must play a

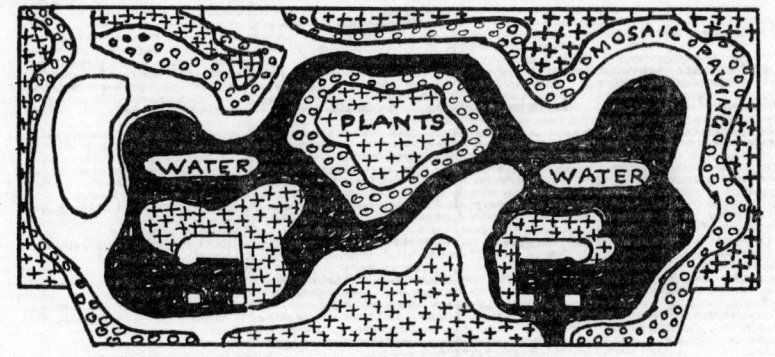

7 (a) Garden in Brazil by Burle Marx

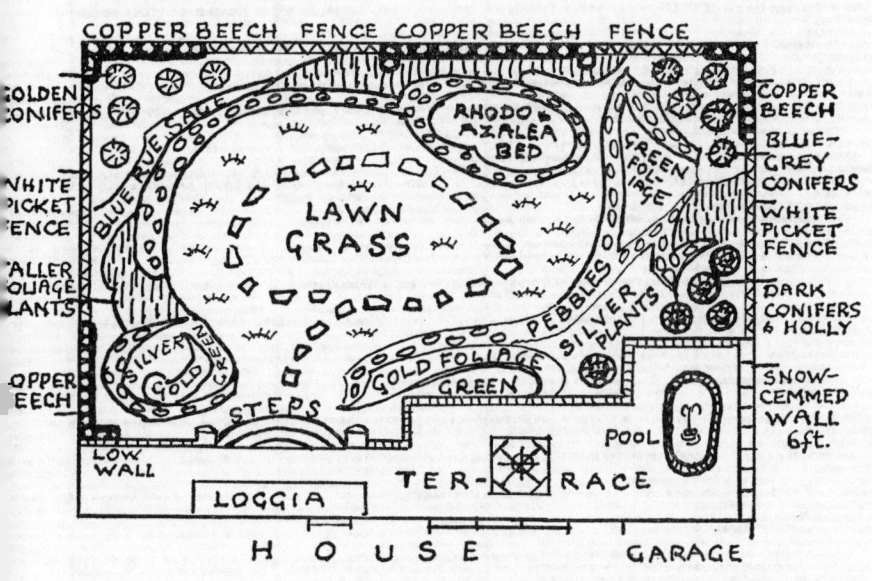

7 (b) 'Free' design in Britain

large part in determining the successful garden, and our grey skies and intermittent sunshine do not lend themselves to the highly dramatic scene. Water, which in drier places with clear atmospheres can be a rich source of blue in the picture, will more often be of a muddy tinge in Britain, and provide ruffled reflections of its surrounding trees and plants. In hotter countries the green of grass is a luxury, a rare item to be prized and fostered, set in other material like a gem stone in gold or platinum. Here in Britain we take it for granted and use it as the frame, not the centrepiece.

It may be of interest to record the results of some discussion with young people about the translation of modern ideas now current in the world of art, if that is possible, into terms of garden planning. A project to be designed and constructed by a teenage family in co-operation with their parents is shown in Figure 7 (b). This is a small piece of land in a modern suburb, but the rectangular shape has not, in the main, been permitted to influence the pattern formed within the boundaries, although those boundaries have been outlined, even accentuated, by the alternation of copper beech hedging in L and E shapes, with attractive white picket fencing.

The terrace behind the house was paved with grey-green Noelite, with an inset pool of oval shape, painted vivid turquoise blue. This is not of a size for swimming, but it was decided to use it for clear water without any plants; the younger members were given an 'Otter' submersible pump with fountain jet attachment, on condition that they kept the pool cleaned out regularly. Nothing looks worse than a clear pool of water which has lost its clarity and become silted up with dead leaves, insects and drowned worms. A 6-foot wall (belonging to a neighbouring house) was Snowcemmed, and its reflection helps to keep the crystal-water effect which was aimed at for the pool.

The focal point, if this irregular design may be said to have one, is a bed of the compact, small-leaved Rhododendrons, including 'Blue Bird' and 'Elizabeth', together with *Azalea mollis*; this is the only brilliant floral colour, except for plants in tubs on the terrace, in the whole of this part of the garden. Although the soil is far from

DESIGNING IN DETAIL

being lime-free, the family is set on having one group of these their favourite subjects. A walled-in site has been excavated, lined with flowers of sulphur, and filled with drainage material, peat, leafmould,* decayed farmyard manure and spent hops. With this burst of colour from about March to the end of May, and various groups of bulbs, there is thought to be sufficient brightness. Later in the season, when their front beds and the gardens of neighbours are filled with modern roses in fluorescent colours, the back garden oasis of quiet foliage provides a restful haven. Although I am doubtful about the wisdom of forcing plants into soil unsuited to their needs, this experiment is the result of thoughtful choice, and one can only hope for its success.

The central path consists of stepping-stones laid in a kind of flattened spiral in the grass, while the rest of the ground is reached by curious shapes made with blue-grey sea pebbles set in cement. These are planned as essential features of the pattern, but they are also of practical value in providing access to the beds. The grass sections here seem to take on something of the special quality which I have described as characteristic of those climes where green grass has to be cherished, with perpetual sprinkling or even built-in underground irrigation. The encirclement by curving patterns and foliage groups, together with the line of stepping-stones, forms here a setting for the green jewel. This lawn will require to be very carefully maintained in consequence.

Apart from the Rhododendrons and Azaleas there are no flowering shrubs in this part of the garden. Perhaps climbers (the redberried *Cotoneaster simonsii* or Pyracantha 'Knaphill Buttercup'— whose yellow fruits are not taken by birds) may in time be allowed to clothe parts of the white fencing, and some species of Clematis could be induced to entwine themselves in the Copper Beech. Groups of trees are arranged in three separate colours: dark Yew and Holly near the pool, blue-grey conifers in the western angle, and golden ones at the south corner, with ground-cover of

---

*Leafmould often has a lime content and should be used with care here.

Periwinkle, the dwarf coral-budded Comfrey (*Symphytum grandiflora*) and dark reddish-purple Bugle beneath them.

A garden room or loggia is attached to the house towards the side of the terrace, which narrows in three stages from the widest part containing the pool, and in front of this loggia three semi-circular steps lead down to the lawn. Beside them a spiral arrangement of small green, gold, and silver foliage plants, many of them fragrant herbs, provides interest at all seasons. For gold plants there are *Saxifraga umbrosa aurea*, Golden Marjoram, and *Chrysanthemum parthenium*; for silver, the lemon-scented Thyme 'Silver Queen', the so-called 'Curry Plant' *Helichrysum siculum*, and *Artemisia pedemontana*, with clumps of the feathery *Chrysanthemum haradjanii* or *C. poterifolium*. The bright green and scented Chamomile (*Anthemis nobilis* 'Treneague'), *Mentha requienii*, creeping *Euphorbia cyparissias* and even the old cottage plant *Oxalis floribunda* are used in contrast to the gold and silver of the others. The latter makes delightful compacted mounds of brilliant emerald in my garden, and if I do not want the shocking-pink flowers these are easily removed.

The taller plants, which are shown on the plan by vertical lines, are of mixed colours, from the bright silver of *Artemisia ludoviciana* and *A.* 'Lambrook Silver' (Plate II b) to the handsome blue Rue and blue-green *Euphorbia wulfenii*, the plum-purple of 'Red' Sage, the bronze feathery foliage of Black Fennel, and the various greens of Hostas and Hellebores. The making of such an unconventional garden provides interest for a family, but once the pattern has been established the maintenance often falls to the adult members. It is therefore as well to see that the main lines are set out in the more permanent material—in this case the grass, pebble paving and stepping-stones. Segregation of plants into unusual shapes, when they impinge one on another, is a difficult business; but in the case of Figure 7 (b) this is almost confined to the small plants near the steps. The pattern here might well be established by miniature 'hedges' of Winter Savory, Santolina, or even a dwarf Lavender, to divide green from gold and gold from grey foliage.

If irregular shapes of this sort annoy you, it is clearly not the type

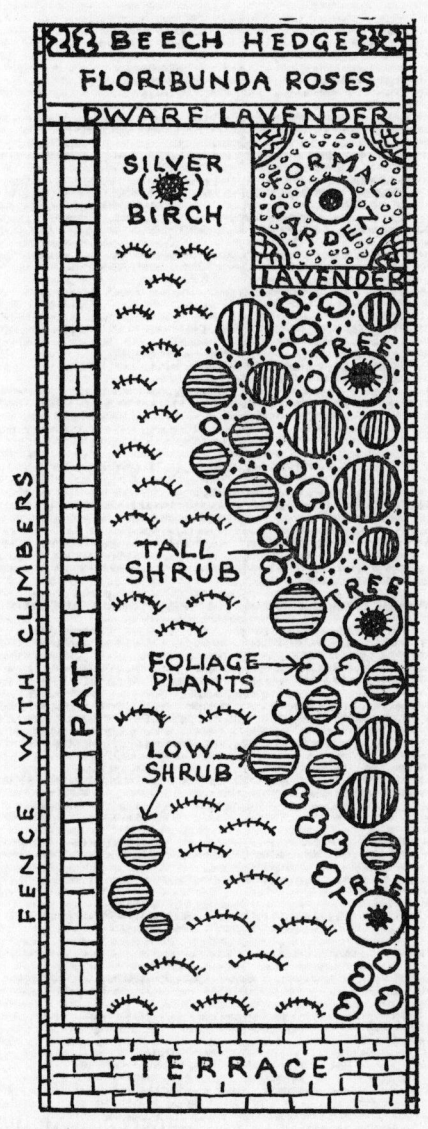

8 Simple design for a narrow garden

of design to choose. It is useful to be sure of what you disapprove, as that narrows down the field and makes selection easier. Another type of irregular planting, suitable for a small strip of ground, is shown in Figure 8. This appeals to many people, and is simpler to set out than the last example. It consists basically of a rectangular 'frame', formed by hedge, fence, screen trees or a combination of these, with a terrace for sitting-out near the house, and a path close to one boundary. A large part of the remainder is grassed, with a generous grouping of shrubs on the side opposite to the path. The shrub border is curved out to occupy more than half the width of the lawn, and then dwindles away towards the far end. This gives a feeling of mystery and makes the beholder curious to see what happens beyond the bulge—in this instance, a little formal garden. A few small shrubs may be spot-planted in the wider part of the grass, fairly near the path. The individual gardener interplants with ground cover; with *Erica carnea* (if the soil contains lime), Calluna and Daboecia if it is lime-free; with bulbs; Hellebore and Hosta; annual seeds and bedding-plants, or whatever else he pleases. A prostrate carpeting shrub which is almost weed-proof with me, *Cotoneaster dammeri*, spreads quickly and has good red berries and glowing autumn foliage. One of the few subjects that will penetrate this plant is the Hyacinth. A group of throw-outs from a pot have pushed through year after year, and the exercise has caused them to slim and grow taller, so that they are now half-way between a wild Hyacinth and a cultivated fat spike. As I do not care for the latter out-of-doors, this compromise has turned out well.

A point which must be remembered when planning and planting any garden is that commonly described as 'aspect'. Most good nurseries classify their climbers as 'suitable for a north wall', or 'requires a sunny aspect'. The only trouble about this system is that the less experienced gardeners are sometimes confused by the fact that the wall or fence on the northern boundary of their property is the one with a 'south aspect', and is often known as the 'south wall', while the southern boundary faces north and is therefore (to the plantsman) a 'north wall'. Once the distinction between geographical location and aspect has been grasped, this difficulty is at an end.

When it comes to planting wall fruit or climbing roses, creepers and the like upon the walls of a house, the colder, north, rooms are of course situated on the northern side of the building, and they face the *northern* boundary wall with its *south* aspect. This apparently simple matter is easy enough to work out; but we sometimes fail to appreciate the need for a moment's thought, and that is how mistakes occur, particularly when plants have been unpacked and are being put in quickly while the weather holds.

Which brings me back to the importance of planning on paper before anything is done to the ground. At Sissinghurst, the Nicolsons were for the first three years hampered by the vast accumulation of debris and the small amount of hired labour available for its removal. So Vita Sackville-West (Lady Nicolson) wrote: 'It was not until 1933 that any serious planting could be undertaken, but this was perhaps as well, because during those three impatient years we had time to become familiar with the "feel" of the place—a very important advantage which the professional garden-designer, abruptly called in, is seldom able to enjoy. A hundred times we changed our minds, but *as we changed them only on paper*, no harm was done and no expense incurred. Of course, we longed to start planting the hedges which were to be the skeleton of the garden, its bones and its anatomy, but had we been able to do so in those early days I am sure we should have planted them in the wrong place.' The italics here are mine, for surely this freedom to change our minds *on paper* is the marvellous bonus given to those who take the trouble to make plans in advance of their garden construction and planting.

Some say, 'It is all very well if you can draw, or have had some training at this sort of thing. How can anyone without talent or training hope to make useful diagrams?' Naturally it does require a little practice, and equally true is it that a simple rectangle is easier to plot than an irregular shape. You do not need skill or training to make the diagrams shown in Figure 1. The land may be measured without going to the expense of buying a surveyor's measuring tape, for a length of rope with knots at foot, or even three foot, intervals (knots made with the aid of a school ruler or dressmaker's tape-measure) is adequate for the approximate figures here needed. There is no need to be able to draw straight lines at right angles to the sides of the diagram, because squared paper can be bought quite cheaply, and these squares are used both to calculate scale and to supply ready-made lines, to be thickened where required by means of pencil and ruler. The curved path need not be drawn freehand—a length of string placed on the paper is manipulated to give the shape, and then traced in with pencil.

Before we moved to the bungalow shown at Figure 3, planning on paper was used for another purpose. On a drawing of the rooms I placed little cut-out shapes representing our furniture, drawn to scale, and thus the rooms were arranged beforehand and surplus furniture disposed of in advance of the removal. Even carpets were laid—on top of the furniture, and cut from tracing-paper, so that it could be seen just how much and where heavy pieces impinged on them. This was before the days of fitted carpets, and when they were taken up annually to be 'beaten' it was an advantage to have little or none under the big chests-of-drawers, or tallboys. Later, I have used this technique for preliminary planning of gardens. Transparent circles for trees, laid on top of paths and beds, show how much shade will be developed when the trees have matured. Again, most good nurseries give approximate dimensions of trees and shrubs after they reach maturity, and this information is helpful to the planner. A great deal of useful knowledge may be gained from careful reading of a good plant catalogue, such as Jackman's *Planter's Handbook*.*

Measuring up the irregular shape of the Sussex garden in Figure 3 was a little harder to do. I am not sure how professional surveyors would go about this task, but I began with the bungalow. It is fairly easy to measure a building, especially a small, new one of that sort, with walls all set at right angles to one another. Old houses were often fitted to the most oddly shaped sites, and in consequence are

*George Jackman & Son, Woking Nurseries Ltd., Woking, Surrey.

DESIGNING IN DETAIL

found to have curved fronts, or rooms with an obtuse angle at one side of the door and an acute angle at the other. Our bungalow gave no such trouble, having been planned on a drawing-board with T-square and rule. When the measurements had been made, I decided to use the scale of one-eighth of an inch to a foot, and drew the plan of the building on a large sheet of paper. Kitchen paper in a roll is good enough for the job, especially for a first try. When the rough is completed, the final draft is easier to make accurately on squared paper.

I continued the work of measuring, by projecting the four walls—using rope and pegs—until these met the boundary fences. The distances from house to paling were then measured, and marked in on the plan. Two dots to the south proved to be equidistant from the house; then these were joined, and continued until they ran off the paper. The other side was plotted in the same way, but it ran away outwards towards the road and inwards to the river. So far this seemed easy, and looked right as compared with the actual ground; but how were the curved frontage and river bank to be established? I tried the same idea, using four points along the front of the bungalow: the outside walls were continued by means of ropes and pegs until they met the frontage, and two parallel lines drawn from the inner wall of the projecting room and from the front door, until they met the front paling. This provided four points along the frontage, from which the curve could be drawn in, freehand. A check on the correctness then suggested itself. A line from each corner of the building was stretched diagonally to the corresponding corner of the front garden and measured, for comparison with the shape arrived at by drawing my curve through the original four points until it cut the side lines. The diagonal measurement was so close to that on my plan that it seemed good enough. The whole plot had now been outlined on paper to the scale given, plus the compass-points, and planning could begin. (Figure 9.)

If the house was built for you, or bought new from a contractor, it is usually possible to obtain a copy of the ground plan, which will save trouble. Or, if there are schoolchildren around, the exercise of measuring and plotting their house and garden on paper would give them an outlet for knowledge acquired in the maths lesson. The garden planned on paper will not, unless one owns an observation tower or a helicopter, ever be seen quite as it now appears, and there is need to guard against being carried away by enthusiasm for some intricate network of line-drawing which might be impracticable to translate into grass, paving and plant forms. It is desirable to cultivate a kind of double vision, looking down in a godlike manner upon the plan and yet imagining, if not a worm's-eye view, at least a man-high one of each unit in the design. All this should take account of the compass-points too.

Because the technique is difficult to begin with, it is sound policy not to embark upon laying out the entire garden, but to construct it in sections, one part at a time. This gives everyone a feeling that something is being done, while allowing the worker to feel his way

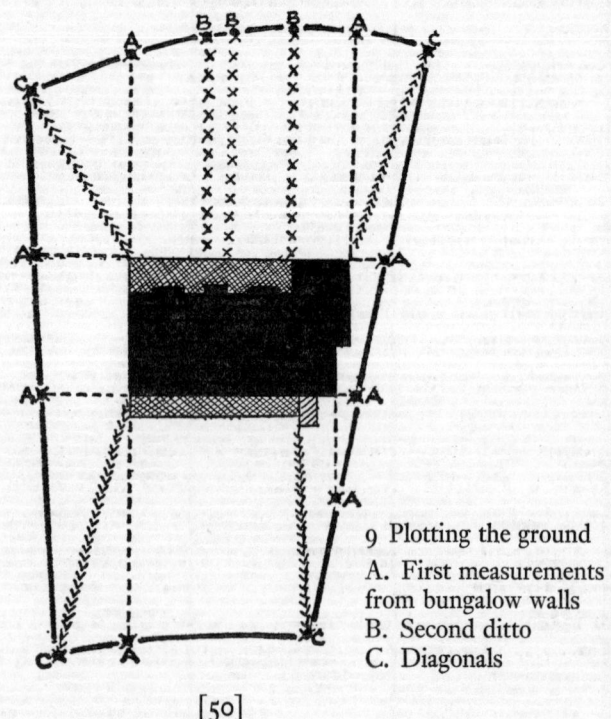

9 Plotting the ground
A. First measurements from bungalow walls
B. Second ditto
C. Diagonals

DESIGNING IN DETAIL

gradually and to gain valuable knowledge of his particular piece of land. Even so, surprises will inevitably occur. The soil itself will often vary in quite a small area, and there may be several microclimates in one mini-garden, either natural to the site or produced by the manner in which walls, shrubs, hedges and trees have been disposed. Although not a newcomer to gardening, I was taken by surprise in recent years when the setting up of three wattle hurdles to screen a small sun-bathing lawn in my walled herb garden—a place of hot, well-drained soil on a southern slope—converted the bed to the north of the screen from a place for Mediterranean-type plants into the cool, damp home suited to Bergamot and its relatives the Mints and Pennyroyal.

It follows that any splitting up of ground into compartments, whether this is done by hardware or by living growths, creates warm or cool patches, and, in the case of fence or wall, space for climbers with north and south faces—or east and west aspects, as the case may be. To break down the process still further, it may be said that each large plant creates some shade for a smaller subject under its wing. So the gardener may tuck in the little Cyclamen, or the Lily-of-the-Valley, or Solomon's Seal, or 'Bleeding Heart' in the solid shade created by *Viburnum rhytidophyllum* or a holly bush, while keeping the rock rose and the golden Marjoram on the sunny side. The fascinating business of making the best use of existing conditions, and creating others at will to suit what you desire to grow, is never-ending, and the education of the gardener requires a long lifetime. In a world where so much emphasis is placed on youth, good gardeners still improve with age, like port wine.

PERSONAL TASTES

WHAT A controversial word, *taste*. Except on the tongue, we are seldom agreed about even its basic meaning, and much less are we able to define our own tastes in a way comprehensible to other people—perhaps not to our own satisfaction either. Yet they are real and important attributes of life and cannot be brushed aside. Sometimes we say that we know what we like; but hesitate and grow vague when questioned in detail about our likes and dislikes. Unless we really do know exactly what kind of garden we like and want, certain preliminary approaches to the problem may be helpful.

First of all a list can be drawn up of what we must have (or cannot do with) in our new garden. If there are children, we must surely provide room for them to play, and we cannot hope to raise rare or delicate plants within their reach. If there are very small children, then we cannot have a pool—or nothing larger than a puddle—because of the danger. If we aim to specialize in alpines, we must have a sheltered and well-drained place for them, and cannot allow trees to drip on the plants. If we are determined to cultivate a quantity of fruit and vegetables in a small area, then in all probability we must forgo a lawn; although a broad grass walk might be managed between two strips of kitchen garden. And if the family is addicted to outdoor meals, we shall be expected to make a good paved terrace for sitting out, and perhaps a garden room, summer-house, or arbour as well.

In Britain there is inevitably the question of pets. The dog—well, it may be the intention of the owner to take it out for regular walks and forbid the use of the garden; but sooner or later the regime will break down, and it is best to acknowledge this from the start. Young dogs, and bitches of any age, are fatal to a lawn. Nobody wants to see fresh green turf with large brown or yellow spots on it. If a strip of rough grass is provided in some unobtrusive place, and the young creature trained to make use of it, that habit will continue throughout its life. Most dogs prefer longish grass, so that an older one can usually be trained to use this instead of the lawn. Cats are unmoved by praise or blame, but they take notice of carbolic disinfectant powder sprinkled around seed-beds in springtime. Other people's cats can be deterred from using one's garden for sanitary purposes by a well-aimed hose jet, or water slung from a bucket. Their amorous clinches (audible though invisible in the dark) do even more harm to plants than the digging of dead-wells. Spent electric light bulbs—hurled, not at the offenders, but at a wall or hard paving near by—will go off pop and cause considerable alarm at night. Sometimes the fond owner will keep his pet indoors after dark, to avoid further explosions. In terms of garden planning, it is worth making a census of the local cat population. If this seems unduly large, a barrier of wire-netting may be installed round the seed-beds. This will be particularly awkward to surmount if it is not strained taut, but allowed to wobble.

The larger quadrupeds, if such are included among our family treasures, should be confined outside the garden boundaries. Lesser ones, among them rabbits, guinea-pigs and mice, must be kept in well-made hutches with securely fastened doors. If rabbits and guinea-pigs are taken out for airings, a portable wooden pen with wired top is essential, and its placing on the lawn should be strictly taboo. A peppering of small brown or yellow blotches on greensward is just as disfiguring as fewer, but larger, circles made by puppies and bitches. The patch of rough grass which has already been suggested for the latter will serve also for the rabbit run, if the land has been levelled to prevent escapes under the sides of the pen. Grass must be clipped to a couple of inches for rodents to eat. After their presence the dog, bitch or pup will be attracted by the scent, and this is all to the good when both types of pet share the same 'comfort station'. In my own family a disused conservatory behind the house was given to us for pet-keeping, on condition that the creatures were not spread around the rest of the demesne. Although we children adhered to our side of the bargain, this concession came to an abrupt end when a visiting adult of portly figure fell through the tiled floor into a rabbit bury neatly prepared for his doom. The tremendous burrowing power of even a small rabbit makes the permanent outdoor wired rabbit-run a grave hazard to the keen gardener. A wire barrier must be put down below the soil to a depth of 2 feet, and this is apt to rot away unseen. The same trouble occurs when fences are wired to keep wild rabbits out, as the wire above ground may still look in good condition when that below the surface has perished. As a child I was entirely on the side of Beatrix Potter's Benjamin Bunny; but the fierce gardener, Mr. MacGregor, has gained much support with the passing years.

One of the most attractive small pets, visually speaking, is the pigeon. Unfortunately it is too destructive to be allowed loose in a small garden. Kept in an aviary it is a pathetic prisoner, deprived of free flight, and loses most of its decorative value as a live garden ornament. Even if one's own tame white flock is too well bred and well fed to damage plants, it will act as a decoy to others—often wild birds with no scruples whatever. Pigeons on the wing are best left to those with farms or large estates, where depredations can be absorbed without the disastrous results that occur in smaller gardens. This being a sore point with me, I overcame the frustration to some extent by modelling static pigeons in white plaster as substitutes for the real thing. (See Chapter 9.)

Strange as it may seem, the humble and immobile vegetable may also be the subject of argument, even of acrimony. This concerns the arbitrary line so often drawn between 'kitchen' and 'pleasure' gardens: a respectable tradition which one may like or dislike but not ignore. In rural districts the old cottage mixture, which admitted no class distinctions as between the Scarlet Runner and the crimson Carnation, the cabbage and the Crown Imperial, continues placidly to produce homely effects which seem to delight many visitors who would not tolerate such arrangements in their own gardens. At first sight this is just one more example of a 'them' and 'us' attitude of mind, suggesting that what is all right for them would not do for us. It may be, though, that something deeper and more subtle plays a part—the great (if unconscious) skill with which the country cottage gardener makes pleasing pictures from his jumble.

That is not easy to achieve anywhere, and particularly difficult when the shape of the ground is a rigid rectangle set in an urban row of houses with similar plots. A pleasant irregularity of land, hedging and trees frequently gives the cottage gardener an excellent start, and sets the key for his planting. I have tried to make classless societies of plants in sophisticated settings, but never with much success. A tentative experiment in Canada consisted merely of inserting groups of 'Continuity' lettuce between clumps of dark blue Lobelia—a scheme which at first tricked the eye because, in their reddish foliage, both plants were alike. But my neighbours could not have been more horrified had I put a line of Brussels sprouts along the road.

Since that day I have seen in England large plants of the Variegated Kale used boldly between flowering plants and shrubs with commendable effect, and more commonly the handsome Globe Artichoke is admitted to the back of a herbaceous border. The increasing interest in flower arrangement and the consequent search for unusual foliage may have been responsible. Perhaps the same art will gradually do away with segregation altogether. Herbs are already accepted as ornamental garden subjects in many quarters, and indeed nobody could fault the stately Fennel, green and bronze; the various coloured Thymes; the several Marjorams, green and gold; Savory and Hyssop; Sweet Cicely, Angelica, Lovage and other umbellifers; and of course the fancy Mints, with Bergamot and Pennyroyal.

Most of us accept apple trees here and there amid flowers, but bush fruits are apparently taboo as yet. In my present small herb garden there is one excellent fruiting bush of Black Currant 'Boskoop Giant', which provokes more criticism and stares than anything else. It is a comely shrub, well pruned and attractive, to my mind, at all seasons. It turns a deep yellow in autumn, smells good at all times, and the musky scent blends well with Thyme and Sage, Bergamot, Lemon Verbena, Curry Plant and Lavender. Why, then, does it cause so much fuss? Were I to substitute a bush of *Ribes sanguineum*, whose smell is unpleasing to me and which makes a less valuable foliage plant in autumn, and with no edible fruit, this would be approved without question. I do not even drape the fruiting Black Currant in netting or old lace screens, but allow the birds to take their pick. So this appears to be an instance of unthinking prejudice. Ours is said to be a permissive society, with barriers tumbling (and some new curtains going up); but the gardener in the main prefers conservatism. Provided that only what is good is conserved, I have no quarrel with that—which brings us back to the matter of taste.

At the Cotswold garden shown in Figure 6 can be seen good examples of what are called 'open' and 'closed' plans. I have not yet mentioned the latter section, which is in the small piece of ground in front of the single-storey stable. This (now made into living quarters) adjoins the kitchen of the house, set at right angles both to it and to the next-door cottage, so that between them the three buildings form an E-shape without the centre bar. The fourth boundary of the enclosure, to the south, is a wall of some 5 feet in height. As the neighbouring cottage turns its blind, windowless back, the only break is caused by a wrought-iron entrance gate and pathway from the road outside.

The main part of this garden has already been described. It is composed of 'open', informal plantings to harmonize with an established orchard, leading the eye through trees to rolling farmland beyond. The enclosed courtyard, when entered from a broad terrace behind the house, is a complete change from that scene: a cosy, sun-drenched place of little paved paths with creeping thymes, sedums and *Anemone pulsatilla* in the crevices. In the centre a wrought-iron well-head and bucket is set above a little circular lily-pond, there being no well. A purist might quibble at bucket-and-chain installed purely as an ornament; but, as this was brought from a former home and not purchased specially, I would dismiss that objection. In size and shape it is exactly right for its new position, giving a strong, vertical emphasis where a tree would be out of place. Some small clipped bushes of box give solidity at a lower level.

On the wall of what was the stable a flourishing *Hydrangea petiolaris* is lovely at all times, with rough reddish stems, the coarse cream lace of its flower heads, and (in a good season) golden autumn foliage. It is accompanied by a self-clinging climbing spindleberry. This Euonymus keeps its evergreen foliage fresh in the worst of winter weather, is developing a silver variegation, berries abundantly, and is a wall shrub well worth growing—if you can get it. It looks like *Euonymus radicans* 'Silver Queen', except for the berries and the rampant growth. I have not before seen an evergreen Euonymus which berried and climbed with such vigour.

Placed in front of these climbers, the stone sink from the cottage kitchen has been filled with a layer of drainage material, followed by a mixture of loam, sand, leaf-mould and peat, and planted with *Lilium auratum*. In this sheltered spot they reach in a good year a height of 8 feet and fill both courtyard and the rooms opening on to it with their scent. They were planted in some 18 inches of soil in this very deep trough, and have had more added as growth progressed; being stem-rooting, they have multiplied. They are slightly shaded by the climbing Hydrangea, by its large sprays leaning forwards over the trough, and are kept moist in dry spells with rainwater from a butt. The owner does not believe in subjecting them to the mineral and chemical content of the piped supply. They amply repay her care—see Plate V b.

Mrs. Money has adopted the usual segregation of vegetables and fruit, which are sited at the top of the orchard and screened with a beech hedge. Her exception to this rule is the edible rhubarb

(*Rheum rhaponticum*), grown in a large clump at the lower edge of the orchard, in full view of terrace and flower garden. Not a lover of the succulent stems, she allows the plant freedom to flower—which it does abundantly, throwing irregular creamy plumes up to a height of 6 or 7 feet. Even in late autumn the seeding spikes, now sorrel-red, are a decorative element in the scene: but one that is in perpetual danger from jobbing gardener and guests, who think it a kindness to chop down and clear away all spent material. Those of us who prefer to have a winter garden furnished with seed-heads are ever at risk in this way.

It may fairly be said that good taste has been used in the making of this garden, and it is there for all to see when open to the public under the National Gardens Scheme (Gloucester section). Within an acre of ground the designer has gratified her liking both for the cosy, miniature, formal arrangement, which in modern language may be called a 'room' garden, and then, beyond this enclosure, for the open, natural planting which becomes progressively more natural as it approaches the boundary with farmland. Each sector is in perfect harmony with the chosen site, and nothing looks as though it has been imposed on nature by force. Obviously a garden is an artefact; but the degree of artifice employed in the making must be adjusted to its setting if it is to give a completely satisfying impression to the viewer, who obtains here a splendid contrast, together with a valuable shock of surprise as he passes from one part to the other.

When discussing tastes, we must not forget those possessed by the plants themselves. The first Great Divide runs between the lime-haters, which must have acid soil, and the lime-lovers or lime-tolerant, which need not. I say *need* not, because many lime-tolerant plants will thrive among ericaceous companions that belong squarely on the acid side of the fence. Lists of plants soon weary the eye, and are better in an appendix where they can be ignored until required. But I believe it is generally true, as a rule-of-thumb, that plants with 'needles' or leathery leaves of narrow shape, mostly dark green, will appreciate acid soils. Think of heathers and whins, Scots pines and bracken—though the latter is not very dark in colour. The Rhododendrons which associate with these other subjects are not narrow-leaved, but they do have a leathery texture. I remember particularly the great specimens of *R. sinogrande* in the gardens of Inverewe, Wester Ross. I used to pick up fallen leaves much larger than my own feet, and so tough that we thought of re-soling sandals with them.

Generally speaking, the silver foliage and golden plants are more at home in alkaline soils and prefer drier, warmer climates. So far as I know, dry soils are seldom acid. (Soil experts may disagree, however.) Apart from soil and climate, there are less obvious tastes among plants which must be of interest to the keen gardener. How many like to have their roots underneath a rock or stone—plants far removed from the little alpines for which rocky anchorages are commonly provided. I believe this liking may be partially responsible for the success of so many self-sown specimens. Their seed may have fallen on stony ground, but quite often the small roots creep below a helpful lump where moisture is retained through drying winds of spring, and so the seedling thrives better than its fellows sown in a bed that has been carefully raked free of stones by the gardener.

It is not difficult to prepare lists of sun-lovers and shade-fanciers, and of unfussy plants which will do well in either situation, but certain families prefer a little of both. The Clematis does particularly well if rooted in a shady spot whence it may climb up into full sun. The scarlet-flowered Flame Flower, *Tropaeolum speciosum*, flourished at Inverewe with its roots on the shady side of a clipped hedge of *Rhododendron ponticum* and its flowers poking out against the sun. This lovely plant is exceedingly hard to grow in the southern part of Britain, however much care is paid to its position and nurture. It may truly be said to have a taste for the North.

Most of us know that there are groups of plants which grow right in water, such as Water Lilies, Water Hawthorn, Flowering Rush, Reed Mace and Arrowhead. Others prefer the damp verges of pond or river, and some will spread from bank to shallow water; I can recall *Iris laevigata*, a hardy blue Iris from Japan and Siberia, which seemed equally happy in shallow water and on damp ground at Inverewe. This plant was at one time confused with *I. kaempferi*, also Japanese, which cannot stand being in water during the winter months, as the roots will then rot. They are very much alike, but *I. kaempferi* has a midrib to its leaves which can be felt more easily than it is seen. The Sweet Flag (*Acorus calamus*), a native British plant which in past times was used as a medicinal and aromatic herb, grows well on boggy verges but seldom produces its quaint brown 'horn' flowers unless its root is right in the water. The gorgeous Kingcup is equally happy in or out of the water; our native *Caltha palustris* looks better in a semi-wild layout, and the cultivated variety, *C. palustris flore pleno*, makes a fine show in more sophisticated water-gardens.

Bog Primulas are a host in themselves, and the native herb, Bistort (*Polygonum bistorta*), likes damp ground so well that it sometimes threatens to swamp everything else. The plumy Astilbe, Meadowsweet, and Rodgersia mingle happily with Hosta and Hemerocallis (Day Lily); if there is plenty of room, the impressive elephantine foliage of *Gunnera manicata* will thrive in boggy places too. Shrubs for really wet ground are fewer, but willows and Dogwoods are at home there, and the curious corkscrew Hazel, *Corylus contorta*. The New Zealand Flax, *Phormium tenax*, will do in moist soil, given a mild climate. We made hedges from this and the purple-leaved *P. tenax purpureum* at Inverewe; but as the plant belongs to the Lily family, perhaps it is wrong to call it a shrub. The gay, slow-growing Alder, *Alnus incana aurea*, is well worth trying.

Plants with a taste for poor soil on well-drained and sunny banks are just as numerous as the damp-choosers. Hypericum—the old Rose of Sharon or St. John's Wort, so often seen in dank shrubberies, will flourish in sun and grow in very poor soil. The taller *H. patulum* will also do well, and the shrubby Potentillas. *Caryopteris clandonensis*, an aromatic grey shrub, is covered with mauve-blue flowers in August. The cascading yellow Broom, *Genista lydia*, will thrive here, and another group of Brooms, named *Cytisus*, particularly like dry and hot conditions. *C. praecox* begins flowering in mid-April, and for the seven or eight years of its life will probably retain its compact shape. The smaller *C. kewensis* blooms in May. Then there is the sturdy silver-grey *Senecio laxifolius*, the woolly-leaved Jerusalem Sage (*Phlomis fruticosa*), and most of the Hebe tribe, known to older gardeners as Veronica. Of the aromatic Rosemary, Lavender and Southernwood, it can be said that they are more fragrant when grown on hot, poor soil than in lush situations. But they do not care for being blown about.

It is doubtful whether any trees—or even smaller subjects—have a definite liking for wind, but some will certainly tolerate it better than others. The gardens at Inverewe, which are now world-famous, were made by Osgood Mackenzie just over a century ago on a windswept sea-girt promontory in the north-west of Scotland, described by his daughter Mairi as having 'nothing between it and Labrador'. The only shrub in sight in 1864 was a dwarf willow about 3 feet high. Trees were put in as shelter belts, and the young owner then waited for over fifteen years before beginning to plant his garden. A thick planting of Corsican Pine (*Pinus nigra* var. *calabrica*) and Scots Pine (*P. sylvestris*) made the first line of defence, but the native Scots Pine was less tough than expected, and in after years Mackenzie advocated *Pinus montana* with Corsican Pine.

Within his defences he later placed Beech, Birch and Larch; Rowan (or Mountain Ash), Wellingtonia, Douglas Fir, and various kinds of Abies, Cupressus, Thuja and Oak, together with the Gums (Eucalyptus) which are now one of the glories of the place. An unusual Oak, *Quercus sessiliflorus* var. *variegata*, has become a very handsome tree and was recently described in *Garden News* as the finest variegated plant the writer had ever seen. Below the trees, that obvious source of quick shelter, the native *Rhododendron ponticum*, was planted liberally and has provided masses of dense cover for more tender subjects. The late Mairi Sawyer (*née* Mackenzie) having discovered its drawbacks—not least the admixture of thousands of 'Ponti' seedlings with those from her rarer species Rhododendrons (a jumble which it was once my task to sort)—

said that she would have preferred hedges of *Griselinia littoralis*, *Escallonia langleyensis*, and *Olearia hastii*. (Plan of Inverewe, Figure 13.)

Lower down still, used as ground-cover rather than shelter, *Pernettya mucronata* (Prickly Heath) with its plentiful, large and long-lasting berries in mixed colours of white, pink and crimson, is one of the most attractive plants known to me, whether it is seen growing out-of-doors, in a pot, or used as cut-flower decoration. But this treasure, so often sold at Christmas time to unsuspecting customers with alkaline soil, will only thrive in acid soil; so the pot-plant dwindles and dies when put out in an alkaline garden. It likes sun, and care must be taken to procure some male plants among the female ones in order to obtain berries. So far nobody has put a hermaphrodite form on the market.

Seaworthy shrubs recommended by another expert (Christine Kelway) and which do not require acid conditions are Gorse, Tamarisk, Sea Buckthorn, *Elaeagnus ebbingei* and *Senecio monroi* from New Zealand, *Hebe dieffenbachii* and *H.* 'Blue Gem' and *Atriplex halimus*. For tree-planting on bleak coasts she suggests *Pinus nigra austriaca* and *Cupressus leylandii*, the latter being frost-proof. One seldom sees the Monterey Pine (*Pinus radiata* syn. *insignis*) mentioned, although at Inverewe it grew right at the edge of our sea-loch 'with its toes in salt water', as the owner described it.

From trees and shrubs on windswept coasts to subjects fit for inland woods may seem a far cry; yet of course the same plants will mostly do even better when given kinder conditions. Only the Sea Buckthorn (*Hippophae rhamnoides*) seems to prefer a tang of salt in the wind.* One of the many things noticed by that great gardener Gertrude Jekyll was the value of the common Laurel as a small woodland tree. She had 'a rather strong dislike' of clipped laurels in a shrubbery, but admired their smooth grey stems 'like elephants' trunks or some kind of grey serpent' when she saw them growing wild and untouched by man in her local Surrey woods. 'They all seem to be about the same age, and must have been planted early

*Male and female specimens must be planted if the amber fruits are to set.

in the century, for they were already old trees when I was a child.'*
The Squire who ordered them little thought that a famous gardener
would praise his plantations long after he was dead.

Miss Jekyll also refers to plant companionships—a curious subject which is often met with in old herbals. There one may read of the reported dislike of Basil for Rue, which were said never to thrive together; or of the power of Chamomile to act as a 'herb doctor' for the cure of sick plants near which it is set; or Bacon's dictum that 'Rew doth prosper much and become stronger if set by a fig-tree'; or of the maternal care taken of other herbs by Elder (the Elder Mother)—and deem it all to be entertaining fiction. Surely the sensible Miss Jekyll would not indulge her imagination in vague fancies? Yet she writes of what seems to be an affinity of the Northern Hard Fern (*Blechnum boreale*) for the Holly tree. 'I do not know if it is the same elsewhere, but I think of three damp hedge-banks with wet ditches at the foot, where there are both Hollies and Blechnums; in most cases where a Holly occurs there is a Blechnum just under it. Two of the hedges are three miles apart, and the third is six miles away from the nearest of the other two.' She clearly thinks the subject worth pondering. A young student of horticulture or botany might choose to make a special study of plant hostility, or concord—long and difficult though it would certainly be.

Woodland plants often have a tough time in our cultivated gardens. The delicate Woodruff, which smells so powerfully of hay when dried, belongs to shady places. Today it is in demand as ground cover, and may frequently be seen perched on dry banks in the sun, where (if it survives at all) it becomes but a poor, parched shadow of its real self. The Foxglove also suffers from being taken out of its rightful place, in semi-shade spiring up towards the sun. The Lily-of-the-Valley usually obtains better treatment, possibly because it refuses to accept sunbaths and drought. But the Primrose and Polyanthus—how commonly the cultivated forms are bedded out in some sunny border near the house, to give 'spring colour', only to wilt and wither too soon. How much finer the Polyanthus

* *Home and Garden* by Gertrude Jekyll (Longmans 1900).

looks at the foot of small trees in flickering light and shade, as it is seen, thickly planted, in the Nut Plat at Sissinghurst. There it makes what the Nicolsons called 'a Persian carpet effect' when in bloom, and afterwards the leaves stay green for some time, until other foliage rises up and veils their decay.

We are here concerned with matters of taste, and I believe that in using cultivated species of the Primrose family in the semi-wild Nut Plat, rather than wildings from the woods, the makers of this garden displayed great refinement. Apart from the villainy of robbing wild places of their dwindling treasure, it is really *not* quite right—and never looks it—to introduce wild plants into an artificially contrived garden, even if the creation is a group of woodland trees or (as at Sissinghurst) a plantation of local cob nuts and filberts. There is always a hint of falseness about the transplanted Primrose and Bluebell, and still more when plants of Edelweiss and Saxifrage are brought to a rockery from some mountain region of Europe. It is hard to say why, for so many plants have been grown for us from seed found by plant-hunters all over the world. But it does seem better to raise them in cultivation from the beginning, and that is true also of our native subjects.

PART TWO

5

TREES AND SHRUBS

NOW THAT so many gardens are small, and the great deciduous trees associated with our landscape are being felled in such large numbers, the deft use of vertical growths inside our fences has become an even more important matter—both for the possibilities of extending the range and quantity of plants that we can accommodate, and for the benefit of height and vertical emphasis that would otherwise be missing. What a deprivation it is! One or two small flowering trees are seldom adequate. This aspect of gardens deserves just as much attention as is commonly given to pool and patio and paved path.

It might be a blessing if the Poplar came back into fashion, for it is easy to grow and makes a valuable 'exclamation mark' when competently sited. *Populus bolleana* is perhaps the best to choose for a small garden. It could reach a height of 20 feet in seven years. But poplar roots can be destructive of foundations, so this tree should be kept well away from buildings and garden walls. Everyone who visits Sissinghurst must notice the groups of Lombardy Poplars at the boundaries of the demesne, which seem to echo and complement the great central tower. If the scene is visualized without those Poplars it is startling to discover how much they would be missed. An excellent specimen tree for small gardens, the Silver

Birch also makes a fairly slim and upright shape. Then there is the Lime, an old inhabitant of the English garden, which may be pruned or pleached. The Lime Walk at Sissinghurst has charm and dignity at all seasons. *Tilia corallina* has red twigs, *T. euchlora* yellow ones, and *T. petiolaris* has pendulous branches and silver linings to the dark foliage. It is also very sweet-scented. If I had room for one of the larger trees I would choose a Lime, if only for the murmur of bees in the blossom.

Given enough space, the handsome 'Incense Cedar' (*Libocedrus decurrens*), which is seen to perfection at Westonbirt, makes a splendid green column. Presumably this Libocedrus was named 'decurrens' to describe the unusual arrangement of its fanshaped sprays, which run round the trunk spirally. It seems to me to give better value as a green fastigiate conifer than the commoner Lawson's Cypress, *C. erecta viridis*. It needs room, so that the ridged chocolate-coloured bark on the short length of unbranched stem shows up against the vivid emerald foliage, and the spiral form is displayed. These charms are lost if planting is too close to other trees.

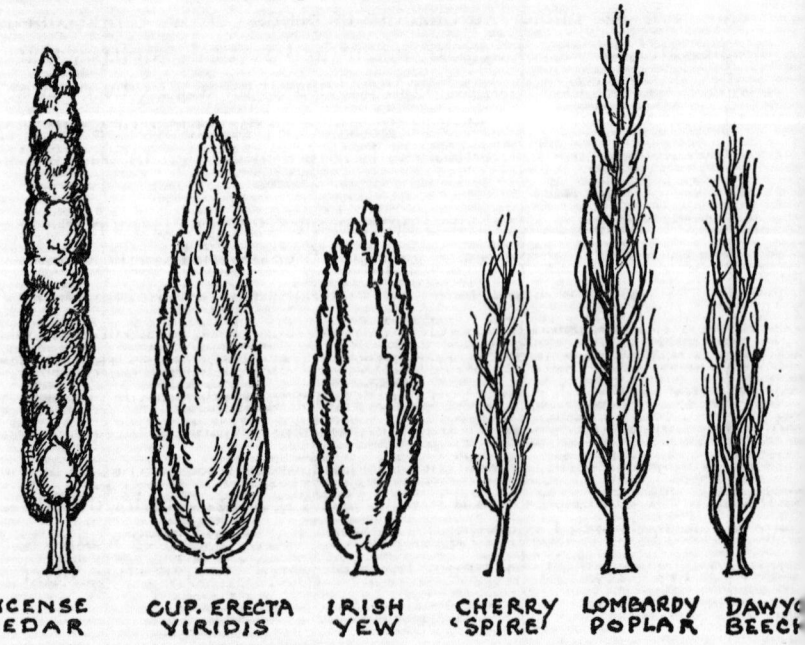

INCENSE CEDAR — CUP. ERECTA VIRIDIS — IRISH YEW — CHERRY 'SPIRE' — LOMBARDY POPLAR — DAWYCK BEECH

TREES AND SHRUBS

A difficulty experienced by those who have to plan new gardens is the conflict between a natural longing to clothe the void—and perhaps to create shelter quickly—and textbook advice about the amount of room which should be allowed for development of the growing trees and shrubs. In spite of the expense, it is not a bad plan to overplant quite deliberately in the beginning, and cull the unwanted subjects after four or five years. At Moyles Cottage, Quenington (referred to in Chapter 13), there were Golden Poplars and various kinds of Cupressus set close together at a windy corner, and for the first ten years those Poplars were invaluable. Then, when the conifers were well established and romping ahead, out came the Poplars. Even their cheerful colour was not much missed, because golden varieties of Cupressus had been mingled with them. Only with fruit trees is overplanting a mistake, tending to spoil shape and inhibit fruiting—also, the best doers might be found adjacent to one another and it is heartbreaking to take out trees that are bearing well. In my young days in Sussex I devised a cheap way of obtaining shelter, by means of willow stakes gathered when the River Board pollarded trees beside the Rother. These took root at once and shot up to twice their original height the following year. It is tough work getting surplus trees uprooted, but the welcome shelter for early years of a new garden is worth the trouble.

The conifer, whether in miniature for use among alpines, or the slow-growing type of medium height in the more formal parts of a garden, or the larger, fast-growing screen tree, has become enormously popular during the last fifty years. My first memory of the conifer craze is of *Cupressus macrocarpa*, bright green, which between the wars thousands of people with new gardens were planting for quick cover. After a while it began to lose face. As a tree it would on occasion get 'browned off' by sudden cold, and when close-clipped as hedging it grew too dense to admit air, which also led to dying patches. It is still worth consideration as a single specimen tree, if the locality is not too cold.

Today, *Cupresso-cyparis* × *leylandii* is all the rage. It would be a mistake to undervalue this useful subject, which does seem to be reliably hardy and very strong-growing; where there is ample space it will form a good screen quite quickly. Yet, in many gardens of smaller size, it seems a pity to cram in a whole row of 'leylandii' merely because it is such a rapid grower. Unless it suits the site and is going to look positively pleasing, there is little point in having it. A high wooden fence, or burlap slung between posts, could be erected even more speedily; but few would want to look at that. On the whole, small English gardens are in danger of becoming clotted with rather too many Cupressus, Cedrus, Thuja and Cryptomeria than is good for them. The miniatures raised in such variety by Mr. Welch of Devizes (Wansdyke Nursery, Hillworth, Devizes, Wilts.) do not come into this category. It is the larger ones that need clear atmosphere and brilliant sunny climate if they are not to become absorbent and stuffy. We have got rid of the Victorian laurel walk, shrubbery and monkey-puzzle, but we do not want to exchange these for modern Elizabethan blotting-paper.

This criticism I believe to be valid, although the dark Yew, grown either as a tree or a hedge, looks so right in the English garden scene. It has a fine texture, and the sombre colour, even when solidly clipped as hedging, seems to throw up lighter subjects planted in front of it; while the other conifers named compete with the brilliance of garden flowers and shrubs and often overpower them in some strange way. It is a highly personal view, but to me they act as garden sponges which absorb light instead of water.

In the 'free' design of a small back garden for a modern family (Figure 7) there are groups of conifers in three of the four corners—one of gold varieties, one grey-green or bluish, and one of darker kinds, and Taxus with Holly. In this instance there is very little bright colour in the form of flowers. The exception, a bed of early Rhododendrons and Azaleas, is well able to combine with the Cupressus of various colours without being made to look feeble. When their season is past, the conifers—set against Copper Beech—accord well with the silver, gold and green foliage plants that make up the mosaic pattern in this garden. I would nearly always choose to put small groups of similar colour together, rather than spot gold, green and glaucous alternately. The last style is apt to produce a restless effect. It is rather like making a dress of two colours in the same material. When varying the colour it is generally more satisfactory to have difference of texture as well, one smooth and one rough, one opaque and one transparent, or something of that sort. In trees, if it seems desirable to vary the colour in one small group, I would combine more than one genus. *Prunus nigra* might be planted with the Golden Irish Yew (*Taxus fastigiata aurea*) and *Cupressus arizonica conica*, giving variety of texture as well as contrast of colour and form.

Sometimes trees all of one colour please, even though the colour itself does not. In one case, flowering cherries of a bitingly acid pink—possibly that suburban favourite 'Kanzan'—were under fire from the owner of a garden which he had inherited, but not planted. Having been brought up in a red-brick district of outer London, where this cherry made spring hideous to me, I had thought it would be a relief never to see it again. It just does not go with red bricks. Yet it was I who pleaded with the critic not to chop down a double row of these little trees, which were set on a green slope of lawn just far enough away from his house—in this case of *grey* stone—to have a little mystery added to their appearance. They were well grown, of uniform size, and placed so that the widest boughs just met overhead, a finger-tip contact, to form an avenue. It would have been a sin to destroy them. This is one of the joys of looking at gardens carefully. Nearly everything gives pleasure if it is used in the right place and in the right proportion, and so a colour which one had described elsewhere as hideous may cause some eating of words when arranged differently. That group of cherries was saved here by grouping, by the large sweep of lawn, and by a background of quiet woodland. This sort of pink will brook no competition.

Competition between plants is always a hazardous matter in gardens, whether it takes the form of a battle for insufficient nourishment between tree and shrub, or hedge and smaller fry at its base, or the less publicized contest of blossom with blossom for the beholder's eye. Colour is not an absolute, but a relative thing. How often people are heard to say that they take no interest in foliage plants, because they simply must have colour. By colour they clearly mean the primaries, red, yellow and blue, or possibly two secondaries—orange and purple. That green is also a secondary colour, and that the subtle tertiaries derived from a mixture of the others have just as good a claim to be called colour, is seldom understood. Also, professed lovers of primary colour often lose sight of the fact that in close association these tend to cancel out. It is the scarlet pillar-box in the grey street that looks brightest, and a similar result is seen when a few red geraniums are put with the grey of *Senecio laxifolius*, or *Helichrysum siculum*, or a clump of blue-grey Rue. There is a story of the artist J. M. W. Turner and a small, grey landscape of his that was once hung in the Royal Academy. Finding it overpowered by a flower-piece and a sunset scene put on either side of it, he took paints to the gallery and gave the tiny figure in his painting a scarlet coat. That one small dab of red amid greys took the viewer's eye away from all the surrounding 'colour'. He well knew the power of contrast.

He also knew all about proportion, and here we come back to the planting of trees. Small gardens cannot hold large clumps of any but miniature trees; therefore the average group of larger trees will comprise five or seven—not 17. This means that you cannot get a small group of bright colour with a much larger one of blue-grey or dark foliage, and if your 'bright' foliage tree—say a golden conifer—is put *singly* with a small group of others, it stands out as a rule in too much of a 'spot'. For this reason it is usually a happier arrangement to put several of the dark colour in one place and a group of the gold in another, unless you vary the kind of tree as well as the colour. I often wish it were possible to obtain samples of foliage to try in a garden, much as the furnishing shops supply pattern-books of fabric. As it is, you cannot even take away container-grown plants 'on approval' —they are too easily ruined by careless or ignorant customers. There ought to be a future for imitation plastic trees on loan, or hire.

So far, colour and size have been given more space than what is called 'habit'. The vertical tree is naturally most popular in small areas, and the wide spreaders least so, especially as the majority of them end up as very large trees: it is hard to think of a small tree with umbrella-like branches. *Malus sargentii* is a good little flowering Crab with tiny red fruits, and it spreads widely, but it is more of a bush than a tree. The white Japanese Cherry Kojima is a fairly wide shape, and so is the earlier Moerheimi. Weeping Ash and Weeping Beech will spread, but these become large trees. We all know the

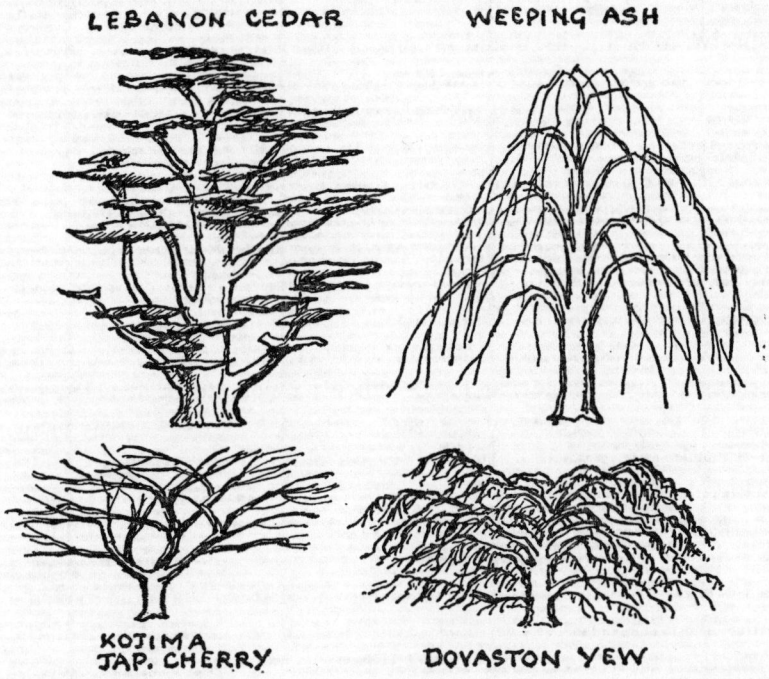

peaceful horizontal lines of the Cedar of Lebanon; the Catalpa (Indian Bean) is a beauty and spreads its branches in a wide circle with age, as does the lovely Dovaston Yew; but none of these could be described as of modest size. Nor can the Weeping Willow, so often mistakenly planted in a little grass plot beside a tiny pool. A really fine spreading tree can be a soothing presence in a garden, but it is likely to overpower the little scheme most of us have to be content with today. The American *Salix purpurea pendula* is the only suitable weeping willow for a small space.

One tree that fits well into most English gardens is the Holly. And how very accommodating that tree can be! If you require a tall tree, it will in time grow almost as high as the chimney. Or, if a small clipped shape is wanted, the Holly can be cut to size. The fancy golden, silver and variegated forms, being slower, are best for this purpose; although I have seen a tall specimen of our native Holly (*Ilex aquifolium*) brutally cut down to a height of 3 feet, and survive to clothe itself and become a neat little shapely tree within a year or two. Most owners of Holly desire it to berry, and so, if there is room for only one, the self-pollinating kind should be selected. *Ilex polycarpa laevigata* (J. C. van Tol) is excellent. If females are put with this plant, it will pollinate them also. Holly makes a splendid hedge; but, at about eight pounds sterling for a dozen plants, few will buy it. Mixed in with cheaper Beech and Whitethorn it produces a sturdy and impenetrable country-style screen. It should be remembered that Holly provides attractive foliage for the house—and not only at Christmas. The flower arranger loves 'Golden King'—which happens to be female—but avoids 'Golden Queen' if she wants berries, for that is a male plant.

People often want to plant trees for autumn colour, and wonder which subjects to select. The American Sweet Gum, *Liquidambar styraciflua*, is one that gives a fine array of reddish-purple and gold foliage in a good season. Although it can become large, it takes a long time about reaching its maximum size. It is pyramidal in shape and has attractive corky bark, with leaves not unlike those of the Maple. Then there is Persian Ironwood, *Parrotia persica*, bold of leaf and hue, which, accompanied by the more delicately coloured Katsura Tree, *Cercidiphyllum japonicum*, grows to perfection in the arboretum at Westonbirt. Both of them may be expected to remain fairly small during our lifetime.

The coarser and commoner Stag's horn Sumach, *Rhus typhina*, turns, briefly, a glowing red in autumn, but has a rather clumsy habit and produces a forest of suckers. If you must have this type of Rhus, the cut-leaved one is prettier. The most worth-while member of this family, *Rhus cotinus*, the Wig Tree or Smoke Tree, is really a broad spreading bush. There is a lovely purple variety (now called *Cotinus coggygria foliis purpureis*), which makes a splendid foil to sulphur yellow Potentilla, Jerusalem Sage, or the blue Clematis *C. heracleifolia* with its Hyacinth-like blossom, or the white *C. recta*, which makes a lovely shower bouquet; this last is too seldom found in the plant catalogues.

To anyone who knows Canada, autumn colour suggests the Maples. It is best to divide these into two quite separate groups when planning a garden. There are the Japanese Maples, *Acer palmatum*, small, spectacular, often with finely dissected lacy foliage. They need moisture and shelter from drying winds, and do best on good neutral or acid soils. Some popular varieties are: *A. palmatum atropurpureum*, *A. dissectum*, *A. dissectum purpureum*, *A. septemlobum purpureum*, and *A.* 'Ozakazuki'.

Then there are the sturdier types which do well in sun with drier soil. *Acer griseum*, the 'Paper-bark' Maple, makes an excellent small specimen tree and gives both scarlet coloured foliage in autumn and wonderful orange bark when the top layer peels off. As a larger specimen tree the variegated *A. pseudoplatanus leopoldii* can be valuable. *A. campestre*, the Field Maple, goes a rusty red in autumn, while 'Wisley Purple' has leaves of dark copper colour all through the season. *A. saccharinum lacianatum*, the cut-leaved Silver Maple begins pale green and white, turning gold in the Fall.

Another form of autumn colour—the berry—is found in the Cockspur Thorn, *Crataegus crus-galli*, together with brilliant autumn foliage. A little tree suitable for a specimen in a small garden, the Cornelian Cherry, has tiny yellow flowers in clusters early in the year, followed by red fruits in the autumn. The variegated kind (*Cornus mas variegata*), green and cream, is unusually decorative. Then for acid soils there is the charming *Sorbus vilmorinii*, with its pink berries in the closing months of the year. The ordinary Rowan or Mountain Ash (*Sorbus aucuparia*) makes a brave show in the early autumn, but birds take the berries very quickly; this pilfering can be avoided if the yellow-fruited variety is chosen. All the Rowans have ferny foliage and dislike lime.

Some rather larger trees which provide autumn foliage are *Robinia friesia* (*aurea*), the golden Acacia which turns a pale orange colour—all Acacias are brittle, and should not be put in a windy place—and the Red Oak, *Quercus rubra*. The Golden Cornish Elm is a neat tree, with yellow foliage all through the season. The Flowering Cherries are not usually selected for autumn colour, but *Prunus sargentii* and its narrow vertical relative, 'Spire', provide pale pink blossom in spring and very good glowing autumn colour as well. There is a Eucalyptus (*E. viminalis*) which, unlike the usual blue-grey gum-trees that spring to mind, is a gold and russet colour all the year, going particularly foxy in the autumn. It is less hardy than some others.

All the subjects mentioned, and many more, would be lovely in the right places; the smaller ones mostly as single specimens and the larger to make a frame for some distant view, or grouped as a little wood where there is space. I can think of few more rewarding assignments than planting a mixed wood with a view to autumn rewards, with some dark Yews between to throw up the brilliance of their companions. One lesson learned in Canada is that too much red and gold *en masse* will tire the eyes and defeat its own ends, memorable though the first sight of whole woods on fire may be.

It is difficult to draw a line between trees and shrubs. Several of the plants already named might be found among the shrubs in a nurseryman's catalogue, even when, as in the case of *Rhus cotinus*, one vernacular name is Smoke *Tree*. The dwarf Japanese Maples will probably be classed as shrubs also. Although the bushy shrub is seldom placed singly in a lawn or centre of small enclosure in the way a little flowering tree is used, it is useful to remember that, when some undesirable shed, pylon, corrugated iron or other object has to be blotted out, a smaller plant near the eye acts as well as a larger one at a distance—and sometimes serves the purpose better.

Certain shrubs look their best when planted in what Gertrude Jekyll called 'drifts', by which she meant a number of similar plants arranged as a long, informal group and not clumped together in a compact patch. The glorious coloured stems of the deciduous shrub called 'Dogwood' (why?), the most usual being *Cornus alba* and *C. stolonifera*, are always most effective when arranged in a drift. As they enjoy damp, a waterside garden suits them admirably, but they are adaptable to drier positions too. In the famous arboretum a less common Dogwood—*C. alba sibirica* 'Westonbirt'—makes a show with stems of vivid sealing-wax red. In general this last is not as lusty as the two first-named. Dogwoods of this type must be pruned hard in spring, to make them produce fresh and brilliant shoots for the following winter. There is a gold variegated Dogwood, *C. alba* 'Spaethii', which gives double value, with its foliage charm followed by red stems, and one, with the cumbersome name of *C. stolonifera flaviramea*, which makes a contrast with buttercup yellow stems. A little drift of this running into larger drifts of the scarlet and crimson-stemmed Dogwoods can be thrilling.

Other kinds of Dogwood are more suited to the single planting necessary in small space, and the Japanese *Cornus kousa* (and *C. kousa sinensis*) both make small, hardy trees, tolerant of any soil. Their 'flowers' are really large white bracts, and these are arranged in decorative layers. Unfortunately the trees take ten or twelve years to produce them. While on the subject of timing, the invaluable flowering Wych Hazel, *Hamamelis mollis*, produces its sweetly scented, untidy little yellow and maroon blossoms in January within a few years of planting—sometimes less—but the spicy Wintersweet, *Chimonanthus fragrans*, takes six or seven years to settle down. Although the former costs more than twice as much as Wintersweet, it is probably worth the price. It likes a cool soil, with peat and leaf-mould, for it is a woodland plant.

I am inclined to think that the well-known flowering garden shrubs—the Berberis, Broom, Buddleia, Cotoneaster, Deutzia, Escallonia, Forsythia, Hebe, Kerria, Philadelphus, Ribes, Skimmia, Syringa, Viburnum and Weigela families—look their best in the mixed border, of the kind that is now replacing the old-fashioned herbaceous border. When such bushes as those indicated are employed to furnish a space without admixture of other plants, the effect is often that of a 'sample' bed in a Garden Centre or exhibition.

The long drift arrangement is splendid when a number of one kind is to be planted, but this requires a semi-wild or woodland setting and seldom fits into the more conventional garden in a built-up area.

The nicest mixed borders are composed of the larger flowering shrubs (and possibly some trained on fence or wall), together with shrub roses; foliage plants (Hosta, Hellebore, Euphorbia, Elaeagnus, prostrate Juniper); aromatics (Lavender, Rosemary, Fennel, Southernwood, Red Sage, Sweet Cicely); with shrubby Potentillas; perhaps groups of Lilies; some of the large Sedums—such as 'Ruby Glow' and 'Autumn Joy'—and the hardy Cranesbills (Geraniums). Surprisingly, certain Dahlias look well in such a mixture, if they are arranged informally in drifts and the colours are pale. The cactus type of flower blends better than the pompon or mop-head. Dahlia foliage in the pre-flowering months looks rather stuffy; it is less noticeable between shrubs, and the plants bloom when the earlier flowering shrubs are over. The mixed border may be edged with Bugle, Variegated Dead-nettle, *Stachys lanata* (Lamb's Ears), Variegated Applemint and other easy carpeters, which will run backwards towards the shrubs and (judiciously controlled) form what musicians would call a bridge passage between one main theme and another: in this case between lawn or path and the major plantings.

Gardeners with lime-free soil, pH 6.5 and below, will be able to grow all the peat-loving plants as well, including the lovely shrub *Pieris japonica*, which bears Lily-of-the-Valley flowers in spring, and spectacular reddish shoots; the Camellias, Enkianthus (which has bell-heather blossom and good colour in autumn), *Siphonosmanthus delavayi* with vanilla-scented flowers, and of course the Rhododendron in all its forms. The natural species are by far the most fascinating, and people who say that Rhododendrons are vulgar shrubs cannot have seen any but the highly coloured hybrids, which mostly have rather dreary foliage. Obviously the Azaleas belong with the Rhododendrons, and then there is the handsome *Embothrium lanceolatum* with its wreaths of scarlet honeysuckle-type flowers in June.

TREES AND SHRUBS

This plant thrives in moist woodland. *Desfontanea spinosa* is evergreen and has scarlet and yellow blooms in late summer, and *Crinodendron hookerianum*, also evergreen, has scarlet hanging lantern-flowers in June. The *Kalmia latifolia* looks rather like a Rhododendron in foliage, but has quaint little bonnet-flowers. It is known as the Calico Bush in America. An enchanting spring shrub for acid or neutral soil is Corylopsis, either *C. pauciflora* or the larger *C. spicata*. These have racemes like catkins, of scented primrose-yellow flowers in March.

For ground cover there is the charming Pernettya, already mentioned in Chapter 4; all the Ericas; the Scottish Lings (Calluna); Irish Heaths (Daboecia); and *Cornus canadensis*, the little Dogwood of herbaceous character which throws new shoots each year. Then there is the Gaultheria; both the American species *G. procumbens* (known as 'Creeping Wintergreen') and *G.* 'Shallon' are the easiest to procure and to grow, but there are others.

There are certain shrubs about which the experts are by no means agreed. One of my favourites, *Azara microphylla*, bears insignificant little flowers, but these give out a powerful vanilla scent which wafts all over the garden in March or April. It is seldom listed by nurserymen, being considered tender; yet it can be seen flourishing in places which are not classed as mild. Vita Sackville-West wrote this about it: 'It is evergreen; it has neat shining little leaves that look as though they had been varnished; it has this tiny yellow flower which is now spreading its scent over my writing table and into the whole of my room... Some authorities say it is not hardy here in Britain except in the favoured climate of Devon or Cornwall. I don't believe this. I have got it thriving where I live in Kent, and I have seen a 20-foot-high tree of it in the rather colder climate of Gloucestershire. So I would say: plant it and risk it.' This shrub does well in leaf-mould, and may be trained on a wall where the early sun will not get at it too soon after a frosty night. I like this Azara because it is such a surprise to sniff the warm vanilla fragrance at a time of year when less exotic perfumes are the rule.

The Sarcococca (Sweet Box) is an unobtrusive evergreen which also gives an unexpected dividend of very sweet scent in the early part of the year. *S. humilis* is only a foot high, *S. ruscifolia* about 2 feet, and *S. hookeriana* 3 feet or more. These are all lime-tolerant, and they like shady places. They spread, as does a much more common plant (properly classified as herbaceous) which develops annual growth of a shrubby type—*Polygonum campanulatum*. This bears bead-like sprays of flowers in apple-blossom pink, a welcome surprise at the end of the summer. Although it runs and makes good ground-cover with shrubs, it is easy to control, being surface-rooting. It likes moist situations and has a tendency to wilt if allowed to dry out.

Those delightful little shrubs, the Daphnes, will not tolerate dry conditions either. They have a reputation for being temperamental; but they are so sweetly scented and so ideal in habit for the small modern garden that it is a pity not to try one or two. The trailing *D. blagayana* with cream flowers is ideal among rocks. *D. mezereum* and *D. mezereum alba* (Bowles variety being the best white) are well known; the species from Japan and China, *D. odora* and its variety, *D. odora variegata*, have pink flowers, are lime-tolerant, and do well in towns. Daphne 'Somerset' is an upstanding and strong-growing shrub, and *D. cneorum* is a low, spreading, rosy-pink plant; a very good form of it is called *D. cneorum eximia*. All of these like to get their roots beneath a rock, where they will be cool and moist.

Certain easily grown shrubs are neglected, without apparent reason. The Bladder Senna, *Colutea arborescens*, has yellow pea flowers over a long season, followed by crowds of inflated seed-pods which survive storms without getting shabby, and in frosty winter sunlight take on an iridescent sheen. It succeeds well in towns. Another easy shrub, *Leycesteria formosa*, sometimes called 'False Nutmeg' although not in the least like a Nutmeg Tree, is disliked by some horticultural experts. I think it has character, and it is very adaptable. In a small space it may only be possible to allow a few stems to develop, but it takes hard pruning and can be treated rather like a raspberry cane; old canes are removed after fruiting and new ones thinned out. The stems are green and smooth, and the drooping racemes of pink flowers, with maroon bracts and dark purple fruits, are decorative. If you have plenty of space, this shrub will soon fill it up. Then there is the lesser-known *Caragana arborescens*, which has yellow pea flowers and feathery foliage, something like a Mimosa with Laburnum blossom. It must be hardy, for it grows well in the Canadian city of Calgary, at an altitude of 3,000 feet with sub-zero temperatures every winter. There it is used chiefly for hedging. I think the plant is ruined by constant clipping, rather as we sometimes see Forsythia mutilated and miserable in this country. The fourth on my list of easy but neglected subjects is the 'Buffalo Currant', *Ribes aureum*. This yellow-flowered version of the ordinary 'Flowering Currant', which is pink or red and to my mind evil-smelling, is by contrast most pleasantly fragrant, has bright green foliage which colours well in autumn, and its April blossom accords better with Forsythia and Daffodil than does the pink and red *Ribes sanguineum*. All four of these suggested shrubs look well in a group together.

Not much has as yet been said about the Eucalyptus. As this tree grows enormous in Australia, and up to 90 feet high in my old home, the Highland garden of Inverewe, it may sound most unsuitable for a small garden. But it can be grown as a shrub, kept down to 6 or 7 feet, when it will produce only juvenile foliage. This happens to be particularly attractive, and the prunings are valued for indoor decoration. Subtle mauve and blue colours appear in young leaves of *E. gunnii*, *E. glaucescens* and *E. perriniana*, while *E. viminalis* has golden and rusty-red foliage at all seasons.

If trees are to be planted below a slope or high bank, care should be taken to ensure that the drainage is adequate. It is not uncommon to find disconsolate gardeners who, having taken great pains to spot-plant young trees in well composted holes, are puzzled by their poor progress. Investigation will often disclose that the prepared pits are acting as sumps for surface drainage, and the trees stand in water. This can usually be put right by breaking up the rock or clay bed below root level, and substituting loosely packed rubble, clinker, ash and such material.

When looking through lists of trees and shrubs it is useful to have the meanings of some common botanical terms in mind.

(a) *Shape of tree or shrub, 'habit'*

decurrens—running along
erecta—upright
fastigiata—pointed
gigantea—large

minima—very small
nana—dwarf
pendula—weeping
procumbens—trailing

(b) *Type of leaf*

aquifolium—prickly
biloba—two-lobed
dissectum—cut-leaved
heterophylla—more than one kind on a plant
macrophylla—large-leaved
microphylla—small-leaved

obtusa—blunt
palmatum—five-lobed, like fingers
pinnatum—a number of leaflets in pairs on stalk
septemlobum—seven-lobed
vitifolium—vine-like

(c) *Colour*

alba—white
argentea—silver
aurea, aureum—golden
coerulea, caerulea—blue
glauca, glaucescens—blue-grey
griseum—grey
lactea—milky

lutea, lutescens—yellow
marginata—bordered
nigra—black, dark
purpureum—purple
rubra, rubrum—red
sempervirens—evergreen
viridis—green

(d) *Flowers and fruits*

baccata—berried
citriodora—lemon-scented
floribunda—many-flowered
globosa—ball-like

grandiflora—large-flowered
macrocarpa—large-fruited
parviflora—small-flowered
praecox—early

CLIMBERS AND WALL-TRAINED SHRUBS

CLIMBERS are used in gardens for many purposes. In Chapter 1 I described a new garden in Sussex, where vertical emphasis was essential to offset the monotony of a wide expanse of levels near the sea; yet even the narrowest of trees would have encroached too much on the view of a wooded escarpment and distant hills. In this design a neat line of wooden posts, arranged in a gentle curve and joined together to form a series of arches, was used to support climbing roses which were carefully pruned and trained to frame the vista without obliterating anything of value.

The pergola is less fashionable than it was then, and climbers, whether perennial or annual, are more frequently used to screen fences and walls; to scramble along balconies, or over sheds, summerhouses and garages; to furnish the walls of a house—perhaps to bring scent and colour to the upper storey windows. Now that many of us have to make do with very small gardens, the intelligent arrangement of vertical growths can become a valuable means of extending the number and variety of plants within our scope.

In addition to the plants normally listed as climbers, and to the fruit trees that may be wall-trained, there are many shrubs which will readily adapt to this form of culture. Some gardeners go a little too far in experiments of this kind. I once saw a young Blue Cedar (*Cedrus atlantica glauca*) planted against a mellow Georgian brick wall some 10 feet in height. The Cedar foliage looked lovely, but before long the roots began to undermine the foundations and the tree had to be removed in haste. Big trees, however attractive when young, are clearly not suitable subjects for training on walls. But the deliciously scented *Viburnum fragrans* will go up like Jack's beanstalk and waft its perfume into a bedroom window without doing any harm to the structure. It looks well at all seasons and has a distinctly architectural quality, while its mahogany-coloured stems and dark foliage harmonize with most building materials.

I have unorthodox views about that easy-going and popular shrub, Forsythia. This is usually grown as a free-standing bush, which soon becomes a tangled thicket of shoots, many coming upwards from the ground until the effect reminds one of the tropical Banyan on a smaller scale. The latter operates in reverse direction, but both plants end up as a grove. If such an arrangement is required for screening purposes, well and good; but too often this shrub is allowed to do as it likes because nobody tries to stop it. Forsythia (whether the thickset, rather gaudy *F. intermedia* var. 'Lynwood' or the older *F. spectabilis*) takes on a much lighter and more elegant character if the 'most for the money' policy is abandoned and the growth is restricted to a few main stems. Exposed to view, cleared of all clutter, these become smooth little grey 'trunks'; and when the flowering shoots spray from a higher level, the yellow bell-flowers, more thinly scattered over the bush, become interesting because they are seen as individual shapes. Specimens that are encouraged to produce a clotted mass of bright yellow too often obtrude themselves violently on the spring scene and swamp the quieter subjects. Judicious thinning will also make Forsythia into an excellent wall shrub: *F. suspensa* is particularly easy to train; but no Forsythia should be subjected to the indignity of being shorn into a formal arch over the front door. Wand-like sprays of bells are its chief beauty, and those who want something yellow to clip should order golden Privet instead.

CLIMBERS AND WALL-TRAINED SHRUBS

A beautiful shrub, one that (except in very mild districts) is happiest against a sunny wall, is the blue-flowered Ceanothus or 'Californian Lilac'. There are really three groups of Ceanothus, all natives of the Pacific coast of America and a little tricky to grow in Britain. The first group, all of which are evergreen, come into flower in springtime and some bloom again in autumn. The flower spikes are smaller in this group than the others, but the colour is usually a better blue. They are the most delicate members of this family, but highly prized because shrubs with blue flowers are particularly scarce at the time of their blooming. They should be planted in spring, as should all these shrubs, and the shelter of a warm wall may be enhanced by paving stones over the root-run.

The next group contains *C. burkwoodii* and a hybrid named 'Autumnal Blue'. These come into flower about midsummer, and are fairly hardy. The really late flowerers are deciduous and the strongest members of their clan; popular varieties are 'Gloire de Versailles' and 'Topaz'. The spring-flowering group comprises natural species, and so these have Latin names. Of recent years one good early hybrid has appeared, called 'Edinburgh'. It is said to be stronger and hardier than the wild ones. All these bushes deserve the warmest soil and the best protection that your walls and fences can provide. Even so, it is necessary to steel oneself to disappointment, for not only the young succumb to winter cold—it is fairly common for a seven- or ten-year-old established Ceanothus to perish suddenly. Pruning of evergreen types should be kept to a minimum, but deciduous ones should be pruned hard in April. It is almost worth while building a *white* house to enjoy the sight of wall-trained Ceanothus at its best.

The grey-tasselled *Garrya elliptica*, a quick grower which is frequently trained up against a support, does quite well on a north wall, and is worth remembering when one needs to be clothed. In the right place it looks its best as a large free-standing specimen bush, if there is adequate space combined with shelter from east winds to grow it that way. The foliage goes brown if it gets caught by frost or cold winds. There is a magnificent free-standing bush of Garrya in the garden of Guincho, at Helen's Bay on the Belfast Lough. I did not measure the tassels, but with rainbows flashing in them in February sun after rain they certainly gave the impression of being measurable in feet rather than the usual 7 to 9 inches. The male Garrya bears longer catkins than the female.

Of course that old favourite known to our grandmothers as 'Japonica' (Japanese Quince, Cydonia, now Chaenomeles), will grow and flower almost anywhere; but I do not think it does itself justice at the foot of a wall in dry soil. My own 'Rowallane' was miffy for over three years in baked soil beneath a wall, and yet it flourished and flowered exuberantly when removed to a slightly damper place. It starts soon after Christmas and continues until May, its flowers a curious red, deep and yet bright, with a hidden fiery glow. There is an autumn dividend of attractive yellow fruit, quite large, which makes good jelly. It is good as a free-standing shrub, with a little central support, and I have a friend in the Cotswolds who has grown it as a fascinating little standard tree. This produces enormous interest and bewilderment among passers-by, being visible from the garden gate. All these Japanese Quinces need fairly drastic pruning if they are not to degenerate into a poor, tangled mat of branches. Mr. Christopher Lloyd advises the gardener to spur back young shoots every time he happens to be near the shrub with secateurs in hand. According to him, all Chaenomeles are shy to begin with: so perhaps my 'Rowallane' might have burgeoned in its fourth year, even at the base of the wall. My point is that it is worth while to try a miffy plant in a fresh place before discarding it.

Of the Jasmines much has been written. The good old yellow-flowered *Jasminum nudiflorum*, known as 'Winter Jasmine', has brightened English winters for so many generations of gardeners that it is now hard to believe it was not known here until 1844, when it was introduced from China. It will grow practically anywhere, and at great speed, so it is useful both as a disguise for unsightly buildings and fences and as a pleasing addition to others. It needs drastic pruning. Old and spindly shoots should be removed and newer

CLIMBERS AND WALL-TRAINED SHRUBS

ones shortened back in April after flowering. It pays for careful training, if you have time and patience to persuade it to fan out gracefully without looping around and strangling itself. Unfortunately it has no scent. Everyone should buy a plant, or take a cutting from a friend's Winter Jasmine. Almost any piece will grow, stuck into a pot or in open ground when the soil is warm and moist. Perhaps we could be a little more adventurous in the use of this and other climbers. A summer-flowering plant, such as the white Everlasting Pea, will combine with Winter Jasmine to give blossom over a very long period, and the flowered shoots of the latter are not too difficult to disentangle when spent. There are interesting variegated forms of Jasmine, gold-splashed and silver-streaked, which give extra value all the year round.

The sweet-scented white Jasmine, *J. officinale*, which has been grown here for 300 years, comes out in June and may continue until September. Avoid the more rampant *J. officinale grandiflora*, which smothers everything else in a short time and has fewer flowers than the old one. This very popular climber (*J. officinale*) is a native of Persia, Kashmir and China. The less common hybrid, *J. stephanense*, has pink flowers and very sweet perfume, but the blossom is short-lived. Its great attraction is the wonderful pinky-gold spring foliage, which must be grown up a host tree or open paling where the sun will shine through it. The colour of those young shoots will be largely wasted if this Jasmine is planted against a wall. Both white and pink look lovely when combined with one of the small-flowered Clematis species, such as *C. spooneri* or the blue *C. macropetala*. The latter may be going over as the Jasmines open, but they accord very well and do no harm to one another.

A wonderfully scented Jasmine, not hardy enough to be grown as a rule out-of-doors, is *J. polyanthum*. It was introduced into Britain in the 1930s, but scarcely had time to become known until after the war ended. If it is planted in an unheated greenhouse it may grow large and flower little, but, when roots are restricted in a pot, one plant will perfume the whole house in February and March. It may be put out in summer, in its pot, and used as foliage on patio or terrace. Otherwise it has little right to be mentioned here, although it did succeed outdoors at Inverewe; but its charms are irresistible. It is easily propagated by cuttings made from young shoots. This valuable Jasmine is also Chinese.

Although foliage of so many plants has been gaining attention in the last decade, it is still difficult to learn much about the colour and texture of rose foliage from the catalogues. To my mind no descriptive lists of plants are adequate unless something is said about stem and leaf, and in wall climbers this aspect is of particular importance. When selecting climbing roses for use on walls and fences it is worth while to find out as much as possible about their appearance when not in bloom. Mildew is a hideous disease, and it flourishes with me on roses growing in the hot, dry soil which is so often their lot when they are planted close to walls in sunny spots. It is therefore advisable to select mildew-proof kinds, and to place them a little way out from the base of the wall, to catch moisture. On the positive side, there is great gain when foliage is attractive, and most of all when, as in the lovely 'Mermaid' rose, it is evergreen. This will do well on a north wall. Others for such a position are 'Mme. A. Carrière' (Plate V a), 'Alberic Barbier', the old favourite 'Gloire de Dijon', the lusty 'Albertine' and the brilliant scarlet 'Allen Chandler': all good doers on north walls. A climbing rose of great vigour, with clusters of small double flowers, is known as 'Orange Triumph'. It is not orange but red, and supposedly named after the Prince of Orange. The red fades in sunlight to magenta or purple shades. Some people loathe this, but I enjoy the oriental colour clash as some blooms fade and others open. The golden autumn foliage, held by my wall-trained plant until Christmas, is indeed an orange triumph, and a bonus to be prized. For a lower span, the delicately scented pink shrub rose 'Queen of Denmark', usually grown as a bush, will do well trained on a sunny wall. It has charming bluish-green foliage and is a rose to fall in love with.

An attractive twining climber, *Celastrus orbiculatus*, has a tiresome name, but it is worth remembering, for the hermaphrodite form (obtainable from George Jackman of Woking) provides sprays of yellow seed-pods, interesting in themselves, which become even more exciting when they split their sides to disclose bright red seeds. This deciduous plant will grow to 20 or 30 feet, and the foliage usually turns a good yellow in autumn. It is very attractive in a host tree, or will look well trained on some kind of trellis. It must be stressed that, unless the hermaphrodite form is selected, two of opposite sex must be planted to ensure fertilization.

The Clematis requires a chapter in itself. Mr. Christopher Lloyd has written a whole book about this genus, in which he specializes at his nursery, Great Dixter in Sussex. The large-flowered hybrids, which everyone loves, have one ugly blot on their escutcheon—a tendency to the alarming and sudden disease known as 'wilt'. But so spectacular are these plants, and so varied their colours and times of flowering, that gardeners will risk calamity many times rather than forgo their delights. The deep purple June-flowering *C. jackmanii* never fails to please, followed by the lilac-pink 'Mme. Baron-Veillard' (August) and the later purple-and-cream 'Lady Betty Balfour', while the obliging 'Nelly Moser', lilac with showy crimson bars, blooms in May and again in September. Of course there are many other good hybrids. This is one woman's choice, if restricted to four of this type. I would have also the autumnal 'Gravetye Beauty', a small-flowered ruby red of great distinction.

Then there are the species, beginning with the rampageous *C. montana*, which needs room and no competitors, although I have succeeded in getting a Winter Jasmine to survive in its clutches. Some prefer *C. spooneri* to the white *C. montana*, and if a pink is required the form known as 'Pink Perfection' is worth getting for the value of its bronzy foliage. In early autumn the yellow bells of *C. tangutica* and *C. orientalis* make a brave show. The first grows in a shower over an old apple tree at Moyles Cottage, Quenington (Plate III b) and the second turns the kitchen wall at East Lambrook Manor into a nest of flowers and silky seed-heads. Then there are species called *C. macropetala*, soft blue flowers in May; *C. balearica* (*calycina*) with yellowish February flowers; and the astonishing *C. florida bicolor*, cream and purple, rather suggesting a Passion

Flower. One could go on and on. The wild Clematis or 'Traveller's Joy' flourishes among bushes and small trees, with its root in the shade, and it is well to remember that when placing a Clematis in the garden.

Hydrangeas are not ordinarily thought of as climbing plants, but *H. petiolaris* is a vigorous and attractive self-clinging climber which takes a year or two to settle and then goes up a house wall in no time. It has foxy rough-barked stems and cream lace-cap blossom. In full sun it may turn a lovely clear yellow in autumn. A related plant, *Schizophragma integrifolia*, has less conspicuous flowers, but these are offset by large white bracts of decorative appeal. Both are deciduous, and will do on north walls. At Inverewe we had *H. petiolaris* climbing 50 feet up a larch tree.

Then there is Honeysuckle, a favourite climber in cottage gardens for generations of country people in Britain. It has one failing—a tendency to attract hordes of greenfly or blackfly, especially when grown in hot places; but early spraying should discourage these pests. There are many varieties obtainable now, of which the Early Dutch and Late Dutch (bred from our native Woodbine, *Lonicera periclymenum*) are the best known and ever popular for their ease of cultivation and sweet perfume. *L. belgica*, the earlier one, blooms in June and July, followed by *L. serotina*, which flowers in August and September. Although this plant will grow in most soils, it is a woodlander and prefers to have some shade and moisture at its root.

The quick-growing evergreen *L. japonica* is useful for screening purposes, but often rather a sparse bloomer, and its foliage dull. The variety known as *L. japonica aureo-reticulata* is worth remembering, for its golden leaves turn pink in autumn and the filigree pattern of gold and pink lace is enchanting. I like to see it left free to wander at will in shrubs, to embrace Wormwood and Old English Lavender, or to filter through a Myrtle or a Bay.

An exotic hybrid, *L. brownii*, lives up to its name 'Scarlet Trumpet', and its glaucous leaves are attractive; but it lets down our expectations in having no scent whatever. Another unusual Honeysuckle, *L. splendida*, 'Spanish Honeysuckle', has very bluish foliage and stems with a waxy surface, and the reddish flowers are truly fragrant. Some people find it a little tender, but it is well worth a trial. It does well on the Tower at Sissinghurst.

Ivies come in many colours, variegations and leaf sizes. The very large cream-splashed foliage of *Hedera variegata* (*dentata aurea*), with soft yellow borders, is extremely decorative; but this plant is a vigorous climber, shooting up to the eaves of a house and often causing trouble in the gutters unless it is watched and checked. Generally speaking, the smaller the leaf the less rampant the Ivy. Most nurseries carry a good selection, so it is not necessary to go into the varietal names here. This plant is equally useful as ground cover.

The good old 'Virginia Creeper' (*Vitis quinquefolia*) so beloved by our grandfathers for training on house walls, has large five-lobed leaves which turn brilliant crimson in autumn. It is self-clinging by a kind of sucker arrangement when established. This will grow in any aspect, but it has come in for some hard words in our time because of its disruptive effect on stonework. It is still acceptable for trailing over fences, to clothe corrugated iron and other eyesores, to scramble in an aged apple tree, or lace a hedge with autumn glory. The small-leafed form, *Vitis inconstans*, once known as *Ampelopsis veitchii*, is less rampant and clings even more tightly to its host. The best form is called 'Beverley Brook'. This can look superb when grown through a hedge of Copper Beech, or up a Silver Birch, where it will catch the sunlight in the fall of the year and glow warmly.

A newer sort, becoming popular with flower arrangers, is of greater interest as an all-the-year plant, although less spectacular in the autumn. *Vitis henryana* has leaves of a greenish purple, with silver and pink veinings. Like the others, it will grow in any aspect and is self-clinging.

The large-leaved ornamental Vine, *V. coignetiae*, has a characteristic wrinkled texture of foliage, and a looping habit which looks magnificent when slung between tree and adjacent stable roof, as it used to grow in the garden of Moyles Cottage at Quenington.

(It had to be suppressed when the stable was converted to a dwelling-house.) Other gardeners train it along large expanses of balustrade or terrace wall, and it has been seen making a glorious background for Rue ('Jackman's Blue') and silver plants. In small gardens *Vitis vinifera purpurea* is more easily managed, and it provides little clusters of black grapes to enhance the purple foliage. *V. vinifera brandt* also bears fruit, and the leaves turn a vivid orange-red in autumn. The last three require some fixing when trained on a wall, and are not self-clinging like the 'Virginia Creeper'.

For an unfailing supply of quick-growing screenery, the so-called 'Russian Vine' (which is not a Vine but a Polygonum) is of value, but it should be planted only where there is plenty of living space and nothing that might be smothered or strangled by this extremely rampageous plant. It bears a foam of opaline white blossom in great profusion, and will flourish pretty well anywhere. Because it is almost a weed we are apt to overlook its remarkable beauty. In spite of its deserved reputation for invasiveness, I think we must admit that it possesses charm. If I had room, I would try *Vitis coignetiae* and *Polygonum baldschuanicum* together, to see if they could live in harmony, or whether the latter would swamp the great vine. The Vitis would need a start of several years.

An evergreen shrub much used on house walls in the past, the Pyracantha or 'Firethorn', is easy and tolerant of most aspects and soils, but the old *P. coccinea lalandii* has rivals in the modern nursery. *P. atalantoides* (*gibbsii*) is liked because the berries are retained for a long time—well into the New Year; and *P. rogersiana fructu luteo*, with orange-yellow berries, is also a favourite Pyracantha nowadays.

Another shrub of long-standing repute, beloved by the great Gertrude Jekyll, the Snowball Tree (*Viburnum opulus sterile*), bears in June white spherical blossoms like out-of-season snowballs, which never fail to interest young children. These look their best against a brick wall, or when allowed to lean upon a dark yew hedge. The greenish-yellow hue of the inflorescence before it is fully open is popular with flower arrangers. The tough and quick-growing *Kerria japonica* is a useful shrub; the double pompon *K. japonica flore pleno* is often wall-trained to a height of some 8 feet. The popular *Cotoneaster horizontalis* will take its flat fish-bone shoots to a similar height with considerable speed, and it complements the red berries by good autumn foliage colour. *C. henryana* has the added advantage of being evergreen, with red berries, and it may be grown either as a free-standing bush or trained on a wall.

Our forebears trained the larger kinds of Magnolia on their house walls. This seems to be a misuse of a shapely tree, unless the climate is too severe for it to flourish in the open, or there just is not room for one grown in its full glory. *M. soulangeana lennei* has large flowers, the outsides blush-rose with paler linings, followed by extraordinary purple pods which open in a wide grin to display vivid scarlet seeds. This will do well on a wall, but as all Magnolias are greedy feeders, it requires plenty of surface mulching. The soil around the root is best left undisturbed, for Magnolia roots are easily harmed by digging. The hardy Moroccan Broom, *Cytisus battandieri*, has silky silver foliage and yellow flowers with a pineapple scent. This will do well as a wall-trained shrub.

For those who require a wall clothed very quickly, there is the vigorous annual *Cobaea scandens*, which will run up to 20 feet in one season. Most of us have to raise it anew each year, but the lucky few manage to preserve it through the winter. It is well supplied with tendrils and may be grown in a shrub or tree without being tied to its support. The bell-shaped flowers are pale green at first, turning lavender and mauve as they develop. In good summers it produces plum-shaped fruits, which turn from green to gold. Another lovely annual climber, the Morning Glory (*Ipomoea*) is suitable for a really hot situation. *I. rubro-caerulea* is a wonderful blue. Unhappily this plant is at present under a cloud because certain foolish members of the community have tried to use it as a drug.

Among lesser-known perennial climbers, the evergreen *Stauntonia hexaphylla* from Japan and Korea is a strong grower. Once this is established it tends to embrace every tree and shrub within reach, but where plenty of space is available it is a useful subject. The small ivory and mauve flowers have a sweet scent, and it sometimes produces an oval berry of purplish hue about the size of a pullet's egg.

Then there is *Clematis armandii*, which should have been included with its family—yet it never seems much like a Clematis to me. It is an individualist, disliking disciplined training and preferring to be left free to ramble at will. The smooth evergreen foliage and clusters of scented white flowers in March and April are lovely when looping over an Irish Yew, around a *Viburnum fragrans*, or woven into the russet stems of *Hydrangea petiolaris*. If forced to grow sedately alone on a wall or trellis it looks like an exotic specimen which has been unnaturally subjugated. There are certain climbers that must be controlled if a garden is to escape becoming a jungle, and the ornamental Brambles are of this group. The Chinese *Rubus cockburnianus* has waxy bark which can easily fool the eye to make one think that a whitewash brush has been at work on it. *R. tridal* has white flowers of dog-rose character with golden stamens, in June, and *R. odoratus* is a rosy purple.

For a sheltered wall the mysterious Passion Flower (*Passiflora coerulea*) is always interesting, with its blue centre and creamy sepals. Sometimes there is a bonus of orange fruits. The climbing white 'Potato Flower', *Solanum jasminoides alba*, goes well with it in a warm and sunny place. The commoner *Solanum crispum*, a more shrubby plant with mauve 'potato' flowers, has a longer flowering season. *Campsis grandiflora*, known to some as 'Tecoma', is a showy deciduous climber with orange-scarlet trumpet flowers—also a lover of warmth.

Wistaria is not planted as frequently as it was in the last century, perhaps because it takes a little time to get settled, and this is an age of speed. If one has the patience to wait, and to give the plant food and water, it is a rewarding climber, long-lived and able to cover a large area of wall. French people seem to love Wistaria, and Lilac with apple-blossom and Wistaria is typical of the French countryside in May. In my aunt's Italian garden near Shelley's *Casa Magni* above Lerici, there was a vast pergola planted with mauve, white, and yellow-flowered Wistarias whose long tassels of blossom hung down almost to the path and had to be parted by hand, like bead curtains, as one walked through. The scent was nearly enough to make me tipsy, and judging by the way bees tumbled around I thought they did get inebriated. Probably these Wistarias were varieties of *W. macrobotrys*, which has particularly long racemes; but the local gardeners, in response to questioning, replied with that maddening Italian vagueness, '*Fiore, Signorina, fiore!*' *W. sinensis* is the more usual choice for a small garden.

A deciduous climbing member of the Magnolia family—not for chalky soil—Schizandra, does well in the walled garden at Rowallane, and likes a north aspect. It is aromatic; *S. rubriflora* bears red flowers. *Actinidia kolomikta* and the Akebias (*A. quinata* and *A. trifoliata*, sometimes called *A. lobata*) were liked by Vita Sackville-West. The first-named is a small plant for east or west walls, and will not be likely to grow above 8 or 10 feet. The flowers are white and unspectacular, but the curious foliage of green, white and pink (splashed by an unseen paint brush) is decorative and just the thing for brightening a dull corner. The Akebias are stronger growing climbers, semi-evergreen, with leaves shaped like those of Shamrock and so particularly dear to people of Irish blood. The brownish flowers of *A. trifoliata* look weird at first, but they 'grow on' the owner like the sound of a French horn. For the dusty violet hue of *A. quinata* Miss Sackville-West revived the old adjective *gridelin*. Lovers of the unusual would do well to obtain a gridelin Akebia—but not to ask the nursery for it under that description. Both Akebias bear plum-purple fruits, and they are easily raised from seed.

A lovely red-flowered climber, *Tropaeolum speciosum*, a sort of Nasturtium with finely shaped foliage, grew with the greatest verve at Inverewe, but will not do anything for us in Wiltshire. According to Mr. Edward Hyams (*The Gardener's Bedside Book*), this Tropaeolum grows up a tree to a height of 20 feet in one season; when the growth is cut down by frost the plant may be kept going by covering the roots, which will shoot again in the spring. Or, says Mr. Hyams, 'it is possible to re-cover your tree with seedling Tropaeolum every year'. He does not say where you are supposed to be living. The experience of Vita Sackville-West accords better with mine, I regret to say. '*Tropaeolum speciosum*, the flame-coloured Nasturtium which does so brilliantly in Scotland and so poorly in England,' she wrote. I would substitute 'southern England', for I have seen it flourishing in Northumberland, and at Hidcote.

Gardeners with lime-free soil have a host of fascinating climbers at their disposal. These are not worth trying unless the soil is definitely lime-free or acid. In the Ross-shire peat *Crinodendron hookerianum* (syn. *Tricuspidaria lanceolata*), the Chilean 'Lantern Tree', grew on the wall of my single-storey gate lodge, spattering the whitened stone with hundreds of scarlet lanterns from eaves to ground level. It is more often seen growing as a bush. We had it both ways, and one bush in my time was 30 feet high. Afterwards it was damaged by falling timber in a gale.

Philesia buxifolia is another red-flowered Chilean climber, with neat box-like foliage—perhaps half way between Box and Yew—which does very well in the moist peaty soil of Inverewe. It always looked particularly comfortable in the enclosure named 'Japan', where it was ensconced in the hairy fibrous trunk of the Chusan Palm, *Chamaerops excelsa* (syn. *Trachycarpus fortunei*). It climbs up a rocky outcrop at Rowallane, and Mr. Hyams refers to a low, stiff mat extending to about 80 square feet of this same plant carpeting some flat rocks in a garden near Glasgow. It is not easy to establish and should be left undisturbed when it does settle. Personally I prefer to see the long, tubular waxy flowers hanging down from vertical growth, as at Inverewe, and feel that as ground-cover this lovely plant is largely wasted.

The Camellia, which requires shelter except in highly favoured parts of Britain, is usually placed in the shelter of a wall or walls without being attached to them. It likes to be in partial shade, in cool, well-drained soil, and is intolerant of lime. The spring-flowering *Camellia japonica* in red, pink, and white flowering varieties is the most showy and best known, being slightly hardier than the slim, smaller-leaved autumn flowering *C. sasanqua*. The latter is a very charming species if it will grow for you. Then there are the crosses between *C. japonica* and *C. saluensis*, spring flowers known as Williamsii Camellias. A recent variety, named 'Donation', is a double pink and very free with its blossom.

SPECIALIZED GARDENS

IN A SENSE all gardens are, or should be, specialized: tailored to the owner's tastes and needs, to his pocket and to the employed labour he can command or the time he himself can give to both making and maintenance. Most of us would agree readily enough with this, but we sometimes leave out the most important factor of all: the landscape and the soil, on which the whole scheme should ideally be based. Gertrude Jekyll wrote: 'Often in choosing plants and shrubs people begin the wrong way. They know certain things they would like to have, and look through catalogues and order these, and others that they think, from the description, they would also like, and then plant them without any previous consideration of how or why.' That this method, or lack of it, still goes on has been borne out by experiences at one of the now popular Garden Centres. It is quite common to find that plants, suitable or not, will be bought without hesitation if they happen to be showing a little blossom, while excellent subjects for the garden in question are rejected because they are not looking attractive at the time.

Miss Jekyll continued: 'Often when I have had to do with other people's gardens they have said "I have bought a quantity of shrubs and plants; show me where to place them"; to which I can only answer, "That is not the way in which I can help you; show me your spaces and I will tell you what plants to get for them".' Advice of the sort she gave is as a rule obtainable in a good nursery garden or Centre today; but customers are afraid of being talked into buying something more expensive than they want to pay for, or else persuaded to have plants the salesman desires to get rid of. Perhaps this gives an advantage to books and articles on the subject, for the writers, being in most cases unconcerned with the plant trade, are above suspicion. For my part I have never been given bad advice by a good nursery. These firms are too jealous of their reputation to supply plants that are obviously not going to do them credit on land for which they are unsuited. Often it is the customer who puts the supplier in a difficult situation. I knew one impatient gardener who wanted a Box hedge 'as quickly as possible', and demanded plants at least 3 feet in height. He was offered smaller specimens and assured that they would make a more satisfactory hedge, but he would not accept these. Large plants were used, at great cost, and there were many failures which left gaps. Here was a firm doing its best to sell cheaper specimens, and failing—to the customer's disadvantage in the end.

Leaving aside the broad sense in which all gardens are to some extent specialized, there are many types of limitation, or specialization, of a narrower sort. These may concern the concept as a whole, or some part of it. The simple informal arrangement of small trees, shrubs and underplanting shown in Figure 8 may have a specialized scheme for the small formal section at the end. This could be used for a herb garden, or a rose garden, an iris garden, a pool garden; or perhaps for a special colour—a white-and-silver or a blue grouping of plants. If that were done there would be a duplication of contrast with the free nature of the rest: one of formal layout, and the other of some form of specialization in the material used.

The Herb Garden

Knowing that I have a particular interest in herbs, some people ask whether the use in a garden of Sage and Thyme, Parsley and Chives, becomes very dull and boring. They are astonished by the variety in my own small space, and cannot believe that these are in fact herbs. It is a mistake to think solely of culinary plants, for the herb garden of old held many a fragrant and decorative delight also, from Lavender and Clove Carnation to the Apothecary's Rose (*Rosa gallica officinalis*), with Lemon Balm (*Melissa officinalis*) and the more tender but exquisitely scented Lemon Verbena *Aloysia triphylla* (syn. *Lippia citriodora*). Then there were medicinal herbs; some handsome, like the lime-flowered Lady's Mantle, the tall woody-stemmed Elecampane with small yellow 'sun' flowers and sculptured foliage, and the silvery Wormwood (the variety called 'Lambrook Silver' is the best); some fragrant too, and some with both advantages. The elegant Fennel: feathery, aromatic, pushing up fresh growth all through the season directly the flowering stalks are cut down, will please eye, nose, and palate. It looks grand, especially the bronze kind, grouped with Rue (Jackman's Blue) and the Red Sage, *Salvia officinalis* var. *purpurea*.

The Mallows belong to a herb family too, as do Goat's Rue and Tansy. The last is still seen in abundance on many a railway embankment, although like other once common wild plants it is fast disappearing from the fields. The very finely cut green 'lace' of Miss Jekyll's favourite variety, *Tanacetum vulgare* var. crispum, is particularly attractive in a garden, and less rampant than the other. The mints are a fascinating world in themselves. The tall and woolly Applemint, good for culinary purposes, towers above quaint mauve whorls of bloom borne by Upright Pennyroyal; the Shakespearian Bergamot; perhaps the minute *Mentha requienii* filling cracks between paving stones. The Variegated Applemint is not very tall, and lolls about among other plants, always gay in its white and silver patterns, while the claret coloured Eau-de-Cologne Mint and gold-splashed *Mentha gentilis* make happy companions. Most unusual of all, the slender grey foliage of Buddleia Mint (*M. longifolia* var. *mollisima*) bears mauve tassels of bloom like a miniature 'Butterfly Bush'.

In America the early settlers had to dye their own materials, using vegetable dyestuffs, and these were cultivated within the herb

The White Garden at Sissinghurst

PLATE I

a The Cupressus path at East Lambrook Manor

b Artemisia 'Lambrook Silver'

b The author at Quenington, with *Clematis tangutica* on apple tree

a Buttress of Golden Privet at Greyfriars, Worcester

PLATE III

Natural pond garden at Inverewe

PLATE IV

b Enid Money with her *Lilium auratum* at Quenington

a Rose Mme. A. Carrière at Sissinghurst

PLATE V

Chusan Palm at Inverewe

PLATE VI

a Herb garden, American Museum, Claverton Manor, Bath

b Sunk garden by Nathaniel Lloyd, Great Dixter, Sussex

Small pool, Tintinhull

PLATE VIII

Shadows on the grass, Sissinghurst

PLATE IX

a The George Washington garden at Claverton Manor, Bath

b The large pool, Tintinhull

Hidcote, Gloucestershire, the cedar

The vestal virgin, Sissinghurst

a Path beside Loch Ewe, Inverewe

b Woodland planting, Inverewe

PLATE XIII

a Rhododendron falconeri at Rowallane

b The old wood, Rowallane

a Angelica at East Lambrook Manor

b Basin at Greyfriars, Worcester

PLATE XV

a Garden in Kensington made by Mrs. Cecily Mure

b Garden in Kensington made by Mrs. Cecily Mure

SPECIALIZED GARDENS

enclosures, becoming known as dye-*herbs*. By adopting this custom we may obtain another range of plants for the herb garden, including the bold Pokeroot with spikes of cream flowers followed by purplish-black berries set closely on the stem; the fine foliage of *Indigofera tinctoria* (Indigo) with reddish-yellow pea flowers; the blue Alkanet; Weld (*Reseda luteola*), a species of Mignonette which yields a yellow dye—this not to be confused with the glaucous Woad (*Isatis tinctoria*). The latter is an easily raised biennial, whose sprays of pendant black seeds are prized by flower-arrangers.

The wild British Iris, *I. pseudacorus*, likes moist conditions. It has been used to produce yellow dye from the flowering tops and black from the roots. Another Iris which is at home among herbs is the Florentine white-flowered *I. florentina*, which stores fragrance in its rhizome. For centuries perfumiers used the powdered 'Orris' root, and our grandmothers put it into sweet bags and pot-pourri. The larger umbelliferous herb plants—Angelica, Lovage and Sweet Cicely, the last with masses of lacy foliage, sweetly scented—are excellent for the back of a herb bed, in light shade and a fairly damp place. Sweet Cicely is perennial, and so is Lovage, whose celery flavour goes well in many dishes; but the splendid Angelica is a biennial and must be raised afresh each year, unless it seeds itself for you. (Plate XV a.)

The pink-flowered Soapwort is apt to be invasive, but it deserves a place because the extract works miracles in the cleaning and restoration of old tapestries and needlework. A double form is known to country people as 'Bouncing Bet'. Another pink flower appears early in May on the native Bistort (*Polygonum bistorta*), a powerful astringent herb with a starchy root often used for food in times of famine. Little globes of pink and mauve flowers are produced by Thrift and Chives, both of which make good edging plants.

Small woody herbs, such as Hyssop—which may be blue, white or pink-flowered—Winter Savory (*Satureia montana*) and Cotton Lavender, the last with either the silver or the green foliage, may be used as low, clipped edgings, as also may dwarf Lavender and Box. In addition to the usual 'Black' Thyme and Lemon Thyme, the fancy gold, gold-variegated and silver Thymes may be used in the kitchen, fresh or dried, as well as for their decorative virtues. The same is true of the Marjorams, and the Golden Marjoram (*Origanum aureum*) makes an astonishingly bright splash of pale gold when grown in full sun. The French or 'Pot' Marjoram (*O. onites*) and Sweet or Knotted Marjoram (*O. marjorana*) are even more sweetly aromatic; but the latter is a native of Portugal and is usually raised from seed and treated as a half-hardy annual.

To the common Sage (*Salvia officinalis*), and the red variety mentioned, which is just as good for culinary purposes, must be added the distinguished *Salvia turkestanica*; this grows to 6 feet and is covered in rosy-purple bracts throughout the summer, lasting until October with me. It looks well with the stately Mullein, Candlewick Plant (*Verbascum thapsis*), together with Moth Mullein, White Mullein, Dark Mullein and perhaps the tall *Artemisia ludoviciana*. Another Artemisia, Southernwood, 'Old Man', or 'Apple Ringie', might, with the old favourite Rosemary, be placed conveniently near a path so that passers-by may take a fragrant pinch between finger and thumb. The Rosemary should be available to the cook, for spearing into joint of lamb or mutton before it reaches the oven.

The last two make sizeable bushes in time, although Southernwood looks neater if cut low each spring. The Lemon Verbena also makes a shrub, and others suitable for a herb garden are the Junipers—either *Juniperus communis* or the little *J. sabina* from which the medicinal Oil of Savin is extracted. Then there is the Elder. Some may exclaim that this bush is practically a weed of the hedgerow. Yet it is a powerful herb, used in times past as food, drink, medicine, and venerated as the Elder Mother of all herbs. Elderberry Rob (a thick syrup for colds); Elderberry ketchup and chutney; wines made from flowers and from elderberries; Green Elder Ointment for chilblains, sprains and bruises; and Elder Flower toilet water—all have been of use to mankind for centuries. If the common Elder is too lusty, the Golden Elder and its rarer relatives, *Sambucus aurea marginata* (gold-edged) and *S. pulverenta* (variegated white) are more compact and make very attractive shrubs for any part of the garden.

Herbs, for the most part, like well-drained land in full sun. Their flavour and fragrance are better when they are grown on rather poor soil. The chief exceptions to this rule are the Mints, with Pennyroyal and Bergamot—these require richer conditions and moisture, and the Angelica, Lovage and Sweet Cicely prefer them. The Lungwort, with silver-spotted foliage and varied flowers, blue and pink, is a herb plant for the cooler part of the garden, too. The fragrances—and they are many—produced by herbs are at their best if the plants are grown in an enclosure, so that the wind does not disperse them. Walls, wattle hurdles, hedges, or a combination of all three are desirable, both to shelter the tenderer subjects and to help concentrate the scents. Rosemary, Sage, Thyme and Marjoram will also do quite well in tubs on a Terrace.

Of the annuals, Borage and Orach are of great decorative value and easy to grow from seed. Borage bears gentian-blue flowers in profusion, with little white centres and black cone-like anthers, the whole plant beloved by embroiderers in the sixteenth century or thereabouts. It figures also in a famous mediaeval French tapestry, *The Lady with a Unicorn*. The young leaves add a cool cucumber flavour to salads and drinks, and the flowers are attractive to bees.

The red variety of Orach (*Atriplex hortensis*) should be chosen in preference to the green, for its transparent crimson foliage, elegantly arrow-shaped, filters sunlight with the effect of stained glass. As a pot herb Orach has been superseded by Spinach, and it is little used by herbalists in medicine nowadays; but as a decorative plant it is worthy of a place in the herb garden or any sunny spot where red foliage would be appropriate.

THE ROSE GARDEN

The Rose Garden is an old favourite, and there is much to be said in favour of growing the modern Hybrid Tea roses and Floribunda roses apart in a separate little domain of their own, for these highly bred types do not blend happily with shrubs and herbaceous plants. I have tried to harmonize them many times, but have concluded that they are too artificial in character, with flowers of large size, or brilliant colour (or both), while their habit, stiffly poised on drastically pruned stems which all good growers have to inflict on them, cannot look natural. Nor are they capable of taking their place in the way of the pleached alley or espalier fruit—that is, trained to extremely conventional forms, but able to act as backgrounds to free plantings of other subjects without clashing.

To most of us the very word rose is so evocative, so full of associations with warm June days, with youth and romance, that it is very hard to stand back and appraise with a coolly critical eye a rose bush in bloom. If this effort is made, if we can forget sentiment, detach our minds and our noses from the colour, texture, shape and scent of the flowers, and examine the bush as a whole, we are forced to admit that by breeding with such emphasis on bloom and stamina the rose hybridizers have not produced a comely plant. The thick stiff stems have no grace, and the foliage provides little in the way of variety. How many flower-arrangers would give a thank you for a handful of rose foliage, taken from a modern Hybrid Tea?

Most of them are women, and the rose-growers predominantly men. It may be that the masculine urge to compete, to produce 'bigger and better' blooms than anyone else, has not been in the best interests of the genus *Rosa*. This is of course a feminine viewpoint, and it is interesting to observe that when a woman (Miss Hilda Murrell) rehabilitated the family nurseries at Shrewsbury after the war, it was the so-called 'shrub' roses, the Gallicas and Musks, the Cabbage and the Damask and the Moss rose, and various modern hybrids of these, which she developed to a particularly high standard. Her catalogue mentions that the popularity of these 'old' roses increases year by year, saying that they are exquisite for picking, 'affording the arranger graceful curves which are notably missing among the modern roses'. Perhaps in time the growers of 'new' roses will improve the foliage and habit of their productions—take a leaf out of the 'old' book, in fact.

SPECIALIZED GARDENS

After saying this, I must admit that one of the most alluring little rose gardens I have ever seen was planted with something very different—with miniature roses, arranged by the same Portland Nurseries of Shrewsbury at the Chelsea Flower Show in 1968. It was fit for small children, or for fairies, but too unspectacular for most gardeners, who would expect a show of larger blooms for their trouble. But perhaps some fond grandfather somewhere in England will make a miniature rose garden with these tiny bushes of China roses and climbers, with names like 'Magic Wand' and 'Pink Cameo', to please a very young granddaughter.

If it is possible when laying out a new garden to include a sunk garden, this may prove an ideal place for the roses. By sloping them down from the tall 'old' roses at the back, to the smaller types of Floribundas in the front, a great bank of roses may be built up. Privacy and shelter in a sunk garden need not all be gained by excavating the soil. The effect of a deeply sunk area is much easier to produce if some kind of wall, hedge or screen is placed round the depression, and the hedge itself, if a width of about 6 feet can be spared, may be composed of the lustier 'shrub' roses. This is not the easiest type of garden to construct, for the matter of drainage requires careful attention, and it may be necessary to install land drains. On very heavy land or in low-lying places subject to flooding it will be wise to avoid it.

If a sunk garden is not within our scope, then it may be possible to select a spot on the level which will lend itself to the formation of a rose garden separated in some way from the rest. A formal paved area in front of the house, with roses set round it, or in spaces left among the stones, can look very agreeable. It is less so if the frontage is of red brick, which would need to be softened and to some extent disguised with climbers and creepers and wall-trained shrubs—see Chapter 6. Unless, of course, the walls are very old and mellow; then they will take almost any colour of rose fairly close without rancour.

When dealing with land round single-storey buildings, bungalows, it is often quite easy to take a section of ground formed in the angle of the house-walls where one room joins another. Should the builder have left an unwanted legacy in the shape of a cement path close beneath the windows, it is not very difficult to rip that out. When the path is remade in a wide arc, there will be a good bed for roses within it, the bushes being backed by climbing roses on the wall. One friend made a wide bed right across the back of his new bungalow for roses. Unfortunately he planted a row of 'Queen Elizabeth' nearest to the windows, and in virgin soil this shot up so tall that the flowers were invisible unless you went close to the windows and peered upwards.

If it is desired to make a rose garden within a large area of existing lawn, then it should be boldly constructed as one section, divided up by paving for ease of maintenance, but not, whatever happens, a series of jam-tart beds cut out of the grass. These never look right; they give a fussy quality to the beauty of the greensward, suggesting a collection of graves in a cemetery; and the maintenance of clean-cut edges is a constant source of friction. Before long, some member of the family will get at them with a sharp edging tool because he or she (usually he) thinks they are not sufficiently neat, and in this way the jam-tarts are enlarged year by year. Such beds are all too easily made—made in haste, and often repented at leisure.

One of the many advantages of the 'old' roses is that they are strong enough to tolerate any amount of competition in the same bed, including complete ground-cover, which the Hybrid Teas are not really happy with. In my youth everyone set small plants, such as Violas in mauve or apricot, at the edges of rose beds. They were not good mixers. The best bedding I can remember with roses—in this case the fat old pink 'Caroline Testout'—was arranged by my grandmother. She raised a lot of pink Larkspur and interplanted the whole bed with them. Their branching, flimsy habit and the way some plants leaned against, or entwined themselves with, the sturdy rose bushes, had a lightening effect on the picture. There was a 'flutter' of the pink butterfly flowers almost down to the ground, balancing the pink cabbages on top.

SPECIALIZED GARDENS

Today some people bed Antirrhinums among their modern roses, but these are rather ponderous looking plants and they do not add grace to the stolid rose bushes. I prefer the fragrant white Nicotiana, with its branching habit, and it enjoys using the stiff rose stems as supports. The white may be mixed with the lower growing lime-green—alas, that variety is scentless. The deep red one looks good with red roses, but the 'mixed' boxes sold by so many garden shops are not beautiful in any position, and should be boycotted by the Society for the Prevention of Cruelty to Gardens—a Society which has yet to be formed.

Detailed instructions for growing all kinds of roses are given in numerous handbooks and gardening papers. One of the best books for gardeners with modest space is *Roses for Small Gardens* by C. E. Lucas Phillips, issued in the Pan Piper series. There is a good chapter on the possibilities for rose culture on chalk in Christopher Lloyd's *Gardening on Chalk and Lime*, in the same series. There are many good Rose growers. A few are named on page 214. Generally speaking, the modern Hybrid Tea and Floribunda Rose is a greedy feeder. The Shrub Rose and most of the climbers and ramblers will make do with lighter soil, although they need moisture and mulches in the growing season.

THE WATER GARDEN

This too may be placed within a sunk garden; if it is informal and surrounded by marginal aquatics it could perhaps be made on low-lying land where some boggy conditions might be encountered in winter. Even with a water garden, certain troubles may arise from water getting into the wrong place; it has been found, for instance, that the lovely Japanese Iris *I. kaempferi*, which does well in very moist soil in summer, dislikes being wet in winter also. It grows in its native land around the paddy fields, which are flooded in summer and dry out in winter. So it is necessary to find out just how much wet each subject can tolerate.

If it is to house a number of Water-lilies, the main part of the pool must be of a good size. Pools do not look attractive unless at least half of the water is free to reflect the sky and surroundings, and, except for the tiny pygmies, an area of 6 or 7 square feet of living space must be allocated to each Lily plant. Therefore six different plants will require roughly 40 square feet of water, and if the total area is to double that, it means a pool 10 feet by 8 feet. This type of pool should be made with 6 inches in depth of concrete, with about the same depth of composted loam on the bottom (avoid peat, leaf-mould and manure, if new, as these give off toxic gases which make the water foul). Water for the larger Lilies, sufficient to protect them against frost, should be 18 inches deep. This adds up to an excavated site 2 feet 6 inches in depth.

The deep centre is best constructed in a rectangular shape, or square; the shallower margins may be of 4-inch thick cement, with an equal thickness of soil and 4 inches of water; this part (unless in a very formal setting) may be of irregular shape, to give naturalness to the whole. The outer edges must be higher than those of the central pool, so that water (always kept brim full to look its best) flows right over the latter and forms an unbroken sheet to the edges. These should be disguised with slightly overhanging rocks or slabs of paving, which will give some shelter to ornamental fish at midday. All Water-lilies need sun, so that their pool must not be sited in the shade of large trees or walls. A great variety of interesting plants may be grown in and around the pool. Some have been mentioned in Chapter 4.

The Water-lily is the one subject that everyone wishes to grow in such a garden, and the number of varieties now available is bewildering. It is useful to have the Penguin book *Water Gardens* by Frances Perry, in a series sponsored by the Royal Horticultural Society. We are told that until Monsieur Marliac experimented with hybridizing, the only hardy species to be had for planting in outdoor pools was the white-flowered *Nymphaea alba*. The first hardy yellow appeared in 1881, and that was soon followed by red, pink, giant, and double, and dwarf forms. This highly gifted French breeder kept his methods a trade secret. They died with him, so that practically nothing new has appeared since his death in 1911. It may be thought that, as he evolved about seventy hardy Water-lilies in every colour and size (except blue) there really isn't much that could be added to his work.

Cultivation of the Nymphaea has been a surprising story altogether. A pink form of the North American *N. odorata* was ploughed up in a valley that had been drained and farmed for at least a century, and the tubers proved to be viable. It had been known that roots of a Water-lily could survive for a few years out of water, provided that the soil was moist and the crowns shaded from direct sun; but the ability of *N. odorata* to persist for a hundred years or more out of its element is astonishing. It is believed that all plants of this fragrant pink Water-lily now in cultivation have been propagated from one of these 'buried treasures'.

Nymphaeas form treasure of another sort to people in Africa and Asia, where the starchy tubers of native species have been used for food and for medicine. The aborigines use Australian species in similar ways. According to Mrs. Perry, the outer skin of the tuber, containing tannin and gallic acid, stains the skin badly when handled, so that it is easy to understand why our own countrymen took the roots of wild Water-lily for dyeing their homespun wools.

Her book, and the Cement and Concrete Association's pamphlet *Concrete in Garden-making*, will provide instruction in detail regarding the best methods of pool construction. The latter is of course concerned with concrete only, while Mrs. Perry takes in fibre-glass and polythene sheeting as lining material for the smaller pool. Other modern techniques are that of reinforced concrete sprayed on under high pressure, the use of vinyl as a liner, or (most recent of all) galvanized steel. These finishes are for swimming-pools, which are seldom painted now that permanent surfaces make that annual treatment superfluous. One very important aspect of the job is that of drainage. Pools used for plants and not swimming have to be emptied every three or four years for the purpose of cleaning and to get at and divide overgrown plants. The swimming-pool needs a great deal more maintenance, although the researchers have now developed a pill which will control bacteria and algae. The matter of drainage must be considered when a pool is being constructed, and the local authority advised if it is to be emptied into house drains.

The question of where to site a pool is seldom an easy one to answer. Too often in modern layouts the pool seems to have been dumped like a child's toy, by chance, or else somewhat coyly placed across an angle to make a symmetrical plan slightly less rigid. Even if a pool has been provided to amuse children, it should still be integrated into the garden scheme, and not just excavated from any piece of lawn or bed that happens to be little used. Generally speaking, if there is a gradual slope or terracing, a pool looks most natural in the lowest part of the garden, unless the designer has planned an ambitious series of pools linked by running water. Where level ground is concerned, and a pool in an existing lawn is planned, the relative amounts of water and grass should be fully considered. A large, formal pool surrounded by generous grass walks can be very attractive; but beware the little oval or circular one which so easily suggests an old-fashioned hip bath left out of doors by a vanished housemaid.

A small pool cut in a large expanse of grass requires some carefully grouped shrubs or specimen trees, not overhanging but near enough to combine with the shape of the water and produce a meaningful effect of some importance. Above all, pools (like babies) should always be really wanted and lovingly cared for. The pool that has been made in a short-lived burst of enthusiasm, or because the neighbours have one and it seems the right thing to acquire, had better never have been born.

THE ALPINE GARDEN AND THE SUNK GARDEN

There is a growing tendency now to have alpine plants dispersed in various parts of the garden, rather than massed on one special 'rockery'. As that celebrated ex-President of the Alpine Garden Society, E. B. Anderson, has said, it is difficult to describe the

SPECIALIZED GARDENS

conditions under which rock plants grow in nature, because the plant-hunters have now brought within our reach a vast collection from all over the temperate world, from North America and Japan and the New Zealand Alps to the South American Andes; and these may in the wild inhabit anything: fill a crevice at 6,000 feet or flourish on the sea-shore, on a cliff face, on scree, moorland or even in a thin wood. So that in our gardens it may be more satisfactory to choose a series of beds with differing aspects and positions, rather than seeking to suit every plant on one site.

Draughty positions are disliked by all of them; the drying effect of spring winds can be deadly when growth is just beginning, and damp hollows with stagnant air may be equally harmful in winter; while all alpines dislike drips from overhanging trees. Windbreaks of interlap fencing, wattle or growing hedge plants may be established for protection; but if the screen is a living one, roots should be placed far enough away not to penetrate the soil of the rock garden.

Not every lover of alpine plants is able to see them growing in the wild, and so the imagination must go to work, picturing these dwarfs, finely adapted to survive, tightly fixed in cracks and crevices from which the mighty storms cannot eject them. Their thickly matted habit prevents loss of moisture when the drained rock and scree dries up under the hot summer sun. Many of them have to remain for months beneath blankets of deep snow, which keep them drier and warmer than the outside air; but at low temperatures and deprived of light, they can only endure in a state of dormant life which one might describe as a plant coma.

Our climate in Britain is mostly very different, if we except the peaks of Snowdonia and the Scottish Highlands, where human beings do not dwell. The task of persuading these mountain plants to accept long spells of wet and cold with little or no snow cover, followed by the extraordinary vagaries of our spring, when sudden warmth is so frequently followed by bitter winds and rain or hail, is a daunting one. Possibly the very difficulties of the craft, with all its complexities and disappointments, serve to inspire and maintain keenness in the many amateurs who become addicted to the cultivation of alpine plants.

Some people consider this to be an expensive form of gardening, as of course it can be if everything is bought and only the best chosen. But Mr. Anderson has explained how he began to gain knowledge and experience in a modest way, in a small garden some 36 feet by 60 feet, on the shores of Dublin Bay. His soil was almost purely sea-sand, and in that he made two rock mounds, a moraine with water beneath it, a scree, a dry wall, a peat wall and a bog. A few beds in the shade, and a plot of grass completed his garden. On limited means he could import only a small amount of loam, to improve the sand, and some chippings for the moraine. Most of his plants were raised from seed. In that small space he found all the refreshment that a hobby could and should give a man, and it proved to be the beginning of a road that took him to the summit. His story may be an encouragement to the young and ambitious, but impecunious, alpine gardener.

Obviously the designer of a rock garden must be governed in the first place by the requirements of the plants, but the aesthetic aspects seem to go along very well with the practical. Weathered limestone is usually considered to be the best choice of rock, but sandstone or granite will serve, and each stone looks best in its own country. Any hard stone will do, provided that it does not break up easily in frosty weather—though flints are not much liked by the plants. Some gardeners have successfully utilized lumps of concrete, coloured with iron sulphate. The ground must be rammed firm to prevent hollows, and the rocks set well in, not less than half buried with the broadest part downwards, and tested by being stood upon. If they move, they are not sufficiently firm. The small, thin stones set on edge like almonds in a trifle are not only hideous, they are of no use to the plants, so this manner should be avoided at all costs. Owing to the difficulty of handling, it is usual to restrict rock size to not more than 56 pounds in weight, although from the pictorial point of view the larger the better, especially at the lower edge of a slope. Misguided gardeners, having installed an ugly jumble of rock, think

SPECIALIZED GARDENS

it will 'look right when clothed with plants'. The secret is to deploy stone to look well *before* planting begins. Given a well-arranged structure, the rockery will be pleasing at all seasons.

In nature the scree is a mass of broken rock lying at the base of a cliff, and in a rockery it may be copied with limestone chips, crushed granite, small gravel, mixed with moss peat and loam, forming a 12-inch layer above some flat stones. This sort of ground suits those plants which will not endure being wet round the collar-line. Sand and ash beds will also grow scree plants. Dry walls, peat walls (the latter for lime-hating plants), and crazy pavements are all suitable for growing dwarf plants; between paving stones the necks of little plants are well drained, and the roots are cool beneath the stone. In fact, some alpine specialists say that almost every choice plant can be made to grow in a piece of well-made paving. It must of course have good drainage, and is best laid on a slight slope for that purpose.

The sunk garden is usually thought of as a water-garden, and very attractive water looks in such a setting, as seen in the large sunk garden made by Nathaniel Lloyd, father of the well-known horticulturist Christopher Lloyd, at the old manor of Great Dixter in Sussex. Behind it a wall designed by Sir Edwin Lutyens when he restored the house links the buildings, and the sunk garden, with a small pool in a wide setting, informally planted in 'cottage' style, seems admirably in keeping with the oast-houses visible over the wall. (Plate VII b.)

A sunk garden for alpines sounds less practical, for it is likely to be the least well-drained part of a garden, and alpines cannot stand being waterlogged. A friend of mine has solved this problem by making a sloping bottom to the excavated space, with a pond at the lower end. She has built up her rock and scree well out of danger, even in the wettest season, and can grow some of the bog plants at the edge of the water. Her garden, otherwise flat and rather windswept, provided little in the way of an appropriate site for alpines until she decided to try using a lower level. The nearby fence, with light screening by lattice and creeper, provides a small amount of shade without drips, and some sparse shrubs along the edge of the sunk garden add to the protection from winds. Since the garden is placed near the house, in what used to be her lawn, she can step out easily in all weathers to look after her treasures, and, as she says, it is one way of avoiding the task of mowing as you grow older.

8

LAWNS, HEDGES AND PATHS

MOST GARDENERS in Britain want a lawn, and nearly all the others think that they ought to have one. Our climate so favours the cultivation of healthy greensward that it has become traditional. Smooth clipped turf does undoubtedly make a restful setting for brightly coloured flowers, as well as being agreeable to tread underfoot. One of the nicest things about mown grass is the effective pattern cast upon it by trees, especially shadows of orchard or ornamental flowering trees when growth is light and delicately traced by spring sunshine. Plate IX of the tower at Sissinghurst from Vita Sackville-West's orchard is a lovely example of tree-shadowed grass. But the lawn is a time-eater, requiring constant regular attention to keep it in trim, and in these days, when the jobbing gardener has almost disappeared, people in senior age-groups have to consider whether constant mowing is likely to prove a tiresome chore in their later years. The paved patio or terrace provides an alternative for sitting out, and although more costly to install it is practically free of maintenance work for a lifetime. Even the crazy paving with gaps for small plants is, if properly laid, easy to look after.

For those who feel that a lawn is essential, the best advice is to put all the grass into one area if possible, and leave it simple, without messy little beds chopped out of it. If the soil is in good condition and free from perennial weeds, the sowing of grass seed or laying of turves may go ahead; more often the selected site is foul with weeds, clogged with stones, and requires careful levelling. In such circumstances it is advisable to resign yourself to a season's wait before the lawn comes into being. If rough grass is already growing there it must be stripped off, not buried during digging operations. The roughly dug area should be cleared of weed roots, so far as these are discovered, and the larger stones and debris removed, then left fallow for some months, allowing time for other invasive and unwanted plants to put in an appearance, and be dealt with.

These preliminaries are of equal importance whether the lawn is to be sown or made of turf. The turves supplied by nurserymen are usually 3 feet long and a foot wide, not less than an inch and a half thick, and are delivered in rolls with the grass inward. They are laid in the manner of brickwork, with joints 'broken'—that is, the joins of one row coming against the centres of the previous row, and not opposite each other. When laying turf it is advisable to stand on a plank placed on top of the row you have just laid. The turves are butted together tightly, and a bucket of fine soil should be at hand to work into the joints. A wooden turf beater is used, not too heavily, to press the turves to the soil beneath them. After a few days the whole lawn may be rolled. When the surface has knit, a top dressing of lawn manure is beneficial.

This is the quickest way of making a lawn—but I have supposed the site to be really level and the soil in good tilth. The drawback to turf is that weeds may be imported in it, and the customer has little control over the kinds of grass from which it is composed. The weed menace is perhaps over-stressed by most gardening manuals, for by close examination of each turf before laying it is a fairly simple matter to identify and remove tap-rooted weeds, such as Thistle, Dock and Dandelion, and of course the white threadlike roots of Bindweed and the knotty yellow ones of the Nettle. My own most successful lawn was produced with bought turves, and it may be that I am unduly biased in favour of this method. The cost is considerably higher than that of seed, provided that you

LAWNS, HEDGES AND PATHS

do not have to employ labour to sow and watch over the latter kind. A newly seeded lawn is rather like a baby. It demands constant attention and cannot be left to its own devices while the gardener goes off on holiday for several weeks. The first cutting of tender grass blades must be done with sharp shears or scythe, for they are not able to stand up to a mowing machine until they have toughened and grown thick.

Detailed instructions for levelling and draining the site may be found in technical manuals, such as *Your New Garden* by A. G. L. Hellyer. Various mixtures of lawn grass seed are to be had, and the local nurserymen will stock those best suited to your district. The finer grasses, such as Agrostis and Festuca, are usually combined with the coarser but hard-wearing perennial Rye Grass, and as a rough guide to quantity, one ounce to the square yard is usually accepted. April to May, or September to October, are the best months for lawn making, and unless the climate is very cold and wet the latter season is preferable. If turves are used the choice is wider, but the job should be done in open weather when some moisture is expected, and not in a summer heat-wave or in wintry conditions.

People who take great care to level the site and produce a fine tilth raked free of stones sometimes omit to consider an equally important matter—that of drainage. The late Margery Fish, in her book *We Made a Garden*, describes the mistake she and her husband made when constructing their lawn at East Lambrook. In their hurry to get the site levelled and sown they forgot that such heavy clay soil might become waterlogged. It does, and today, thirty years later, it still produces luxuriant patches of moss. It would have paid them to lay agricultural drain-pipes beneath the surface, dropping slightly to a clinker-filled pit at one corner. They also lost a good deal of the best top soil, because they omitted to remove and store it while carrying out the levelling operations. A lot of infertile subsoil came to the top during the process, and valuable humus-laden topsoil was inadvertently buried. It is essential to understand that topsoil is alive with valuable bacteria, which must not be buried or otherwise wasted. One sometimes hears a hopeful gardener remark that ashes left on a bonfire site will ensure prolific crops there. In truth the heat of the fire will probably have destroyed life in the topsoil, and plant growth may be inhibited, not increased as a result. Anyone who cares to go more deeply into this fascinating subject could not do better than to borrow a copy of *The Living Soil* by Lady Eve Balfour, now out of print. The author, who was responsible for the inauguration of the Soil Association, has spent a lifetime in study of the soil. One far-reaching result of her insight and patient endeavour, often against ill-judged criticism, may now be seen in thousands of gardens where the compost heap is giving valuable service to fertility of the land, and improving the health of those who consume compost-grown vegetables and fruit.

The hedge is as deeply rooted in our conception of an English garden as is the lawn of mown grass. A. G. L. Hellyer has said that on the whole we plant too many of them, particularly in town front gardens—which are often so full of hedge that there is hardly room for anything else. We all know the sort of little plot he means. They give me the sensation felt as a small child when some misguided adult put an enormous humbug into my mouth, which could not even be shifted around in the natural process of sucking. But however much we may smile at a tiny front garden with a gobstopper of a hedge between its lips, nobody who has endured life with other people's children and dogs making free of an open-plan American garden could honestly blame the hedge devotees for their obsession with privacy. From the semi-basement of what was called the 'rumpus room' of our Canadian home I hated to look up through the windows, placed at soil level, because enormous dogs frequently relieved their bladders and bowels against the glass. How in such circumstances one longs for a good old English hedge!

Having decided upon a hedge, the choice of plant must be made, and there is a very wide choice. That old stand-by, the oval-leaved Privet, has the virtues of cheapness, hardiness, tolerance of almost any soil, however poor, and the strength to stand up unsupported against wind, rainstorms, and a load of snow that would break many a choicer plant. In its golden form it brightens an otherwise drab scene.

The chief rival of Privet in the small, economical garden of to-day is the bushy Honeysuckle with neat oval leaves—*Lonicera nitida*. It is at its best when kept low, not above 3 feet. Being less resilient than Privet it is inclined to break off or split in rough weather, if allowed to grow taller. A tougher kind, *Lonicera yunnanensis*, is not so easy to get, but is worth pursuing. It bears little, fragrant blossoms in springtime, and is considerably stronger than *L. nitida*. Both of these subjects cost about one shilling and sixpence apiece, and should be planted 15 inches apart. They look untidy unless clipped three or four times during the growing season.

Those good companions of the old English garden, Box and Yew, still have few rivals in my estimation, although a hedge of Sweetbriar might steal the limelight in June. But they cost five or six times as much as Privet, and are rather slow growing by modern standards. Left to itself, the Box will reach a height of 20 feet—at the rate of some 3 inches a year. Yet it will tolerate being clipped into any size and shape, which makes it very popular for topiary work. It is labour-saving in that one annual trim is enough. The little plant known as *Buxus suffruticosa* is generally supplied for edging purposes, and costs 15 shillings for enough to fill one yard, placed in a trench and just touching. It has an aroma that never fails to evoke nostalgic memories of old country gardens known and loved in one's youth.

Other aromatic plants used to form low hedges around the edges of flower beds and herb gardens are the Hyssops (blue, white or pink-flowered), Winter Savory, Lavender, Rosemary, Santolina, and the handsome 'Jackman's Blue' Rue. Fragrant foliage is not the only bonus to be garnered from a hedge. Anyone who has gardened by the sea will know the heady apricot scent of the Gorse in flower under a hot sun, and this plant flowers sporadically over a long period. For an impenetrable barrier, both cattle-proof and boy-proof, the Gorse is ideal, provided that you can spare room for it. It has a tendency to middle-aged spread, and it is uncomfortable to work near, so that plants should be kept at a respectful distance from a gorse hedge. The double form, *Ulex europaeus flore pleno*, is the most showy for garden use.

At a higher level in the social scale, if plants may be said to have one, is the hybrid shrub *Osmarea burkwoodii*, which makes a good hedge with neat, Box-like habit and scented white flowers in April. It stands clipping quite well, and is evergreen. Like most good things it is expensive; but for a short length of screening it is not exorbitant. Then there is Philadelphus, commonly known as 'Syringa', or 'Mock Orange' because of its scent of almost cloying sweetness. From the dozen kinds usually found in nurseries, *P. manteau d'hermine* is the neatest one for a hedge. Another valuable screen plant is the common or garden 'Butterfly Bush', *Buddleia davidii*, which seeded itself all over the ruins of war-torn London. This should only be used where there is room to let it grow tall and spreading. Inside a low wall or fence where fairly dense (and attractive) cover is required, perhaps from road traffic during summer, but not the exclusion of light in winter months, it is an excellent choice, and easily raised by the gardener for himself.

The hedge of Sweetbriar, so typical of English lanes in glorious June, is an enchanting object in the right place. It needs room, and it looks best in a semi-wild country garden. *Rosa rubiginosa* may be bought very cheaply for hedging from certain large nurseries, but if I were making such a hedge I should prefer to buy fewer, and better quality, plants and set them farther apart, say 4 feet or even more. Then I should mix in some Honeysuckle, and perhaps Clematis. The Sweetbriar sometimes gets leggy, and the bottom of the hedge too thin for comfort. This, according to the late Vita Sackville-West, can be obviated by planting against a post-and-wire fence, and tying-in long shoots to the lower part of this fence instead of pruning them off. The Sweetbriar is fragrant as to foliage as well as blossom, and there is the scarlet harvest of hips to be seen, and perhaps used for syrup rich in vitamin C.

Everyone knows the splendour of Beech, with its rufous leaves retained throughout the winter until the newcomers push them off in the spring. I think Beech really needs to be left to grow tall—up to 20 feet—to look its best. I cannot remember the precise height of that very famous Beech hedge in Perthshire, but from the car it towered above us like the ramparts of Edinburgh Castle. It saddens me to see this plant kept down to 3 feet or so; but it is undoubtedly very satisfactory as a small hedge, and this feeling is purely personal. The Hornbeam is faster growing, more twiggy, and on the whole less attractive. Personally I like a mixed hedge, and think we might well copy the mixtures found in the nearest countryside to our garden. The Myrobolan or Cherry Plum, the Holly, the Hawthorn, the Sweetbriar and Honeysuckle would do very well in the West Country where I live, had I room for such a luxury, with some of the small-flowered species Clematis planted on the shady side of the hedge. At Hidcote there is a combination of Yew, Box, Holly, Beech and Hornbeam: 'like a green-and-black tartan', as Vita Sackville-West wrote of it in the *Guide to Hidcote Manor Garden*.

Another form of screening—the wall—should not strictly speaking appear in a chapter on hedges and paths; but the drystone wall, at least, is often closely related to the design of paving and path. Although that type of walling is at home in the Cotswolds and similar stone country, and is very charming with small plants outlining the pattern of its joints, it is worth recalling the opinion of Sylvia Crowe in her *Garden Design* that 'to interpose a terrace wall of rough stone or rock between a rockless pasture landscape and a house of brick or concrete is to divide the house from its setting instead of uniting it'. Sir Edwin Lutyens understood this, and built his terrace walls of brick and dressed stone in the same style as his houses. One such wall is shown in Plate VII b, backing the sunk garden made at a later date within it by Nathaniel Lloyd, at Great Dixter in Sussex. The house and garden were restored in 1910 by Lutyens and Gertrude Jekyll. 'In the Lutyens/Jekyll gardens the interlocking between house and garden is achieved by his architecture thrusting outwards and her planting drifting inwards'.

But how would the owner of a concrete house view the prospect of still more concrete, in the form of a wall, thrusting outwards?

Even that knotty problem has been given an interesting solution by the resourceful Miss Crowe. A picture in her book shows corrugated cement shuttering, set up in curved forms to provide a marvellous effect of light and shade with the sun shining on it. A much older, traditional form of corrugated walling, seen in East Anglia, would be too expensive for most of us now, even if the craftsmen to make one could still be found. Known in Suffolk as 'crinkle-crankle', this serpentine walling was beautifully constructed of brick, the curves being longer and more gradual than the corrugations of the shuttering. Lucky indeed is the gardener who owns a crinkle-crankle wall, with its play of light and shade to suit a variety of climbers, and plants at its base.

On acid soils, the native *Rhododendron ponticum* makes a solid hedge and may be clipped like laurel. This plant was used to provide dense windbreaks beneath shelter-belts of trees in the West Highland garden of Inverewe. *Escallonia langleyensis, Griselinia littoralis,* and *Olearia haastii* would have been more attractive and equally practical, being wind-resistant and tolerant of salt spray. Then there is the Sea Buckthorn (*Hippophae rhamnoides*), which forms a lusty hedge. Provided some male plants are mingled with the females it will bear fruits of an attractive amber colour. The feathery sprays of Tamarisk, a native of sandy wastes, will do in poor dry soil near the sea, but it is not a dense shrub and is better as a mask for some unwanted view than as an excluder of animals or winds. The well-known *Buddleia globosa*, which often retains its leaves until mid-winter, is useful as a screen, and the shrubby Veronicas, now called *Hebe*, and the rather sprawling *Atriplex halimus* makes a grey-leaved hedge which flourishes by the sea. The use of conifers for screening, and that popular subject, *Cupressocyparis leylandii*, have been discussed in an earlier chapter. My best idea for an attractive hedge in the very small garden is the red-berried 'fishbone' Cotoneaster (*C. horizontalis*), because it will grow in very narrow spaces. It should be trained initially on chain-link or spile fencing, but in a few years will stand on its own feet. Small plants may often be bought at reduction by the dozen for hedging.

LAWNS, HEDGES AND PATHS

The subject of paths is one apt to cause more argument among makers of gardens than any other. An amusing dialogue between husband and wife occurs in the late Margery Fish's description in *We Made a Garden* of installing driveways and paths at East Lambrook Manor. In common with the writers of most technical manuals on gardening, Walter Fish required paths to be immaculate and weed-free, so he insisted that all stone paving must be set in cement, with no open joints between the stones. His wife thought this arrangement looked cold and ugly, so she furtively forced some pockets in the cement, using a crowbar when she was unobserved, to make room for little creeping plants. The weeds her husband feared never became very troublesome, and in time the creeping plants worked their way all over the place, with excellent effect. To be too 'house-proud' is not an advantage to the gardener.

When it came to the drive, Mr. and Mrs. Fish made a marvellous job of levelling and putting in drainage material—5 inches of broken brick and rubble, rammed, watered and rolled firm, then covered by 3 inches of finer ash and clinker, similarly bedded down, with the final topping of gravel an inch and a half thick. They took pains to see that the gravel went happily with the golden colour of the local Ham stone with which their house was constructed. 'Some kinds of gravel', wrote Margery Fish, 'are really violent in colour and shriek at everything in sight.' During the lifetime of her husband that drive had to be kept scrupulously free of weeds and loose soil from boots and plants, but after his death Mrs. Fish gave up her struggle and looked upon her drive as a convenient rooting-place for self-sown plants. Many a valued seedling I have found there when it was needed, and it looked far more interesting than the perfect drive of earlier days.

On heavy soils it is essential to dig out and lay foundations of rubble for drainage purposes before laying stone paving, but on lighter ground it is enough to level the surface. In order to keep stones really firm underfoot it is a good plan to put three or four 'joggles' of cement under each piece as it is laid. Grouting between them makes for dullness unless pockets of bare soil are left here and there for plants. When grouting is carried out, it will look its best if care is taken to scoop away a little of the cement before it has set hard, so that the edges of the stones are clear and defined, not smeared over in the way most handlers of cement leave it.

Some of us have to make do with paths entirely made from cement laid down on the site, or from moulded blocks of that material, on the score of economy. The synthetic paving Noelite is made in pleasantly subdued pale colours: grey, sand, pinkish and a good sage-green, labelled grey-green by the makers. Although these paving slabs are made with a rough-textured surface to prevent slipping, and to relieve monotony, the moulded corrugations are necessarily a little mechanical in effect, and when large areas have to be paved it would add greatly to the result if borders and dividing strips composed of cobble-stones laid in cement could be interposed. I have asked the firm whether slabs of cement ready-made with sea-pebbles inserted in them could be made available. In reply, it was stated that the possibility of making such a product was being investigated, but on exhibition sites the firm at present lays sections of pebble in cement to surround or divide areas of paving. For the small gardener this is not difficult to carry out, but supplies of the large sea-worn pebbles are difficult to obtain in small quantities. It would help if Garden Centres stocked this useful material.

Some of the paths I have most admired were composed of peat, littered with pine-needles, and they had pine-logs in the round set in to make risers for small steps. These delightful walks threaded their way in subtle curves through the woodland plantations of Inverewe in Mairi Sawyer's time. Paths of an earthy brown, overhung by plants, are natural in woodland and would look good in a closely planted 'natural' type of garden anywhere. They were largely ousted from Inverewe because of their spongy nature, and where peat does not occur naturally it would be impracticable to import loads to form paths of sufficient depth. But there may be an alternative. The use of dry, sifted sphagnum peat with cement and sharp sand in the mixture known as *hypatufa*, for application to the surface of white enamel sinks, fitting them for garden use, is mentioned

LAWNS, HEDGES AND PATHS

in Chapter 9. It is possible that the cement path, or cement paving slabs, could be coloured and textured by mixing in a proportion of sphagnum peat to make an agreeable synthetic path material. I have not yet had time to try out this idea. It sounds better than the old country plan of colouring cement with water in which cow manure has been steeped.

Two questions that arise in the setting out of most garden plans are: How wide should the paths be? and (if the land slopes), Shall we make the path into steps, or retain the slope? A stock answer to the first query is to make paths as wide as possible, in order to facilitate passage of a wheelbarrow, or of the gardener laden with a forkful of rubbish. Personally I would opt for a slimmer barrow, and a path made to match. The ordinary wheelbarrow is a cumbersome tool, even in its lightest form, for the weight and top-heavy character increase as it is filled up to its widest splay. Many a time, when trying to negotiate a laden barrow through confined spaces at Lambrook while helping Mrs. Fish, I have longed for the narrow, straight-sided handcarts we used at Inverewe. These had two wheels, and one leg at the rear to rest on when stationary. They took far less energy to push than the ordinary barrow, held plenty of rubbish, and travelled along the woodland paths easily. The wide expanse of path, made specially to take an ordinary large wheelbarrow, is seldom attractive in a small garden and it takes up valuable plant space. How much better to substitute a narrow handcart!

One compromise between the narrow, secret path and the wide, easily negotiated pavement is made when plants are encouraged to sprawl out over a large section of paving on either hand. When the time of autumn clearances, or spring weeding, digging, planting, or mulching comes round, the plants may be pushed aside or judiciously pinched back to give easy, if temporary, access. In the picture of the vestal virgin at Sissinghurst, a wide strip of paving is nearly smothered by 'Lamb's Ear', *Stachys lanata*. (See Plate XII.)

As for steps, these often provide interest, and they are more comfortable to stand on when admiring plants than is a sloping path. The latter can be a menace when such useful adjuncts to gardening as balls of twine are dropped—to roll away at speed and possibly land in the pool or in a prickly hedge-bottom. But, unless the risers are very low and the treads wide enough to take a barrow or handcart, steps are highly unsuited to the passage of wheeled traffic. If the garden is narrow, and one path is all it can take, it is necessary to make up one's mind whether steps must be ruled out, or whether the use of a barrow is to be so infrequent that it may be wheeled along the lawn, without causing material damage to the turf. A more imposing flight of steps than the one here intended has been made in the garden of Moyles Cottage, Quenington, allied with dry-walling and a large paved terrace. (See Chapters 2 and 13.)

Some admirable paths of gravel have been made in the replica of George Washington's garden in the grounds of Claverton Manor, near Bath—now the home of the American Museum in Britain. As the picture (Plate X a) shows, the gravel reaches almost to the top of the neat stone edging, and plants are allowed to spill over on the stony surface, like waves of an incoming tide. This garden is of great interest to the designer, and contains many an old-fashioned plant, very well used in large clumps without crowding. We cannot all procure a summer-house as elegant as George Washington's schoolroom, with its silvery shingled roof; but the white picket fence cut at the top to form slopes that give the effect of curves, could be used decoratively in a number of small schemes. The modern design shown in Figure 7(b) has sections of similar fencing used alternately with sections of Copper Beech hedge, making a striking contrast of light and dark.

ETCETERAS

'"The time has come", the Walrus said, "to talk of many things: of shoes—and ships—and sealing-wax—of cabbages—and kings—".' Should you be inclined to think that only the green vegetable here named is relevant to a garden book, this narrow view needs to be greatly enlarged. In fact, for my purposes the homely greens and roots, except in so far as I have considered the class distinctions which currently debar them from our flower borders, have been deliberately omitted from my scheme. The kitchen garden, together with the orchard proper (excluding old fruit trees used as backgrounds to flowering plants, or as hosts for climbers), has been so well covered by a vast literature of practical gardening that it would ill become me to add to the pile. In any case, this is a book about the design of what are sometimes classified as 'ornamental gardens'.

Under that heading the ships may sail in, or even approach under their own steam. As one drives around the country lanes of England, it is amazing to see how many old salts, having swallowed the anchor, remind themselves pleasantly of days at sea by watching a weather-vane in the shape of a vessel which swings at anchor with every puff of a breeze. Some go even further than the local blacksmith to have their nostalgia for the sea assuaged. A front garden in the main street of a village near Bath is nearly filled by a large topiary man-of-war, steaming proudly alongside the busy road. Although I am the daughter of a naval architect, and myself served in a naval department of what was then the Admiralty, I would not like to commit myself as to her class. She evidently belonged to the King's navee, before we had a Queen, and in another decade or two may be the sole survivor of the old-fashioned warship armed with guns designed to fire shells and not objects known as 'missiles'.

As for royalties, the plant world is stuffed with them. Not only are there the old vernacular names, such as Kingcup, King's Spear, Queen Lily and Queen-of-the-Meadow, but denizens of that Wonderland created by modern nurserymen: the hollies Golden King—which is female—and Golden Queen, a male plant.

Then there are gardeners with a fancy for shoes. I have seen a whole row of wooden sabots used as plant-pots for small treasures on a low garden wall. My own foible is even more bizarre: I confess to using sealing-wax as a quick means of fixing new, temporary name-cards to old painted wooden labels. Does any gardener ever have enough *new* painted labels? Is it not a chronic disease to want an unsullied one and fail to find it? And what a chore the repainting of used labels can be! I prefer sealing-wax, and a slip of card or plastic stuck over the old tag. It will not last for ever, but by the time it disintegrates I have probably learned the name of the new plant and no longer require a label for it.

So far from the 'many things' of the Walrus being superfluous in a garden, I sometimes wonder if there is anything at all that has not been, or could not be, used by the enterprising gardener. The breakfast egg does not at first glance seem particularly promising; but with the top neatly sliced off, the shell carefully cleansed after the meal, and a few holes bored in the base with a knitting-needle, the ingenious person makes an excellent pot for a seed to grow in. Invalids and small children obtain endless pleasure from those little boxes in which eggs are packed at the poultry farm, each hollow containing a clean egg-shell, into which John Innes or similar compost is spooned—naturally, with a plastic egg spoon. If compost is considered to be messy, vermiculite may be substituted, or even sawdust or blotting-paper. We can all remember the marvels of 'mustard and cress' flourishing on damp flannel in the nursery.

The egg-shells can be made into a charming Easter garden, if the tiny species crocus are planted, one to each shell, with a sprinkling of grass seed added so that the many flowers that spring from each corm seem to be set in a lawn. The fruit-eater may like to raise plants from pips of apple, orange and lemon; others make little forests of cacti and succulents, or propagate pot-plants, such as scented-leaved Geraniums, in these home-made pots. Competitions for the most ingenious egg-shell gardens have become popular in Women's Institutes and similar institutions, and they are invaluable objects of interest to bed-ridden or long-stay patients in hospital, and to both the handicapped and the normal child. They seem to have been invented by that famous gardener Fred Loads. When the egg-plants become pot bound it is a simple matter to crush the shell and plant the contents outdoors, if hardy, or in a larger pot if not.

In the 'free' design for a modern family garden, described in Chapter 3, there is a mosaic decoration on the paved terrace, based on the compass and showing the orientation of the land. This was a combined effort made by the whole family from fragments of broken china set in a slow-drying cement. The children later collected a larger quantity of shards for a more ambitious project—a mosaic mural to go on the white wall beside their pool, based upon the signs of the zodiac. As children will, they begged with the greatest tenacity once their interest had been aroused, importuning strangers for broken china in places where none but the most brazen adult would have dared to set foot on such an errand unaccompanied by a childish escort. The reply of an imposing lady in an expensive antique dealer's shop sounded very like that of Edith Evans in *The Importance of Being Earnest*, the unforgettable 'A *handbag*?' being here replaced by an incredulous 'For your *garden*?' when the request was voiced. Provided the china is used in really small pieces, the curvature found in shards from bowls and cups does not matter, it will in fact add to the texture of the finished mosaic.

The essential point to remember about etceteras is that you

should feel the need first, and then set about making or obtaining the article you have in mind. To acquire objects in haphazard fashion, and then try to place them in the garden, will almost certainly prove fatal to the success of your design as a whole. The purpose of design is to create a harmonious whole and not a collection of bits and pieces. I am convinced of the absolute truth of this principle, even though it has at times come into conflict with my besetting passion for white pigeons. Frustrated, as I have indicated, in my longing for the live birds, I modelled one in clay and set about having it cast in plaster, to produce counterfeits which might, when rendered weatherproof by paint and varnish, be placed in groups on grass or paving. I soon discovered that, while the living birds look good wherever they pitch, static clay pigeons must be posed in exactly the right places, and that these would alter during the growing season and from year to year, as the garden changed.

Carefully used, such home-made ornaments—which cannot, owing to the limitations of fired clay or cast-making, be *too* naturalistic—are a great improvement upon the sickly realism of plastic gnomes and the unidentifiable birds of commerce. Here is a useful outlet for the creative ability of children, who are often adepts from an early age at handling clay. The local pottery or brickyard will usually help with the firing of clay in a kiln, and it then becomes tough and permanent. The 'found' object, such as a large stone shaped by wind and weather into something resembling an abstract sculpture by Henry Moore or Barbara Hepworth, can be of value in the right place, as can a fallen bough or piece of tree-trunk in writhen form, naturally bleached and strangely alive in death.

The garden trough, tub, pot, urn, or 'planter' is an etcetera of great importance in many a modern scheme, and there are enough types available to fill a chapter. Personally, if I cannot have old stone troughs or sinks, I prefer good terracotta pots of the simplest shape to the rather spineless objects moulded in cement and beloved by municipal gardeners. Copies of old lead containers made in fibreglass by Verine are excellent in the right place, if you can afford them, and they are wonderfully light and strong. But they seem to need a background of dignity and style, which generally suggests a venerable house of Georgian or earlier date. In association with modern buildings they are apt to look merely pretentious.

When staying on the Italian island of Ischia, I admired the amazing variety of terracotta pots produced by Fabbrica Mennella and lined up along the seafront in their display yard to tempt every garden-maker almost beyond bearing. For which of us, in these days of air travel, could transport vast troughs and jars weighing half as much as ourselves? Many of these desirable souvenirs are decorated in low relief with legendary beasts and birds, and with

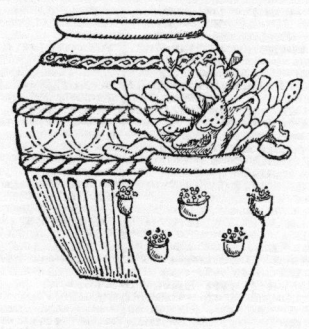

classical *ovolo* and *guilloche* patterns. In London, where all things may be bought—at a price—it is possible to get similar pots from Provence; or there are the simple English ones made in north Devon by Brannam of Barnstaple. This firm makes one pot, 15 inches high and 19 wide at the top, with a simple band of scrolling branch and leaf which has classical charm. They have also a 'strawberry pot', with little pouches clinging to the sides of a large, tall jar, but the four rows, although giving room for more plants, are less satisfactory as a design than the uncluttered Italian model, which has only two rows. It was in Ischia that I first saw broken pottery, in this case glazed tiles, used in garden decoration. The gardeners were engaged in making some steps out of concrete, a material which they found dull compared with the princely marble which was squandered on peasant cottages and garden terraces until rising costs of labour made it too expensive. To compensate for the variations of colour in the living marble, and for its sheen, those gardeners created spontaneous little patterns with pieces of broken tiling, and when an old well had to be renovated with cement they stuck in the remaining shards to cheer that up.

The fashion for stainless steel sinks has rendered thousands of the glazed white type superfluous, and these may be picked up cheaply from builders' yards. As they stand they are horrible, quite unsuited to garden use, unless perhaps in a greenhouse. But there is a way of disguising them very satisfactorily, as was described by the celebrated alpine gardener, Joe Elliott, in a lecture given to the Royal Horticultural Society in April 1967, and reproduced in that Society's *Journal* for October 1967. The method of covering these sinks is as follows: after removing all traces of grease, the outside and a few inches of the inside are coated with a bonding material, either Polybond or Uni-bond. This is left until it grows tacky, and then a layer of what is called Hypatufa is applied, a quarter of an inch thick. This is made up by mixing one part (by bulk) of cement, one part sharp sand, and two parts dry, sifted sphagnum peat. I do not know whether Mr. Elliott invented this stuff, but it is an invaluable aid to the impecunious gardener, and if he did think it up he deserves a medal. It is also possible to cast the whole trough from similar material. An article by S. E. Lilley describing the process will be found in *A Handbook of Rock Gardening*, issued by the Alpine Garden Society.

That eccentric poet and gardener Alexander Pope (1688–1744), must have been one of the most ardent users of etceteras ever born. His garden beside the Thames at Twickenham is no more; only the famous grotto beneath the road still exists, though shorn of many trappings. It belongs to St. Catherine's Convent, Pope's Villa, Twickenham, and may be seen by appointment on Saturday and Sunday afternoons. Poor Pope! He was tiny, physically deformed, and plagued by a host of chronic illnesses, and yet in making his beloved garden he experienced a kind of ecstasy. 'I am as busy in three inches of Gardening as any man can be in three score acres. I have a theatre, an arcade, a bowling green, a grove,' he wrote in 1725,

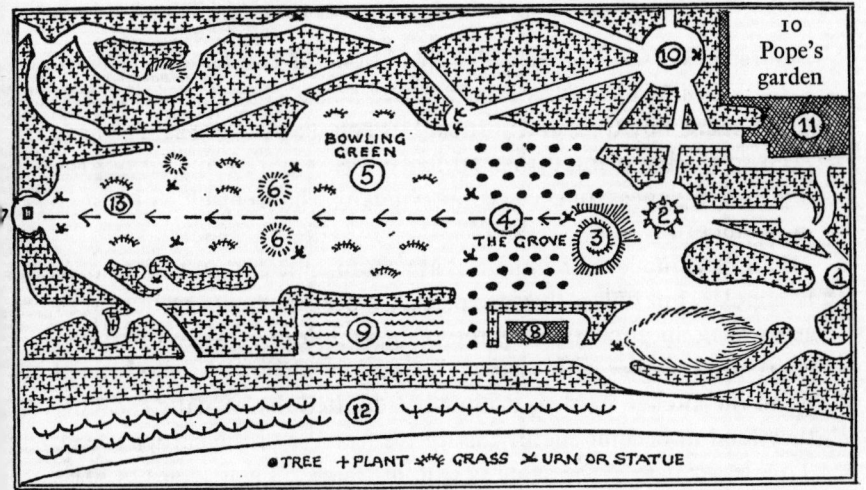

1 Entrance 2 Temple 3 and 6 Mounts 4 Grove 5 Green 7 Obelisk 8 Stove
9 Vineyard 10 Orangery 11 Gardenhouse 12 Kitchen garden 13 Vista

and he was constantly adding to his treasures up to the time of his death. I have not been able to discover any mention of the precise area his 'three inches of Gardening' covered; but, so far as can be judged by the plot occupied by his villa on the plan, his land must have been some 800 feet long by about 250 feet wide.

Within that space he arranged no fewer than three statues, four busts, four lead urns, 16 stone urns and a shell temple, together with an imposing obelisk in memory of his mother. He designed his plantings to increase visual distance by means of false perspective, a device used in recent times by Mr. and Miss Matley Moore in their small town garden at Greyfriars, Worcester (see Chapter 13). Pope planted dark cypresses round the obelisk, which stood at the end of his main vista. He explained to his friends that 'you may distance things by darkening them, and by narrowing the plantation more and more toward the end, in the same manner as they do in painting'. He described the picturesque nature of the garden as being 'just like a landscape hung up'. It is interesting to us, over 200 years later, to notice that the free-flowing shapes of the shrubberies in Pope's scheme have an affinity with abstract painting today, and are not unlike those of the modern garden shown in

Figure 7. We do not possess illustrations of the larger pieces of garden furniture, such as Pope's 'stove house', but this was clearly well screened by trees and shrubs. His boundaries were said to have been so thickly planted that no fence was required to shut out the inquisitive glances 'of every country fellow who went by with a pipe in his mouth'.

Our little modern greenhouses are cheap, efficient, and enormously popular, but unless they are placed so near the house or bungalow as to form an appendage to the main building, or placed within a courtyard together with washing line and dog-kennel, or else hedged off in the kitchen garden, it must be admitted that visually speaking they tend to become highly disruptive features of the garden scene. To a lesser degree the same is true of frames. Their panes of glass catch the light, and sharp rectangular lines of construction do not blend in with surrounding plants. Now that many modern materials do not require constant painting, it should be easy to disguise outlines of greenhouse and frame either by training creepers over the house itself or by erecting a light trellis close to it, while frames may be bedded down within low hedges of Box, *Lonicera nitida*, golden Privet or aromatic Lavender and Rosemary. Even a thin screen of foliage, enough to break up the hard outline without cutting off light, is of the greatest benefit to the picture.

When it comes to painting garden sheds, greenhouses, seats, frames and plant tubs or water-butts, such etceteras are enormously improved if the common white paint (or the crude green beloved by municipalities) is abandoned in favour of grey-green or olive-green, which blends in with natural foliage instead of hitting the eye with a bang. The manufacturers of paints as yet pay very little attention to gardeners' need for colours provided in ready-mixed brands. One exception is called 'Cotswold Stone', which looks particularly well on garden furniture in association with buildings of Cotswold or similar stone. Unfortunately it is not easy to get, but it is worth taking trouble to obtain this colour. It is a great improvement on those dead greys so often described as 'stone colour', for it has life in it, but is unobtrusive.

ETCETERAS

Although the makers of plastic buckets are at last producing these useful articles in a pleasant olive green colour instead of the screaming yellows and reds which have been on offer for many years past, the extremely useful plastic-coated wire trellis has yet to follow suit. The white, which is suitable only for white or cream coloured walls, is invariably partnered in Garden Centres by trellis of a gluey kind of 'grass' or 'emerald' green, unlike any self-respecting grass and far removed from the precious stone. Do those firms concerned with garden sundries never place their wares outdoors and survey the result critically? Most articles seem to have been thought up in offices or designing studios far removed from the places where they are to be used.

Although here included among the etceteras, a compost heap is really an essential to any garden, however small. In my tiny herb garden there are two bins side by side, each about 2 feet square; while one is full and coming to maturity the other one is used, turn and turn about. They are built up with planks, slipped into slots as the piles grow. All garden refuse goes into the bin (except for woody prunings and the bad perennial weeds, which are burnt); this is supplemented by the household waste of purely vegetable nature. Some people add meat and fish, but that may attract rats, and the prowling cat sometimes disinters it and makes a great mess. I keep shelter 'blinds' of polythene sheeting over the top of each bin. They are fixed to the back and slope down towards the front boards, with stout rods run through hems at the lower edges to keep them from blowing up in the wind. A compost heap needs ventilation, moisture and warmth, but should never be allowed to get sodden. Well-made compost is friable and clean to handle, like hop manure. The material is built up in layers, thinly spread, large leaves and stems being cut up into smaller pieces, and lawn mowings sprinkled carefully in between the other items. Thick layers of grass form impermeable sodden layers and are not desirable. At 12-inch intervals a good layer of soil or mushroom litter goes on my heaps, and when the bin is comfortably full I apply *Fertosan* herbal activator. The best book on this subject, *Commonsense*

Compost Making, by M. E. Bruce, has recently been revised by Lady Eve Balfour of the Soil Association and is obtainable in a new edition issued by Faber and Faber. The compost heap may be easily and conveniently built within a screen of wattle hurdles. Wattle admits air, and so makes an ideal container, and it always looks pleasing. Honeysuckle and Jasmine grow over mine.

The more ornamental etceteras, such as sundials, bird baths, urns and bird tables, need very careful choice and siting. It is a good plan to take the attitude of 'when in doubt, do nothing'. If a need becomes pressing, inspiration as to the type chosen, as well as its siting in the design, is likely to develop with the desire to own the article in question. Birds, it should be remembered, leave droppings around their feeding and drinking places, so that it is a mistake to put these near garden seats. Plants bespattered with bird-lime are unhappy-looking objects, and a piece of paving which may easily be hosed down is a more practical choice than a flower bed. Our own wild birds are fed beside the compost heap, and that is convenient for the person who tips green household refuse into the bin and bread and fat scraps on the feeding table. This consists of a stout post, made from 3-inch-square timber, creosoted, with 5 feet above the soil and 1 foot below it. On the top a small wooden tray is permanently fixed. This has drainage holes, and an ordinary rectangular enamel pie-dish exactly fits into it to take the food. In hot weather it is an advantage to be able to wash such a dish, to prevent smells from traces of meat or fat left by the birds.

If the introduction of such permanent ornaments as the sundial and the urn is left until the main design has been laid out, this will be an insurance against overdoing these accessories; but it may be that some additional planting suggests itself to accompany the hardware. I am thinking not only of the plants to be put into a planter or urn, and the dwarf Lavender or 'Mrs. Sinkins' Pinks to surround the base of the sundial, but of plant accents to complement the latest acquisition. In the re-designed front garden mentioned in my first chapter (see Figure 2), the gardener who removed a diagonal cement path installed by the builder later added on his lawn a plinth made from two or three courses of stone, to hold an old copper retrieved from a friend's wash-house. Having established this focal point on his lawn, he then felt the need for some 'echoes' round about it, and satisfied that want by planting eight small fastigiate conifers—*Juniperus communis hibernica*. These were placed in the angles of the rose beds and on either side of the stone stepping-places made between drive and grass, and near the front door. This gardener took time to think things out. He was quite sure what his particular design really demanded to complete the picture before he added the finishing touches. All really successful gardens are compounded from three ingredients: natural features, plantsmanship, and thought. The greatest of these is thought.

OLD WELL, ISCHIA

PART THREE

10

SOME FAMOUS GARDENS IN ENGLAND

1 HIDCOTE

HIDCOTE IS situated in Gloucestershire, not far from the Warwickshire border and Shakespeare's country. The small and lovely Cotswold towns of Broadway and Chipping Campden are a few miles away, reached by winding and hilly lanes; Bredon Hill, made familiar to poetry lovers by A. E. Housman, is visible from the garden. Major Lawrence Johnston, an American who made his home in England, acquired the Manor of Hidcote in the early years of this century—some authorities quote 1905, others 1907. The pleasant stone house, built in traditional gabled Cotswold style, with its own farm, snugly placed in the tiny hamlet of Hidcote Bartrim, at that date possessed practically nothing in the way of a garden. One fine Cedar of Lebanon and a few Beech trees formed the nucleus of all the planting that now goes to make up this very well-known garden, carved by one man from the English fields surrounding his home.

It was a highly original conception; one that has had great influence on other gardeners and their work in more recent years—for this was the very first of the so-called 'room' gardens. As the landscape architect Miss Sylvia Crowe points out in her *Garden Design*, the influx of new plant material at the end of the Victorian era and in our own century encouraged a love of collecting and cultivating plants for their own sakes. Gardens became horticultural workshops, where men employed their leisure hours growing rare plants, or developing larger specimens of common ones, for private pleasure or for competitive shows. In the midst of all this, the importance of designing the garden as a pictorial composition was largely overlooked. Plantsmen's gardens, as Miss Crowe says, are commoner than any other sort in England today, and they too often lack stability and repose. 'The very diversity of their planting is monotonous *because its contrasts are on too small a scale and too often repeated.*' No garden designer can afford to ignore that criticism. It is worth writing up in letters of gold before we begin to lay out our scheme. Miss Crowe goes on to point the moral by saying that these modern English gardens seem to lack the distinction between open space and dense planting to be seen in good French designs, with their open avenues and flat parterres surrounded by thick bosquets, and shown in our own landscape school in earlier years, when trees in clumps and belts were set against open sweeps of grass.

At Hidcote an attempt has been made to solve the problem of housing a great variety of plants without restlessness of effect, by building a series of 'green walls' out of high hedges and trees, within whose enclosure lies a series of small open-air rooms and connecting passages. The 'in and out' principle of architectural composition has informed the way progression is engineered at different levels from one compartment to another, and a pattern of solid and void is contrived by very close planting in some sections, contrasted with sparse furnishing of others. As the gardens are sited some 500 feet above sea-level, on the windy wolds, the enclosure system is an eminently practical form of gardening as well as a satisfying one from a pictorial point of view.

The late Vita Sackville-West wrote of Hidcote as being a cottage garden on a most glorified scale, covering in fact 10 acres and thus quite outside the cottage range so far as size goes. 'It resembles a cottage garden, or rather a series of cottage gardens, in so far as

1 Entrance court
2 Theatre lawn
3 Pool
4 Mrs. Winthrop's garden
5 Stilt garden
6 Kitchen garden

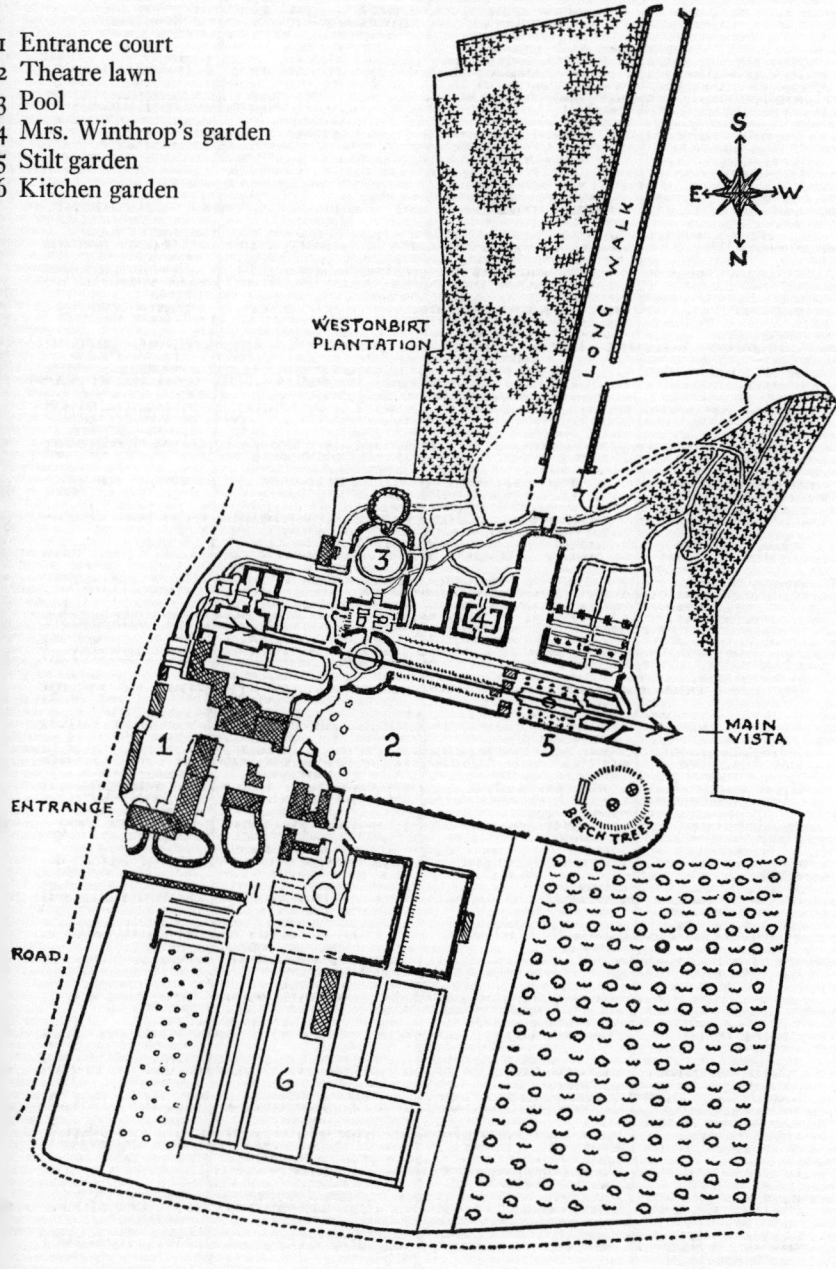

11 Hidcote

the plants grow in a jumble, flowering shrubs mingled with roses, herbaceous plants with bulbous subjects, climbers scrambling over hedges, seedlings coming up wherever they have chosen to sow themselves.'

Entrance is made through a forecourt which has around the walls and verges *Schizophragma integrifolia*, Magnolias, *Solanum crispum*, the large-flowered 'Hidcote' variety of Hypericum, which was raised in this garden, *Viburnum carlcephalum*, some species Clematis, and much else. The way leads past the kitchen garden and glasshouses, screened by hedges to the north, to a great expanse of grass known as the 'Theatre Lawn', where some original Beech trees are enthroned upon a mound with spring bulbs at their roots. This is the largest 'open' section in the whole design, and by contrast with its spacious peace the plunge into the close-planted 'Old Garden', reached from the south-east corner of the lawn, is like diving into a Devon combe after walking on Dartmoor.

From this enclosure—really a whole series of small 'rooms'—the principal vista leads the eye through the 'Stilt Garden', bordered by pleached Hornbeam, to openness beyond. Because of rising levels, the view is not of distant landscape but of sky. Only when the far end is reached can Bredon Hill be seen. So enticing is this long walk that, were I condemned to crutches, it would still compel exploration of the full length. The whole design, as Miss Crowe says, is an invitation to explore. 'None of the main vistas at Hidcote is terminated by a feature. Instead of giving the eye something on which it can rest and be content, they lure it on by an air of mystery, by the knowledge that there is something round the corner.'

A point here which appeals to the inquisitiveness latent in most of us is the narrow width of so many steps and paths; often they seem to hint 'You are not really *supposed* to come this way'. So of course that is the way one determines to explore, where it is out of the question to proceed two abreast, and the 'Indian file' of childhood gives nostalgic pleasure to those of mature years. Even a slight feeling of guilt may be experienced, just enough to increase enjoyment. There is surely a lesson here for every designer, however

SOME FAMOUS GARDENS IN ENGLAND

small his garden may be. We should not put all our cards on the table, but keep people guessing; give them mystery and some sort of surprise.

One of the drawbacks to public ownership of gardens is the increased traffic that ensues, and the idea often held by those responsible for their upkeep that walks must necessarily be widened to accommodate the visitors in parties of two or three or more abreast. In some cases this idea may be fairly harmless, in others it is less so, and it could easily have been the ruin of Hidcote if applied there. When a garden is becoming overcrowded, why not proclaim a quota system, or form a queue, as is so often done at busy seasons when stately homes, museums—even Coventry Cathedral—are open to the public? The spoliation of places of interest because too many wish to enjoy them is both tragic and ludicrous. It was summed up ironically by the oldest inhabitant of a famous village in these words: 'The old "Bull" has gone, the forge has gone, and Church Cottages are going; we're just waiting for the church to go when they finish widening the road. So many people wanted to see our village, it couldn't hold them all.'

Although we can all appreciate the clipped Box and Yew at Hidcote, many will think that Box is too expensive and Yew too slow-growing to be used in the smaller modern garden. While it is true that small plants of Box cost about 6/- each, and similar plants of its common rival, *Lonicera nitida*, may be had for 1/6, it must be remembered that the latter needs at least half-a-dozen clippings each year against one given to Box. Neither does the latter get 'browned off' the way Lonicera is apt to do, nor is it brittle, so it will endure people bashing against it without breaking. The smaller the garden, the fewer plants are required, so make sure that you get the best. For low hedges or 'edgings', Box is undoubtedly the better of these two. Yew, which makes a superb background to flowering shrubs and plants, is not as slow as most people imagine; but it must be confessed that it needs a good deal of food, and grows with a middle-aged spread. Considerable width must be allowed for a hedge of Yew.

It is evident that Major Johnston admired the great Holford arboretum at Westonbirt, situated near Tetbury in the same county of Gloucestershire. An area to the south of the enclosed gardens at Hidcote has been planted with *Sorbus hupenesis* and *S. vilmorinii*, which look so lovely with their pink and crimson berries in the Westonbirt Silk Wood; with various Maples and Oaks; with the American Sweet Gum (*Liquidambar styraciflua*); with the broad-leaved Holly and the Chilean Bamboo; with *Nothofagus antarctica, Fraxinus mariesii*, and other interesting subjects. They were chosen for their berries and autumn foliage colour, and most of them are seen also in the Holford plantings. This accounts for the fact that at Hidcote this section has been named 'Westonbirt'.

Hidcote is often called a 'plantsman's garden', and an expert plant-fancier its owner certainly was; but Major Johnston seems to have been unusual in contriving to disguise this fact from all but the hawk-eyed few. He could always see the wood as well as the trees, and chose his plants for their suitability and character, without worrying about whether they happened to be rare or not. Having selected a plant, he gave it considerable freedom to do as it pleased: a trait that appealed to Vita Sackville-West. She spoke of a narrow path beside a dry-wall at Hidcote—the gardener called it a 'rock garden', although it resembled nothing she had ever seen by that name. At the foot of the wall ran a ribbon of *Campanula portenschlagiana bavarica*. 'This, after the Hidcote principle, had been allowed to spread itself also in brilliant patches wherever it did not rightly belong. Out of the dry-wall poured, not the expected rock plants, but a profusion of Lavender (the deep Hidcote variety and "Hidcote Giant") and wands of Indigofera . . .' Again that refreshing unexpectedness.

The Hidcote Hypericum has already been mentioned; Hidcote Lavenders are another result of Major Johnston's plantsmanship, for which all gardeners must feel grateful. The profusion of dark purple spikes, and the compact habit of *Lavandula* 'Hidcote' make it ideal for any small garden. It is a long-lasting plant, not easily broken apart by wind or snow. Gardens also owe a debt to Hidcote for the early-flowering climbing yellow rose that bears Major Lawrence Johnston's name, although this was not raised in Gloucester but in France, by Monsieur Pernet-Ducher. It was nursed, unknown, at Hidcote for many years before Mr. G. S. Thomas brought it out and named it in honour, as he says, 'of its careful keeper'. This vigorous rose has a good scent and attractive foliage of a clear green. It is one of the best yellows for a warm, sunny spot.

We have wandered through Hidcote without once mentioning water. There is a stream, and a large brimming pond which almost fills the 'room' in which it is placed. A great circular mirror, reflecting the foliage and the sky, watched over by plump little topiary birds with cocked tails—very young peacocks, perhaps. Elsewhere I remarked that this pool garden alone would satisfy me, and those are no idle words. It has power both to soothe and to excite interest, however long you stand and stare at it. What more should a mortal ask? Yet the square garden beyond, planted with yellow peonies, golden hops, Lady's Bed Mantle and Evening Primrose, named after the owner's mother, Mrs. Winthrop, is equally enticing. If it be not too greedy, I will opt for both of them.

Does it sound unpatriotic in this land of lovely gardens to confess that I am much addicted to the American gardener and his work? One can discern something in common between Hidcote and the great eighteenth-century reconstructions at Williamsburg, the George Washington Garden at the American Museum near Bath (Plate X a), and in the contemporary ideas of Mr. Lanning Roper—all of which possess qualities at once fresh, enlivening, and basically simple. That artless hymn of the early settlers seems to express the mood: 'It's the gift to be simple, it's the gift to be free . . .'

2 Tintinhull

Tintinhull House, a small manor house not far from Yeovil in Somerset, was built in about 1600 in unassuming style, and had a grander façade added to its western elevation a century later. This is of dressed Ham stone from a local quarry, with carefully spaced windows, four pilasters—the two central ones supporting a pediment—and a handsome doorway.

Of garden there is no record until Dr. S. J. M. Price, a distinguished botanist, came to Tintinhull in 1900 and laid out a series of formal enclosures. It is believed that the solid paving of the long path leading from the west front to the fountain garden dates, like that façade, from 1700, together with the walling of the small pleasance near the house known as 'Eagle Court' because stone eagles stand on piers guarding the exit. The great Cedar of Lebanon may be contemporary also, for this species was introduced into England in 1676.

In 1933 the place was bought by Captain and Mrs. F. E. Reiss, who had come south from the Andoversford district of Gloucestershire and were familiar with the Hidcote garden, then over a quarter of a century old. For the next 28 years Phyllis Reiss devoted all her thought and energy to the maintenance and improvement of the Tintinhull garden, which she did with conspicuous success. Captain Reiss died in 1947 and Mrs. Reiss in 1961, having given her house and garden to the National Trust some seven years earlier. She lived in the house and cared for her garden to the last, and when she knew that life was nearly at an end for her she planted a young cedar tree where it will at some future date be ready to replace the old giant. The great Elizabethan mansion of Montacute is not far off, and any garden lover who visits that would do well to make time for Tintinhull also.

The whole flower garden (excluding the kitchen garden) is no more than 1 acre in size, and yet it gives an impression of spaciousness which makes it hard to believe that the area is only one-tenth that of Hidcote. Although it is to some extent a 'room' garden, and although we know that Mrs. Reiss was familiar with Major Johnston's work and an admirer of his ideas, I think it would be misleading to pretend that they resemble one another closely. Tintinhull is far less of a cottage garden, less homely and intimate, and has a slightly severe, remote quality—of a sort to engage rather than repel. This is not a place in which to pipe up that old settler's hymn. Rather would it set me dreaming of classical times, of the glories of ancient Greece and Rome. Perhaps a villa stood on this site, with a garden not unlike that of today, where some exiled Roman strove to cultivate the vine and the fig, and astonished our simple forefathers with the first topiary work they had ever seen.

One feels that Phyllis Reiss had been either imbued with the classics in her youth, or born with a classical bent to her mind. When I mentioned this to Margery Fish, she remembered that her friend had once talked of placing a row of busts on pedestals along the Yew hedge. Mrs. Fish indicated some distaste for this scheme, and Mrs. Reiss replied that it had proved prohibitive from a financial point of view—otherwise she would have carried it out. 'She gardened like a man—ruthlessly throwing out anything that did not conform to her ideas; she never allowed sentiment for individual plants to interfere with her over-all plan.' Mrs. Fish added that, unlike most working gardeners, Phyllis Reiss liked to *sit* in gardens, and when being shown a strange one her first task would be to find a good place to sit down. Probably her capacity for contemplating her own garden helped her to decide exactly what planting she preferred.

Public admission to the garden is ordinarily through a courtyard to the east of the house, which has big gates opening to the street. Tucked away in a corner near the house door is an aperture in the wall through which one enters the north garden. This informal, grassy space is dominated by the immense Cedar of Lebanon, with its small successor growing beneath it. These are situated at the far side, away from the building. On the opposite boundary, close to the house wall, several Yews—smaller, darker and more shaggy than the clean-limbed Cedar—form a bosky kind of colonnade, and a neighbouring Magnolia in the lawn contrasts well with the rich depth of the conifers. Although there are so few trees, this section is mysterious, for I find myself thinking of it as a woodland garden. Could it be that land where powerful trees once grew has some faint emanations left behind, intangible and invisible, but able to create a woody sensation in the mind?

While this asymmetrical part of the design is perfectly in keeping with the older, humbler and less formal style of the north elevation, I prefer to have a first sight of the garden by means of the house door opening on to the steps from the classical western façade of 1700. There one steps down to a grey terrace and so to the long paved walk between small domes of clipped Box, planted so that two-thirds of their circular skirts are on the lawn and the remainder now overlaps the path (Figure 12). I noticed that this arrangement, which seems perfect at ground level, causes me some irritation when viewed from an upper floor window, for the bushes suggest pawns that have slipped off their squares on a chess-board. I want to push them back, and it made me wonder if we take enough trouble over the planning of gardens in general with the bedroom (or upstairs sitting-room) aspect in mind.

From the terrace, the path running between those Box bushes carries the eye along a delightful vista through the Eagle Court and the next enclosure—a rectangular 'room' with an apse-shaped lawn and beds of Azaleas—to the pond and fountain garden at the far end. A finely placed rounded *Quercus ilex* (Evergreen Oak) tree in the south-west angle of the middle room echoes in its own fashion the dark mass of the great Cedar which towers over the north-east corner of the land. This vista, this paved walk, and these three fairly small sections or 'rooms' are the core of Tintinhull, and could serve of themselves to make a self-contained and satisfying garden. Here, then, is a useful study for those who have long, narrow strips of garden to plan.

At Tintinhull there is more to come. As your eye roams along the path from the west front there are signs that a small outlet in the north boundary will lead elsewhere, and when the visitor has passed through Eagle Court and the central garden between the clipped Boxes, another vista on his right suddenly opens up an entirely different conception. This is a modern section, made on the site of an old tennis court by Captain and Mrs. Reiss in the 1950s in memory of their nephew killed in action during the Second World War.

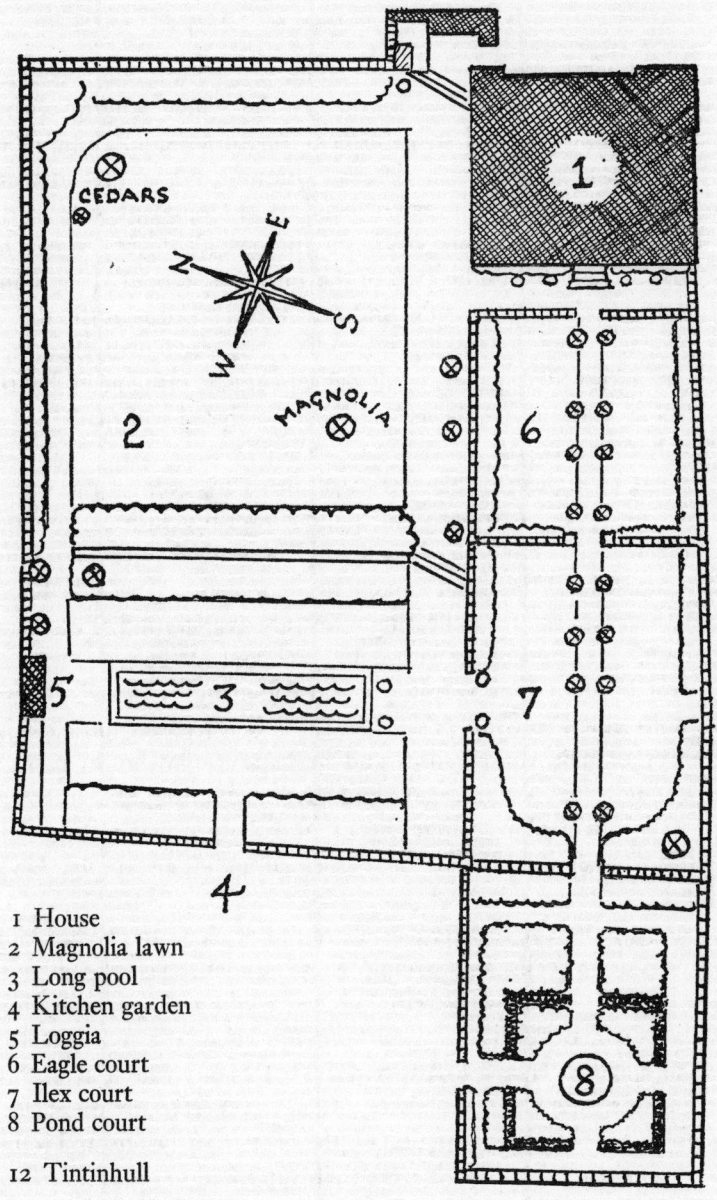

1 House
2 Magnolia lawn
3 Long pool
4 Kitchen garden
5 Loggia
6 Eagle court
7 Ilex court
8 Pond court

12 Tintinhull

A long rectangular pool, large enough to swim in but occupied solely by goldfish, stretches for nearly the whole length, with a paved surround, parallel strips of lawn on either side, and a stone loggia, flat-roofed and with classical columns, set at the northern end. The columns are cleverly echoed on the opposite side of the pool by neat little pillars of Irish Juniper (*Juniperus communis hibernica*) (Plate X b). This part of the garden is so open, bright and gay, with its clear water reflecting rain-washed skies on the day of my last visit, that I named it 'Arcadia'. I learned then that Mrs. Reiss had travelled widely and was obviously influenced by the gardens of Italy and Greece, which she analysed and made use of to suit her own needs.

It must be a cheerful place to stroll or sit in, even in the winter months. In spring there are bulbs and flowering cherries; in summer the roses flanking the loggia, the vases filled with Geranium and Agapanthus, the great mixed borders against the side boundaries, added to the sky-reflecting water, are exhilarating. The plantings here have been made with deliberate contrast between the east and west borders. One is full of warm colouring, with reds, flames and pinks allied to coppery foliage, the other a pastel mosaic with a shower of pale yellow roses and herbaceous flowers in delicate mauves and pinks—white also—and silver Artemisia, backed by the dark Yew of a flanking hedge. Scent, and the profusion of growth, provide what Sylvia Crowe has described as 'an enveloping sense of the joy of creation'.

In addition to the recurrent background of Yew, and the binding effect of stone walls and paving, these gardens have been given unity by the planting of certain subjects again and again—such as *Senecio greyii*, Bergenia, *Lathyrus latifolius albus* (White Everlasting Pea), and white Japanese Anemone. That plant, which as a child in a London suburb I saw far too often, never gave me pleasure. I was given to critical examination of plants at an early age, and found this one wanting. Little girls were then supposed to love all flowers, believing them to be made by fairies. I probably held that view, being accustomed to seeing 'little people' around, but in spite of this familiarity (or perhaps because of it), felt sure that fairies, like other individuals, had their off days. The Japanese Anemone, whose wiry stems and 'plastic' texture of petal repelled me, must have been invented at a particularly uninspired moment. In the Tintinhull garden I met it afresh, and saw it to be a classical, aloof sort of plant, appropriate in this setting—where it is used as part of a design and not meant to be handled or approached too closely.

A narrow opening in the hedge to the west of the long pool provides a glimpse of kitchen garden, where a 'florist's shop' of massed bloom, grown for cutting between fruit trees, suggests a peasant market somewhere in Europe. If we penetrate this gaudy array of colours and then slip through another gap, to the south of this enclosure, we receive the maximum contrast of effect on arrival in the little pond court, whose white and silver plants come upon the eye like a cold shower on skin which has been cooked in a very hot bath. We are now in the final section of that chain of 'rooms' already described as leading westwards from the early eighteenth-century façade of the house.

Compared with the light, open space of 'Arcadia', this is a cosy little parlour. Even the fountain in the pool is a miniature whose thin jet has the character of some parlour game, while the leaves and cups of water-lilies in the small circular pond remind us of a Jane Austen tea-set arranged on a tray. The surrounding beds, filled with finely cut silver foliage and delicate white flowers, are the lace curtains and chintzes of our withdrawing-room, and at the centre of the end wall there is a seat.

From this we get one of the best vistas in the whole garden, looking eastwards past the big Ilex tree, up the long paved walk between the neat Box domes, and below the aloof eagles with their stone wings heraldically displayed, to the lovely west front of the house (Plate VIII). This has an unusually varied and subtle blend of colour, even for the versatile Ham stone, from palest waxy-candle at the top, through parchment, Devonshire cream, honey and toast to amber, bronze, and finally a dull maroon-purple, like claret spilt down the south corner at terrace level. The pattern of paving in the old stone path is a bold and simple one of rectangular shapes placed end-to-end to form borders, enclosing large squares with smaller squares set diamondwise inside them.

There are very few man-made curves in this garden, and those few in exactly the right places. The stone copings on the old brick walls between pillars in Eagle Court form graceful, unobtrusive supplements to the convex pediment above the entrance door, and elsewhere a shallow flight of curved steps leads from the Yew colonnade to Arcadia, providing an ampler, built-in echo of the movable earthenware vases which are the only artefacts not composed of straight lines in that rectangular design.

Sylvia Crowe, who knew Phyllis Reiss well and admired her garden, has written of Tintinhull that, of the slightly larger gardens divided into 'rooms', there can be few better examples than this. 'Although it is larger than the average garden of today, the principles are applicable to smaller areas. The relationship of closed and open spaces, which runs through all the classic gardens, can still be translated to the smallest site. Because one should be dominant over the other, grass walks and borders should not divide the space equally between them. Because there should be clarity of design, the open space of lawn should not be cut up or dotted with planting. Although Tintinhull is a country garden, it is almost wholly in-looking and owes very little to the surrounding country, and in this it has something in common with many of the newer gardens of today. It is also applicable because it is divided into several parts, each complete and satisfying in itself, although combining together into a united whole.'

In other words, those who have eyes may glean ideas and inspiration for laying out their own gardens—of whatever size and wherever situated—by studying how it was achieved at Tintinhull.

SOME FAMOUS GARDENS IN ENGLAND

3 SISSINGHURST

This husbandry, this castle, and this I
Moving within the deeps,
Shall be content within our timeless spell,
Assembled fragments of an age gone by . . .

Those lines are taken from a poem called *Sissinghurst*, written by the poet, novelist and biographer V. Sackville-West, who, after a long and honoured career as a writer, finished her days by acquiring equal or even greater fame as the maker of what is now one of the loveliest gardens in England. There is a 'timeless spell' at Sissinghurst Castle, and she was instrumental in perpetuating it. With her husband Harold Nicolson she bought the place in 1930 and set to work restoring what remained of the buildings, and making out of mounds of rubbish and weeds a living work of art that would outlast them both. Here the writer describes her first impressions: 'The place when I first saw it on a spring day in 1930 caught instantly at my heart and my imagination. I fell in love, love at first sight. I saw what might be made of it. It was a Sleeping Beauty's castle running away into sordidness and squalor, a garden crying out for rescue. It was easy to see even then what a struggle we should have to redeem it.'

Before long it was theirs, and the couple began to take command, camping out in the half-ruined tower and helping an old man and his son to clear away the rubbish that littered the ground—a task that took two years. The planning of their garden has been mentioned in Chapter 2. It was very much a marriage of two different approaches: the one (Harold Nicolson's) restrained and classical, the other romantic and exuberant in the extreme. It was indeed fortunate for them and for the nation, which since 1967 has had this property as part of the National Trust for its enjoyment, that Mr. Nicolson was there to plan the 'bones' of the garden, and that his wife was fully in agreement with his ideas. Her planting was to be carried out 'within the confines of utmost linear severity'.

Soon they were planting hedges of Yew and Hornbeam, Limes

in what became Harold Nicolson's spring garden, climbers to clothe the walls, herbaceous plants, and bulbs. Later on, writing of the hedges, Vita Sackville-West said: 'Yew is without question my own favourite, and it is not nearly so slow-growing as most people imagine, but it has two drawbacks: it is poisonous to cattle, so you cannot plant it where your own or other people's cows are likely to browse on it; and it is expensive, so you cannot plant it unless your purse is deep.' In 1953 she wrote in the Royal Horticultural Society's *Journal* of what have now become the enormous (and seemingly venerable) Yew hedges of Sissinghurst: 'I look back now with amusement on those very tiny Yews—when first planted in 1933, one by one, separate, a row of little Christmas trees; when, in impatient despair, I could not imagine that even within my own lifetime they could cohere into a dense thick hedge 10 feet above my head. Yet so it is. I cannot see over, I cannot push through.' She was tall, and I doubt if the hedges were quite as much as 10 feet above her head; but certainly they were taller than she—those plants which had been only 18 inches high in 1933.

It would be interesting to know what those plants cost the Nicolsons before the war. In 1966 Mr. Nigel Nicolson kindly allowed me to look through some garden notebooks in his mother's Tower Room, but this detail did not appear. Today a good nurseryman quotes a price of 144/- a dozen for Yews of the smallest size, that is from 18 inches to 2 feet in height. In the garden notebooks were entries which caught the eye, such as 'Order one mermaid for boys' bathroom'. Presently this is complemented by: 'Aunt Eliza coming from Barr in the spring. Put with mermaid, boys' bathroom.' And then 'move *Iris sibirica* by the lake to a place where it will not be eaten off by the cows'. We all keep garden notebooks, but I doubt if any are so readable as this. Suddenly we are in the realm of poetry:

> '*Two swans are on the lake.*
> *They speak the very essence of my love.*
> *Pure, plumed, majestical.*'

SOME FAMOUS GARDENS IN ENGLAND

I had had curious, intermittent, brief glimpses of the writer—always fascinating—and found her abandoned garden notes intensely moving. In 1935 we had the loan of a cottage at Smallhythe belonging to Ellen Terry's daughter Edith Craig, and Edy took me to hear Vita Sackville-West, whom she knew, give a lecture on *English Gardens since Roman Times* in the town of Tenterden. Afterwards I was taken up and introduced, and hearing that I rode about the lanes on a bay mare, Vita issued an open invitation to visit her. I was too shy; but kind Edy invented a message for me to take, and armed with that excuse I went. I remember V. S-W. standing in the garden against her rose-pink Elizabethan tower. Both tall, both English, yet with soft overtones of something foreign. Both she and her castle possessed Bacon's 'excellent beauty that hath some strangeness in the proportion'.

Nearly twenty years later, when I was staying at Inverewe, very sadly after the sudden death of Mairi Sawyer, I opened the Lodge door one morning to find Lady Nicolson and Sir Harold (as they had now become) wishing to see the gardens. I took them round myself, and was impressed by her quick eye which took in not only the rare wonders of the place, but little things that passed unnoticed by the crowd. 'This common Lobelia in the drive—what a marvellous blue it is in your peaty soil!' It was—blue like the deepest Gentian, but I was so accustomed to the colour that I passed it by every day without stopping. Vita Sackville-West stopped for every worthwhile plant, however small and common it might be.

She loved names. Sometimes as I wander and sniff my way among the shrub roses that disport themselves so freely at Sissinghurst around the circle of Yew which Kent people dubbed the *rondel*, I ask myself whether the names of 'Chapeau de Napoléon', 'Hippolyte', 'Nuits de Young' (was that called after Young's *Night Thoughts?* she asked), 'Reine des Violettes', 'Tuscany', 'Cardinal Richelieu', 'Rosa Mundi', 'Souvenir du Docteur Jamain'—the rose which she found and rescued, the Cabbage Rose, the Moss, the Centifolias, the Gallicas, Musks and Damasks, attracted her almost as much as the plants themselves. She loved them and she loved their names, which she somewhere describes as suggesting 'a honeyed southern dusk'.

She defined the shrub rose as 'anything from the so-called "old" roses to the more recent developments such as the hybrid Musks. The one common denominator should be the character, which, as Mr. Graham Thomas rightly insists, leads us to regard them as flowering shrubs rather than roses in our own modern conception.' After her death, Alvilde Lees-Milne wrote that the free and generous planting of these roses at Sissinghurst was significant and had been copied by many. 'None of the stiff, garish-coloured hybrid teas is to be seen here.'

But the gardener did not spare self-criticism. Vita Sackville-West described her rose garden in 1959 in these terms: 'The area is walled on two sides by high brick walls covered by Fig trees, Vines, and some of the tenderer climbing roses such as the yellow Banksia and *Rosa anemonoides*. Beds are spacious and somewhat jungly. The jungly effect certainly makes for luxuriance in mid-June, but it has its drawbacks and I have often wished we had not crammed the roses so close and had left more room between them with stepping-stones, for as it is the innermost ones are difficult and prickly of access. Ignorant amateur impatience is to blame. One can hope only that others may profit by one's own mistakes.' She goes on, with down-to-earth practicality, to say that all her roses are fed with pig manure in the autumn.

Sitting alone in the Tower Room in 1966, I found the writer enjoying more names in that garden notebook—names of the Vine, which she loved to plant recklessly in her garden. 'Tokay Frontignan.' 'Primavera Frontignan.' 'Golden Drop.' 'Muscatel.' 'Reeves' Muscadine.' 'Black Prince.' 'Dutch Sweetwater.' 'Royal Muscadine' ('Golden Chasselas', the sixteenth-century *Chasselas de Fontainebleau*). I could hear her low voice enunciating these words as she wrote them down, together with a note that Vines for the courtyard wall must have 'red leaves not purple'. Then there are some entries about roses. 'Rose Prince Camille de Rohan. Best deep red. Smells good.' She always had little jars of flowers on her desk, particularly scented ones, and would have enjoyed the good smell of Prince Camille de Rohan. This work-room still seemed full of her presence, and it was difficult to credit that she was dead. Yet there was the tablet at the foot of her stair to prove it:

> *Here lived V. Sackville-West who made this garden.*
> *Born at Knole 9th March 1892 Died at Sissinghurst*
> *2nd June 1962.*

Her marvellous garden has gone the way of her earlier home, Knole, both now being in the care of the National Trust. Gardens such as this are delicate creations, easily misunderstood and fudged up into something quite different and inferior; but Sissinghurst is fortunate in that the two Waterperry-trained women gardeners who were working for Lady Nicolson, as they call her, before her death are still in charge and will keep the spirit of her masterpiece alive. They speak with great affection of their late employer. 'Lady Nicolson seldom left this place. She made a few sorties abroad, but she wouldn't stay a night away from home in England if she could avoid it. She was seriously ill with pneumonia in 1961. When she had to stay in bed at that time, also during her last illness in 1962, we took it in turns to see her every day, to discuss work in the garden.' Miss Pam Schwerdt and Miss Sybille Kreutzberger must have been a great comfort, and the Principal of the Waterperry Horticultural School told me that Lady Nicolson called them her 'treasures'.

The garden is certainly a treasure chest: a series of mysterious secret chambers—The Tower Lawn, The Rose Garden, The White Garden (see Plates I and XII), The Cottage Garden, The Herb Garden, The Lime Walk, The Nut Plat—opening out of each other with quirks of design that keep you guessing. It would not surprise me if some day I went into one of these 'rooms' and found no way out. Seen from the top of the tower the plan of this garden looks as clear and simple as could be; but when you reach ground level the mystery returns. The classical logic of the basic design is overlaid by something deep, secret and beguiling. (Figure 4.)

Perhaps this springs from the antiquity of the site, from the 'obtuseness' that bothered Harold Nicolson when he set his classically-nurtured mind to work out a scheme, and from the romantic spirit of Vita Sackville-West, who had been absorbed in her youth by the great house of Knole and its traditions. The 'feel' of Knole, inside the buildings, is matched by the 'feel' of the garden at Sissinghurst. They are fruits of the same tree, and the Sackville blood, sap of that tree, ran strongly in V. S-W. This castle, which she purchased in a ruined state, had been built about 400 years before by Sir John Baker, whose daughter Cecily married Sir Thomas Sackville, first Earl of Dorset, who received the house and lands of Knole from Queen Elizabeth I. Sissinghurst had double claim to be 'home' to the Honourable Victoria Mary Sackville-West, only child of the third Baron Sackville.

My last view of her castle came from a winding lane as I walked away towards the main Cranbrook road. It was a fine afternoon in November, crisp and clear and sunny. I lingered beside a gap in the hedge and looked back. There stood Vita's fairy-tale tower —mellow, time-worn, but invincibly gay—humming to itself a little tune that seemed to proceed from the very marrow of the bones of England.

What ideas can Sissinghurst provide for the designer of a small garden today? I think the absence of any attempt to be 'grand', even though this *is* a castle, is particularly noteworthy. In Plate I the great earthenware vase in the White Garden is shown raised up on a brick platform, and round its base a clutter of flower-pots hold scented-leaved Geraniums and other small plants. The effect is one of casualness, quite as oriental as the great jar itself; this came originally from China, but was found in Cairo by Sir Harold. What a pleasant homely effect such informality has upon the beholder, so characteristic of Lady Nicolson. She really *was* aristocratic, and had no truck with assumed airs of grandeur in herself or her surroundings.

In the same White Garden is a modern statue of a vestal virgin by Rosandic, cast from a walnut carving which is in the castle.

This statue is not displayed proudly in some central position (where so many of us would put any fine work of art we happened to possess), but set at one side in the shade of a silver willow-leaved Pear, so that the sylph-like figure seems to grow from the trunk (Plate XII). This throw-away technique is essentially right for the immature maiden, and I am not suggesting that the eighteenth-century statue of Dionysus down by the moat would also have looked better placed beneath a tree. It is the ability to throw away some treasures and to display others, to achieve exciting contrasts and some measure of surprise, and the eschewing of the obvious, that make this garden timelessly enjoyable.

The use of pot-plants outdoors in a garden scheme attracted Miss Sackville-West, and has a very long tradition behind it in Europe. At Sissinghurst it is employed in many different ways. The owner liked to look closely into certain plants, and would often use stone troughs raised to eye-level, or large jars, to contain these subjects. The four urns in the entrance court, which came originally from Bagatelle, a famous rose garden near Paris, she had planted with *Campanula isophylla mayii*, whose blue-grey foliage and hanging lavender-blue bell flowers repay close study. They are far more deserving of a site on or near one's eyes than are the more commonly used zonal Pelargoniums or Petunias.

In 1966 I saw a large pot of *Erythrina christa-galli*, the 'Coral Tree' of Brazil, placed in blazing sun outside the White Garden below a marble plaque showing three jovial clerics, who have presumably given the name to 'Bishop's Gate' at that spot. The savage dried-blood colouring of the Erythrina was almost hurtful after the coolness of the White Garden. Such a contrast is like mustard on the plate—a little adds zest to the dish—and with portable pot-plants the condiment is easily placed at the right moment.

Away out beyond the Nut Plat is a fine herb garden which should on no account be missed. It makes the very most of a great variety of herbs, all labelled for the interest of visitors. The enclosure is sheltered and warm, so that the fragrances are well concentrated, and there are seats where visitors may rest while the quiet, subtle charm of herbs has time to act upon the senses. Here is a great variety of herb plants, some of them too little appreciated today. That old blue-dye-producer, Woad, is one of these. With its glaucous foliage and pendant black seed-pods, it is worth cultivating for its decorative value, apart from its claim to fame in the history books as the warpaint worn by the Britons who met Julius Caesar.

Then there is the white Florentine Iris, delicate looking and fragrant, whose rhizome gives the Orris Root used in past centuries for perfume. The moth-repellent 'Camphor Plant', a grey-leaved tall subject with little white daisy flowers; the ferny and aromatic Sweet Cicely; clumps of Rue with metallic blue foliage; a Calamint (*Calamintha nepetoides*), more attractive than the wild one which grows in my paths and doesn't mind being trodden on; Liquorice, which suggests a small bush of wild rose; and handsome but wicked plants of Henbane, all are worth study.

Although not actually in the herb garden, a little lawn near by, made from creeping Thyme, is an idea which can be used with success in many a small garden. It is neat, it requires very little attention, it grows into a thick weed-suppressing carpet, it is aromatic, and gives a sheet of crimson (or whatever colour of Thyme you select) in the summer flowering season. The possibilities of Sissinghurst are legion, and in a few pages they cannot be listed in full. One can only indicate broadly the opportunities that exist, and hope that garden-lovers will be able to see for themselves.

11

INVEREWE

INVEREWE, when I knew it, was not so much a garden as a way of life. In going to this remote Highland fastness on the northern coast of Wester Ross, a twentieth-century city-dweller took a longer trip than the 700 miles travelled by train and car. It was also a journey backwards—far backwards in time—a journey, it seemed, to the very beginning of the world.

It is now over 100 years since the widowed Lady Mary Mackenzie of Gairloch bought the lands of Inverewe and Kernsary, where her son Osgood (born 1842) was to make his world-famous garden. Here in 1864 they planned and built the first mansion house on the promontory known in Gaelic as *AmPloc Ard*—The High Lump. The peninsula was hardly a fruitful looking site at that time. With gales and salt spray coming in off the ocean, with only the thin, low line of northern Lewis between it and Labrador, this was a bleak place indeed.

The land was a mass of Torridon red sandstone, with a covering of black peat varying from 1 inch to 2 feet in depth; the only vegetation it nurtured consisted of short heather, crowberry, and two small willow bushes. In order to make gardening possible, Osgood Mackenzie went in for afforestation. He put in hundreds of little fir, larch, beech, birch and oak trees within a screen belt of Corsican

Pine and Scots Pine, and thick hedges of *Rhododendron ponticum*. For the first five years very little appeared to be happening, and the critics did their best to discourage the young man. But those trees were 'growing downwards instead of upwards', as someone said later.

When the house was completed, Lady Mary and her son took up residence at Inverewe and watched the green plumes growing up around them. Although the whole place was alive with game, very little real damage was done to the plantations. Grouse (according to Osgood Mackenzie) did no harm; Black Game picked out the leading buds of young Scots Pine and made them bushy; brown and blue hares took off some shoots from Austrian Pine and Oak; but on the whole the trees and game co-existed satisfactorily. The rabbit plague had not yet begun, and there were fewer roe deer—those stealthy and determined robbers feared by the Highland gardener today.

At the start trees were planted for shelter, and nothing unusual was put in, but when the Wellingtonia came into fashion Osgood was tempted to try four of them. In his old age he liked to relate how, when pits were dug for planting these near the house, spades clicked ominously on the bed-rock, and after a wet night 'all we achieved was four small ponds'. An old man was detailed to fetch quantities of soil from another part of the demesne, and the young trees were installed hopefully in the pockets prepared for them. Forty-three years afterwards their owner recorded with pride that they had made 60 feet of growth and measured 8 feet in girth at a man's height above the ground.

This man deserved his triumphs. He had to wait 15 years while the shelter-belts were establishing themselves, before he began to cull some of the commoner trees and replace with the species he really wanted to cultivate, among them Douglas Firs, Copper Beech, Sweet and Horse Chestnut, Arbutus, and several kinds of Eucalyptus. Small clearings were made, enclosed in deer fencing, and planted with a variety of tender subjects that were known to succeed in the mild areas of Devon, Cornwall, and the west coast of Ireland.

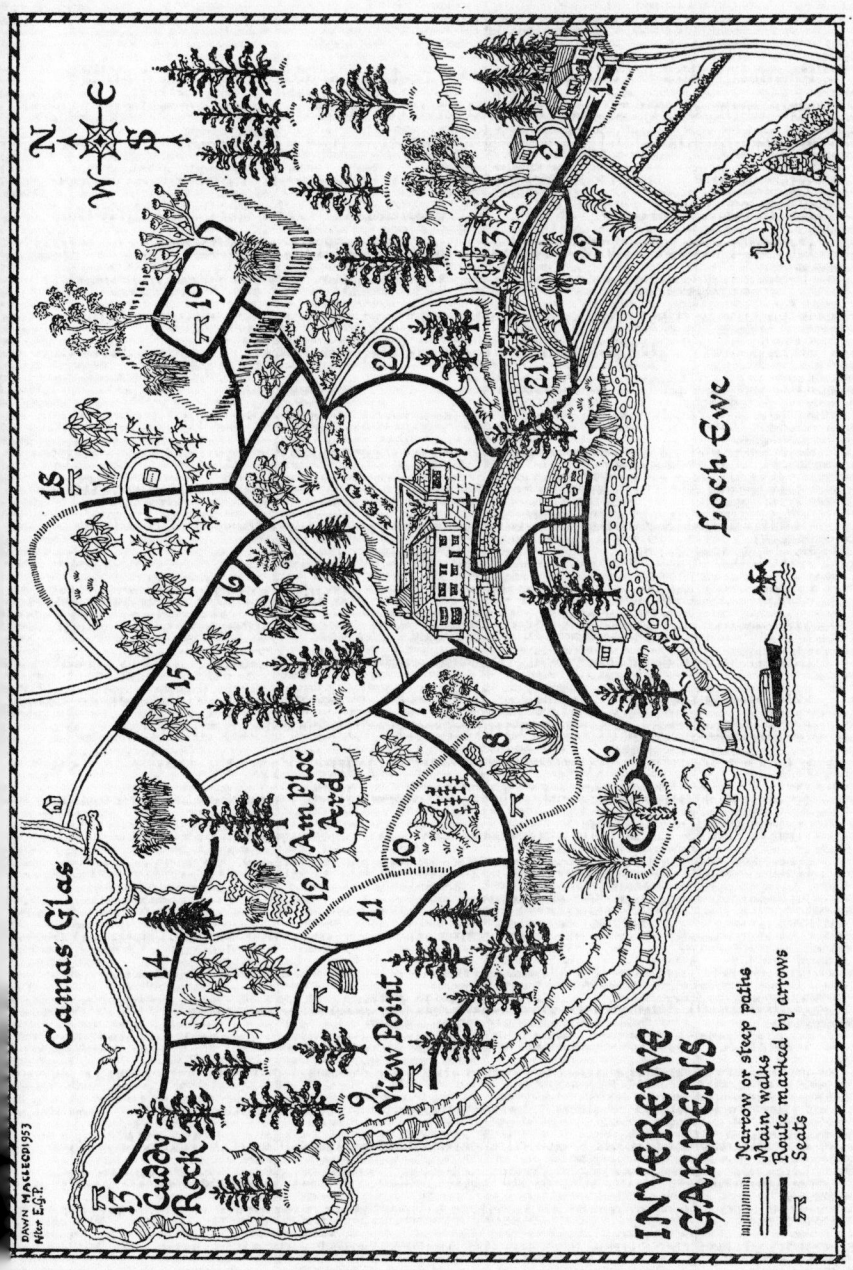

1 Lodge 2, 3 Drive 4 House 5 Rockery 6 'Japan' 7 Grove 8, 11, 12 Water gardens 10 New Rock 15, 16 Rhododendrons 17 'Peace Plot' 18 Coronation Knoll 19 'Bambooselem' 20 'America' 21, 22 Walled garden

Plants of this sort had never before been tried in the Highlands—although many Scottish landowners copied the idea when the achievements of Mackenzie at Inverewe became known. He wrote with natural pride of his pleasure at being able to show a visitor from Kew Gardens his fine Tricuspidarias, Drimys, Embothriums, Leptospermums, Metrosideros and Mitrarias; also the Australian Tree-fern and the Tasmanian Apple-berry (*Billardiera longiflora*) with its wonderful blue fruits. These and many other unusual plants were 'all flourishing at Inverewe, thanks to the Gulf Stream and lots of peat and shelter'.

He made a walled garden, where fruit, vegetables and flowers for cutting would be grown, on an old sea-beach down by the loch—the only level strip of land free from rocks. The soil here was a mixture of three parts pebble and one part black earth. The men who dug it had each a girl or boy alongside him to gather up and remove the stones, which were replaced by good soil from the bed of Loch Ewe and from old turf dykes, giving a rich layer of humus. Above the beach level a terrace was carved out of the hillside, and a great retaining wall built against the rock. This was the place for fan-trained and cordon fruit, interspersed with the warmth-loving scarlet 'Bottle-brush' (*Callistemon citrinus*) and 'Parrot's Bill' or 'Red Kowhai' from New Zealand, which we called 'Lobster-claw' because the flowers were shaped that way. Neat rows of vegetables were planted side by side with the brilliant Kaffir Lily (*Schizostylis coccinea*) and stately Acanthus.

Osgood Mackenzie's marriage in 1878 was not very happy, but the only child of it, Mairi, grew up to be her father's inseparable companion and fellow-gardener. It is tiresome for those who knew her to come across traces of patronage which suggest that she was merely a dutiful daughter who did her best to carry on at Inverewe after her father's death. In truth she had inherited much of the traditional gardening talent of the Gairloch Mackenzies, had worked closely with him for about 30 years (he died in 1924 when she was 46), to become a highly skilled plantswoman, with creative and artistic ability second to none. Until her death in 1953 she supervised Inverewe and worked alongside her gardeners in all weathers; but her ways were quiet, her mind subtle and her devotion to the place selfless, so that in this age of advertisement she has received less than her just due. She disliked and avoided banal and merely showy plants. The absence (pointed to with surprise by less perceptive later custodians) of modern hybrid Rhododendrons and other slightly garish shrubs like the Buddleia called 'Royal Red', and herbaceous and bedding-out flowers in bright colours, was due to the fact that she disliked such plants and thought them quite out of keeping with Inverewe. Vita Sackville-West, who is said to have loathed Rhododendrons, was probably thinking of those lumpish banks of what we called 'Suburborhodo', that is, the showy bushes carrying enormous trusses of bloom amid uniform dark green shiny foliage, with which she would have been familiar in the southern counties around Sissinghurst.

Our own specimens, their elegant growths kept carefully balanced by skilful pruning—often very hard pruning too—were given room for each to display itself separately, never squashed into a solid mass. With warmly coloured barks, and finely shaped foliage in many shades of green and bluish grey-green, some of them enriched with linings of gold or silver plush, these were the aristocrats of the shrub world, here seen in great splendour against a background of hill and loch (Plate XIII). Often Mairi (now Mrs. Sawyer) would pause in her work and stand perfectly still looking at her garden. 'Isn't it lovely?' she would murmur, *willing* me to stop and look too, and giving a subdued chuckle of pleasure at all this beauty. She was never too busy to enjoy, and be grateful for, her surroundings.

For several years I spent public school vacations with her, and lived at Inverewe for the last 12 months of her life. We developed that great depth of mutual confidence and understanding which is independent of the spoken word, and spent many happy days working together almost in silence. Both of us loved the sounds of wind and water, of seagulls, wading birds, and the unmistakable soft crooning of the Eider duck. All this, and the fluting of woodland birds too, came to us unsullied by the clank and rattle of machinery, for aeroplanes were seldom heard and even road traffic was light enough for us to speculate on the ownership of any car we did not recognize.

During vacations I had stayed at the big white house—successor to the turreted mansion built in Victorian days, which had been destroyed by fire in 1914. In 1952 I was given a cottage near by, and when Inverewe Gardens were handed over to the National Trust for Scotland in 1953 I moved to the Gate Lodge as first custodian there. With the daily opening to attend to I had less time for garden work, to my dismay; but in earlier months, while living in the cottage by the burn, I had gardened for two whole days each week.

Picture a fine, calm morning in early summer, with small waves coming onshore in tiny splashes perfectly audible from my cottage door in the silence. The mail bus which transports passengers as well as mail to the nearest rail station at Achnasheen, some 40 miles off, has passed on its way to Poolewe village, and there is no other traffic. A thin thread of blue smoke rises from the kitchen chimney of Inverewe House, pale against the dark mass of trees on the High Lump, and away to my left the little white village is reflected in a deep pool at the head of Loch Ewe.

As I walk in past the Gate Lodge and up the drive, with tall gum trees and a wooded brae on my right hand, I can see over the great retaining wall on my left some of the gardeners busy in the vegetable garden far below. That fertile strip made by Osgood Mackenzie nearly 100 years earlier is still in good heart and producing marvellous fruit and vegetables for the hospitable table at the Big House. Giant Himalayan Lilies, with woody stems like young trees, are in bloom beside the drive, together with Camellias, Magnolias, Hydrangeas of vivid blue, and various Rhododendrons, whose flowering season here ranges from November to July. At the western end of the kitchen garden, just outside its gate, a clump of the Chatham Island Forget-me-not, with shiny rhubarb leaves and trusses of blue flowers, each the size of a halfpenny, is flourishing on the diet of herring-fry provided for it by Mairi Sawyer. This plant did not thrive at Inverewe when first planted; but when a newspaper published a correspondent's report about what was clearly *Myosotidium hortensia*, growing among rotting carcases of sharks on the shore of its home in the Chatham Islands off New Zealand, it was decided to give it seaweed and the nearest thing to shark available, which was herring-fry. The Giant Forget-me-not immediately responded, and became one of the glories of this garden.

Soon I find Mairi Sawyer, who had already been at work for an hour after her early breakfast, and we begin a combined attack on an overgrown piece of woodland which is being opened up and planted. Already I have been taught to distinguish between seedlings of 'good' Rhododendrons, which are cherished, and the 'rogue' or wild ones (*Rhododendron ponticum*), which have to be ousted. I believe Mairi really hated that plant, not only for its invasive habits, but because she thought its growth unattractive and its foliage dull. Her natural species from China, Burma and Tibet, each with its distinctive character and leaves of subtle colouring, were as different as Worcester china from kitchen crockery. She often said how much she wished that her father had not employed the 'Ponties' for hedging. Griselinia and Escallonia made equally good shelter belts, were better-looking, and their seedlings were always in demand. The wild Rhododendron multiplied excessively, swamped the less rampant young plants of the species, and nobody wanted it.

It was rare to hear her saying nasty things about her plants, for she liked to pretend that plants meant more to her than people. At times they were much less trouble. But she always seemed glad to have me around, and told me not to make my visits home last too long. For my part, although friends in the south considered me rather young to be 'buried' in that remote place, I should have been content to stay and work with her for ten or more years—as seemed likely, for she was very active for 75. That an eye operation on so fit a person could be followed at once by a fatal pneumonia had not occurred to me or to any of her friends. The patient herself grew restive, and may have felt life slipping away. She sent urgent appeals for an ambulance to bring her home, but doctors refused to sanction the journey from Edinburgh. Given hindsight, one cannot help wishing that she could have died—if die she must—at her beloved Inverewe.

Mairi Sawyer was like a stream that runs underground for most of its course: a deep and reticent character. Her garden, while she was there to care for it, was reticent also, its beauties largely hidden except from those who took time and trouble to find them. There were few obvious vistas; many of the paths were narrow and winding; often the peaty surfaces would suck at high-heeled shoes of any woman foolish enough to walk about this garden in them. The public had always been admitted, in aid of nurses' funds, but little was done to encourage visitors: no advertising, no gimmicks, no show of any sort. This was a wild Highland garden, and you took it as you found it, or else left it alone.

With the handing over to the National Trust for Scotland all this began to change, although at a very slow pace in her lifetime. I was with her on that spring morning in 1953 when Trust notices had to be set up at the gates of Inverewe. Little was said, but her efforts to find niches where they would not show were significant and sad. This did not involve disrespect to the Trust. With no heirs to inherit the place (both children had died in infancy) she must have been glad to think, as she said, that the gardens would be maintained 'just as they are now'. But the act of handing over this garden, to which her life and that of her father had been devoted, of labelling it as no longer a family possession, was inevitably distressing.

One piece of foreknowledge was spared her. She had no idea that, as a result of advertising, daily opening, coach parties, and all the resources of modern transport, the number of visitors would be stepped up from a few thousand to 60,000 annually within a decade. It is now rising to nearer 100,000. To cater for this influx, car parks have been made and a large restaurant built, not on the adjacent land which was left to the Trust, but right inside the gardens. First came the cutting of what one of her faithful gardeners called 'motor-roads' across the garden. Ways for these were blasted out of the rock, and hard surfaces laid down to take tractors, so that stone and gravel could be easily transported to most parts of the 50-acre demesne. Many of the lovely woodland paths were altered out of all recognition, as their narrow windings were considered to be unsuitable for numbers, and ladies lost their shoes in the soft peat.

The National Trust for Scotland is a small body, ever in need of money, and if a well-endowed property can be made capable of earning more, to help other good projects, seemingly it must exploit the possibilities to the fullest extent. Only those who are prepared to make good the needful sums are really entitled to criticize the commercialization of a lovely place—although laments for lost charms are admissible.

In some alert countries—Scandinavia in particular—planning schemes are already being formulated to make access *difficult* to certain kinds of wild open space, on the grounds that those who really care for and need such peace will manage to get there on foot or bicycle, while the crowds in cars pass by to concreted and café-strewn pleasure grounds elsewhere. They believe that as towns increase in size and the racket of modern life becomes intolerable the untouched country will become of vital importance to man. I was glad to hear that the National Trust in Northern Ireland hopes to pursue something akin to this policy—at least to the non-provision of catering and absence of facilities for motor coaches—at the next garden on my list, Rowallane in County Down.

On the subject of useful suggestions to be gleaned at Inverewe, one is forced to think first of those owners of notable gardens who consider the possibility of giving them to the nation. Although the Trust may refuse to accept properties with legally binding provisos attached to them, it can and does take into sympathetic account what is called a 'letter of wishes'. Mairi Sawyer, when she handed over Inverewe in 1953, clearly expected to be in residence there for a number of years, and did not foresee any alterations. She would assuredly have hated and resisted a restaurant inside the demesne, and had any thought of such a development been bruited she might well have left a letter of wishes recording her dislike of such a scheme. All she said to me was, that visitors would have to obtain food in Poolewe village; but as land belonging to Inverewe was left to the Trust extending nearly to that village, she might well have considered the building of a café near the site now turned into a caravan centre. It is clearly worth while for any donor to foresee what may happen, and, if he so desires, forestall plans not in accordance with his taste. The trouble with tourist attractions is that they may begin in a small way and look fairly innocuous, but as crowds multiply so do the café and car park. The restaurant at Inverewe has been enlarged twice since its inception in 1958.

Such considerations are of practical application only to very few people, but most gardeners could have gathered inspiration from the way the Inverewe plantings were handled in Mairi Sawyer's time. One of her pronouncements is of special importance to custodians of well-known gardens. She pointed out that, although many a botanist found material to keep him absorbed for a week or more, Inverewe was 'not a Botanic Garden'. This is a vital, inescapable truth. Botanic Gardens exist to inform, and display material of interest to students (professional and amateur) of plants. Because many of their possessions are intrinsically beautiful, Botanic Gardens are often pleasing to the eye. But the creation of pictures is not the chief object of their attention. In a great garden such as Inverewe that *is* an overriding aim, and botanic interest should be kept firmly in a subordinate position. If a fine artistic creation is put into the hands of a botanic expert his very keenness on the individual plants and their habits may render him less sensitive to the total effect. When we lived on the other side of the Atlantic I was astonished by frequent questions about the *number* of plants grown at Inverewe. I did not know or wish to know. Quantitative considerations, and the acquisition of complete collections of this genus or that, are the business of Botanic Gardens; we had no truck with it.

INVEREWE

We are told that 'Inverewe has very few of the modern hybrid Rhododendrons, and cannot claim to possess a representative collection of Rhododendron species'. But why should it? That comment, and others of the same type, are quite irrelevant to a great garden. Unfortunately little if any study has been made, by those who supervise such places, of the basic underlying needs of a design. Mr. Edward Hyams wrote on the opening page of his recent *Gardener's Bedside Book:* 'The English are good at plants and bad at garden design, which no longer interests them very much; they adopt one of half-a-dozen conventional plans in the layout of their gardens, but their object is to have as many flowers as possible, and a lawn.' This depressing statement seems to be valid north of the Border also. The plantsman and botanist is much easier to find than the creative garden designer.

The eighteenth-century writer on gardens, Uvedale Price, said of Painshill: 'I was highly pleased with a woodland walk, and I was pleased with it not merely from what had been but from what had *not* been done; it had no edges, no borders, no distinct lines of separation. If it be high commendation of a painter or a writer that he knows when to leave off, it is not less so to an improver.' He goes on to say that although no precept is more generally admitted in theory than that of *concealing* the art which is employed, none has been less observed in practice.

Mairi Sawyer instinctively concealed her art, and this led people who had not understood the gift to rush in with what they believed to be improvements after her death. The natural type of garden amid trees in a magnificent landscape is possibly the most difficult of all to make and maintain with perfect harmony and balance. In the first edition of the Inverewe Guide, which I wrote under Mairi Sawyer's instruction (for she flatly refused to waste her time on writing when the garden demanded all her energy), I took these words down: 'Some years ago a great horticulturist visited Inverewe, and I felt extremely shy of letting him see the garden, apologizing for its unkempt appearance. I knew he had 50 gardeners, while I had only two and a half! However, after a "tour of inspection" his parting words were "Don't alter it, it is lovely. It reminds me of some wild corner in Burma or Northern China."' He knew and she knew that gardens are *not* natural; but in that remote corner of Scotland plants from Burma and China and many other places had been made to appear at home. It requires great nicety of touch to bridge over the joins between nature and artifice in such a place. Anyone with a piece of woodland or river bank could have learned how to use it for planting, without spoiling the natural beauty, from a visit to Mairi Sawyer's garden (see Plates IV, VI, XIII).

One of her abominations was the flower of garish, loud or squeaky colour. When later visitors ask me whether the Gate Lodge was in her day surrounded by the gaudily coloured 'Livingstone Daisy' I produce an explosive 'No!' Lots of people admire such plants and have every right to do so. But they are the pop music of the plant world, and so far nobody has suggested bringing a passage of Beatle or Rolling Stone sound into the Hallelujah Chorus. 'A place for everything and everything in its place', my Highland grandmother would say. Inverewe is not the garden for pop plants, and no 'natural' planting can absorb them. Still less is it a suitable place in which to stage what another writer has recently described in print as 'a wholly incongruous (and we hoped temporary) exhibition of pop-art sculpture'. People who have it in mind to leave bequests of money or land to the Trust in Scotland would do well to voice a firm protest against such ill-advised intrusion on one of that country's great treasures. How both the maker and the donor of Inverewe would have detested this abuse of their life-work!

12

ROWALLANE

No stranger arriving in Belfast for the first time, and seeing the gigantic cranes piling up concrete office blocks storey by storey into the sky, would conceive that a green paradisial garden existed only 12 miles from the roar of the City centre. Perhaps in holiday seasons Rowallane seems less of an Eden. I have wandered there only at times when it was officially closed to the public, being allowed access by courtesy of the National Trust in Northern Ireland. But I think that some spirit of peace at the heart of the place must persist, however many people may crowd the green walks.

This garden is not set in spectacular surroundings like those of Bodnant and Inverewe. Here are no wild crags, no sea-lochs, no steep glens or mountain torrents to provide drama. The land, some 300 feet above sea-level, undulates placidly, lightly wooded with such trees as Scots Pine and Beech, and watered by small, clear streams. There are whinstone rocks—some rounded outcrops above eye-level and lesser boulders reclining in the grass. Soil in most parts is but a thin cover for the bony structure, yet it manages to sustain an ample green cloak.

Even in the month of January the demesne gave out a kind, almost luxurious, feeling of happiness and well-being, in spite of intermittent storms of wind and rain. Preoccupation with the 'feel' of a place may appear to be idle fancy: yet those who pride themselves on being 'factual' forget that hard facts are often soft at the core and perishable, while the free-flowing intangible spirit is a river that wears down and outlasts solid rock. The name of the near-by village, Saintfield, suggests that those who walked here in ancient times may have left some traces of their radiance behind. A cartoon in an Irish paper showed the nations wrangling about trade, while Ireland remarked serenely 'In the Dark Ages we exported Light'. At Rowallane this idea comes alive and is seen not to be mere verbiage.

The garden consists of 12 main areas or sections, irregularly shaped and differing greatly in size, leading from one to the other; they are variously divided by walls, hedges, walks, and by natural changes in contours; but few are sufficiently enclosed to be called a 'room' garden. It was once a farm, and in spite of the magnificent plantings, has still some suggestion of agricultural use about it. Its sections are more like small fields and copses that have been filled with lovely trees and shrubs, utterly different from the formal enclosures of Hidcote, Tintinhull, and Sissinghurst.

My guide on the first occasion was Mr. John Hanvey, the Head Gardener, who has worked at Rowallane since the 1920s and clearly understands and appreciates every cranny and each plant in the 35 acres under cultivation. He spoke of his old employer, the late Mr. Armytage Moore, who inherited the property in 1903 and at once began to plan and plant his garden, although he could not come to live at the house until 1917. For nearly 50 years he experimented and developed his garden art, raising many trees and shrubs from seed and exercising his unique gift for using natural features to the fullest extent in the creation of his masterpiece. Then came the war of 1939–45, and from a staff of six men the workers were reduced to two.

By the time the war ended the owner was growing old, his resources were depleted, and expenses, ever increasing, made many garden lovers apprehensive about the future of Rowallane. Finally, in 1954, Mr. Bowes-Lyon, then President of the Royal Horticultural Society and Chairman of the Gardens Committee of the National Trust, approached Mr. Moore to inquire whether he would discuss ways and means of preserving his life-work for future generations to enjoy. With the help of the Government of Northern Ireland the property was acquired, and it is now in the safe keeping of the Trust. It is clear that the original conception of Rowallane has been understood and sympathetically maintained; how easily the reverse can happen is only too apparent elsewhere. And who is responsible for supervision of this unique garden? The answer is, The Honourable Mrs. Terence O'Neill: a lady so modest that she asked me not to mention her. John Hanvey grew indignant at the thought of such an omission. 'I look upon Mrs. O'Neill as my boss!' he exclaimed. Others told me that this inspired and informed gardener is considered to be among the very best in all Ireland. Her husband being Premier at the time, publicity was distasteful, but it is impossible to write of the lovely Rowallane without some brief mention of her work there. Perched above the drive is a fine group of the big-leaved Rhododendrons, including *R. falconeri*, *R. sino grande*, *R. coryphaeum* and 'Grandex'—the latter being a hybrid from Bodnant. In gaps among the trees Mrs. O'Neill has recently planned and planted some appropriate new groups of Rhododendrons, mostly seedlings given to this garden. The whole collection is much too large to be catalogued here.

The first section to be reached on foot from the discreetly hidden car parks is the 'Wall Garden', which has its north and east walls at the usual right angles to each other, but an unexpected curved shape on the south and west, through which there is an opening to the 'Outer Wall Garden'. These two together form an area roughly rectangular, with the curving division between them which breaks up the space in an interesting way and provides good shelter for climbing plants.

Many unusual and tender subjects thrive here. In early summer the magnolias from China and Japan, *M. wilsonii* and *M. watsonii*, both white with crimson centres, and *M. veitchii*, make a splendid group. Related to them is the beautiful shrub *Drimys colorata*, which combines pink, mauve and gold with all the soft subtlety of a midsummer's dawn. A formal corner in the shape of a Celtic cross has at its centre a huge circular bush of the white-flowered *Viburnum tomentosum* in a variety raised here and named 'Rowallane'. Below the trees and shrubs rise immense Cardiocrinums—giant lilies from Himalayan regions, with woody stems and great cream-coloured trumpet flowers in July. At their roots primulas abound, including a vigorous hybrid raised here and called 'Rowallane Rose'. On the wall the so-called 'Chinese Jasmine' *Trachelospermum jasminoides* hangs its polished leathery leaves; it has very fragrant blossom, as have the many white-flowered trees of *Hoheria lyalli* and *H. lanceolata* from New Zealand. Later on the Chinese *Clematis heracleifolia* gives a delightful surprise to September visitors, for its lavender-blue flowers look and smell like spring hyacinths. Here too the popular 'Blue Poppy' and other varieties of Meconopsis thrive.

Growing freely is the little Bloodroot (*Sanguinaria canadensis*). Its orange-coloured sap, a powerful dyestuff, was used by the American 'Red' Indians as a war-paint. The flower resembles a white crocus, with the bud tightly folded in leaves, rising above them as it opens. The first mention of this plant in Europe appears in a Herbal by Cornutis dated 1655. The author had seen Bloodroot in Paris, where it was shown by French explorers lately returned from Canada. It has long been noted for its medicinal properties. Among those attributed to it the sedative and narcotic are commemorated in one of its many vernacular names: 'Sweet Slumber'. Others are 'Indian Paint', 'Tetterwort', 'Coonroot', 'Paucon' and 'Red Puccoon'.

In the 'Outer Wall Garden' there is a good specimen of *Rheum alexandrae*, the foliage plant related to our common culinary Rhubarb and to *Rheum officinalis*, whose bitter medicinal taste was so disliked by children in Victorian times. The flower beds here contain, besides more lilies and Meconopsis, hybrid Rhododendrons together with Nerines and Watsonias. The latter, which are known to travellers as 'Bugle Lilies', flamed among the dark trees and shrubs in September at Inverewe, and were greatly loved by the late Mairi Sawyer. She often told me how she had enjoyed seeing them, on some plant-hunting travels with her father, growing in wild profusion in South Africa.

The Chinese Yellow Wood, *Cladastris sinensis*, and a fine Hypericum, the 'Rowallane' hybrid, companion a big yellow *Euphorbia sikkimensis*. There is also *Hydrangea sargentiana*, with velvety leaves and lilac-and-white flower heads, accompanying *H. villosa*, another fine 'Lace-cap' Hydrangea with handsone foliage, and flowers a mixture of powder-blue and lavender. In summer the lovely Eucryphia, which always suggests a tree smothered in 'Mermaid' Roses, follows a red Chilean 'Firebush' (*Embothrium lanceolatum*), while the 'Handkerchief Tree' (*Davidia involucrata*) flutters its white bracts in the wind.

We leave these wall gardens by an iron gate and cross some rough ground to the 'Spring Garden', looking downhill over Azaleas, triflorum and hybrid Rhododendrons. Although named for its spring glory of blossoming tree and shrub, with bulbs flowering in the grass, this section is vivid in autumn too. *Prunus sargentii*, Enkianthus and Fothergilla (American Wych-Hazel) all turn into fiery pillars before losing their leaves to the oncoming winter. The main walks and winding paths of Rowallane are cleverly designed to lead one on with pleasure in the going. Edgings are casual, and often a bend leading through a narrow gateway makes it imperative to see what happens next. (See Plate XIV a.)

The main walk leads gently downhill to 'New Ground', and beyond that to the rock garden and an imposing outcrop named 'Bishop's Rock' because of its resemblance to a mitred bishop enthroned against the sky. From this path, which is a winding mown track through rougher grass, there are more magnolias to be seen. *M. mollicomata* flowers while still young, on leafless branches in spring; its companion, *M. campbellii*, takes about 30 years; but, when its large pink 'Water-lily' blooms do appear and are seen against a clear blue sky, most gardeners consider them worth waiting for. Here too is the fragrant white *M. sinensis* from western China, and the Chilean *Philesia buxifolia* (syn. *P. magellanica*) whose waxy red bells, which at Inverewe grow on a fibrous trunk of the Chinese palm, are here seen against a big rock.

As John Hanvey and I passed down towards 'New Ground', and

the interwoven curved lines of path and wall which are such a feature of this garden began to make their impression on me, I was dimly aware of its affinity with something studied long ago. When we had climbed a slight rise and I was able to look down on the pattern as a whole, I recognized those whirling intersecting lines— developed from the natural formation of the ground by Mr. Armytage Moore—as having a distinct resemblance to the interlacing patterns of Celtic art, seen at their best in the famous *Book of Kells* in Trinity College Library, Dublin. A sketch of the ground-plan of Rowallane, used here by kind permission of the National Trust in Northern Ireland, suggests that very little alteration would be needed to transform it into a capital letter B in character with the P from the *Book of Kells*. This sets one speculating as to whether landscape affects the subconscious mind of a designer and is subsequently echoed in his work.

In the section of garden still known as 'The Hospital', where former occupants who farmed this land learnt to shelter weakly lambs and ailing calves because it was the warmest spot, there is a splendid free-standing specimen of the Chinese Wych-Hazel (*Hamamelis mollis*), placed there because it was transplanted from Rostrevor when a fair-sized bush, and to succeed with such a move it was deemed necessary to give it the kindest conditions. It was smothered in bloom when I saw it in January. John Hanvey cut a spray for me, a delicate twig with shaggy little maroon-centred bobbles of flower bursting out of the grey bark in such an improbable way that the uninitiated might have thought it to be artificially contrived. But one whiff of its heady fragrance would have put a stop to that idea. I was also handed a sprig of the small white-flowered *Rhododendron moupinense*, which stood up to wind and rain well, and a branch of particularly fine 'Pussy Willow', *Salix gracilistyla*.

Drimys winterii also flourishes in that enclosure, and *Desfontainea spinosa*, with its showy yellow and red blossom. To most of us in the British Isles this plant from South America suggests Christmas holly. The Drimys, grown today for horticultural interest, has a long

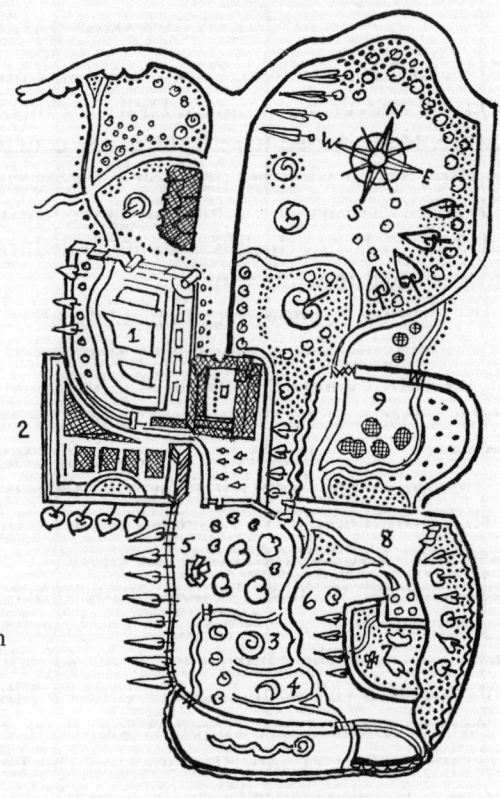

1 Wall garden
2 Outer wall garden
3 Spring garden
4 New ground
5 Trio Hill
6 Old wood
7 Hospital
8 Stream
9 Paddock

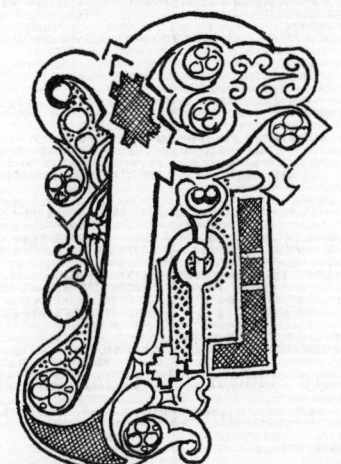

14 Irish design
(above) Rowallane (below) from the *Book of Kells*

history of service to man. Bark from it was brought into England in 1579 by one of Sir Francis Drake's captains, whose name was Winter. He had used it with success to counteract scurvy on board his ship, and it soon became noted for its curative powers. In the eighteenth century Sir John Hill described in his *Herbal* a purge called *Hiera picra*, which was compounded from Winter's Bark and Aloes steeped in white wine.

In addition to more recent plantations of shelter belts, and to some aboriginal Scots pines, Rowallane is attractive to tree-lovers for its many good specimens of unusual subjects. The Dawyck Beech, a fastigiate tree well suited to smaller gardens, and the Southern Beech, the Camellia-like Stewartia (*S. monadelpha* from Japan, *S. koreana* from Korea) together with many species of Acer and Sorbus grow here, also a variety of conifers. In The Hospital we saw Tasmanian Cedar and the yew-like alpine Totara from New Zealand, while beyond in The Paddock grow other kinds of Beech; the flowering *Prunus serrula tibetica*; an American Chestnut (*Aesculus parviflora*), and the Himalayan *A. indica*, which has white flowers blotched with yellow and rose in June or July. Towards the drive, in Avenue Ground and Home Wood, there are good specimens of Weeping Spruce, Umbrella Pine and the Chilean Hazel *Gevuina avellana*, as well as more Eucryphias and Magnolias and the Japanese *Trochodendron aralioides*, which bears bizarre flowers of a bright green.

Before we left the gardens I discussed with my guide the various types of walling to be seen here, mentioning a section in the Cross Garden composed of brick and undressed stone, three or four courses of each laid alternately, which seemed unusual. This remark led John Hanvey to show me a stranger kind of walling. Thick glazed tiles, made with bull-nosed edges, were sandwiched between courses of brick. The tiles protruded from the surface of the wall, and had holes bored through them at intervals of a few inches. These were made to take twine, and this wall had permanent facilities for training climbers at each level from top to bottom—a gardener's dream.

Last of all I was shown a secluded summer-house built by Mr. Moore as a memorial to his devoted housekeeper. 'He was so upset when she died that he cried like a child', I was told. Somebody always has to go first; no doubt after long and happy years of service to a kind master she would have been equally upset to lose him. The words 'master' and 'servant' wear no ill-favoured looks in such a relationship. A tablet inscribed with this faithful friend's initials bears a tribute: 'A. Q.—Blest are the pure in heart.' That may now be regarded as a memorial both to the servant it commemorates and the employer who chose it.*

Of the lady who is today responsible, under the National Trust, for the careful maintenance of the lovely garden he made I am not permitted to write in any detail. The fact that such a ban has been imposed is of significance where the life-work of one person needs (and here receives) the greatest delicacy of touch to preserve its character. This is work rather akin to that of the accompanist, always adjusted to the singer. It is not a job for those who enjoy self-advertisement. Some people, offered the custodianship of a famous garden, will rush in talking of all the 'improvements' they intend to make there, and lay about them like a young wife rearranging furniture. Unhappily, living plants cannot be replaced so easily, and a few ill-judged changes may spoil a whole conception. Plantsmanship has nothing to do with this. Sometimes the botanic expert does the most harm.

Rowallane has been fortunate—how fortunate only those who have grieved over the result of less tactful operations elsewhere can fully appreciate. The late owner, The National Trust, and the thousands who come here to enjoy the gardens have good cause for gratitude to the Honourable Mrs. Terence O'Neill, who so skilfully cares for this piece of Irish soil.

---

*An article on Rowallane and Hugh Armytage Moore by R. C. Jenkinson appeared in the R.H.S. *Journal* for September 1964.

13

SMALLER GARDENS IN TOWN AND COUNTRY

1 East Lambrook Manor

I FIRST MET Margery Fish in the garden of her Somerset home during a brief dry spell in a damp and chilly autumn day. It was that dour kind of weather when even the stoutest plants may quail a little, as though they sense the approach of winter and are withdrawing into the innermost recesses of their being. The wet garden held much of interest, and I loitered with more thought of plant discoveries than of creature comforts, but their owner quickly drew me into her sixteenth-century manor-house for warmth and refreshment. It was a welcoming place, its wide oak door giving direct access to the chief sitting-room, where a mattress of ashes, several inches thick, smouldered on a great open hearth. All around us timbers of soft pinkish-brown colour, like the gills of a field mushroom, leaned in attitudes so relaxed that it seemed the house must exist to support them, not they the walls and roof.

We went up to bed by means of an elm staircase whose shallow risers and wide treads appeared to have sprung naturally from the flagged floor without the aid of men and tools. This kindly house reminded me of a plump old nanny, dressed in a plain habit and white apron, looking down protectively on her charges from a rosy well-soaped face. Thoughts of the comfortable nurseries and nurses of childhood led me to imagine what a good nanny Margery Fish herself might have made, had she been born a quarter of a century earlier and in another walk of life. But a nursery of a different sort, filled to the brim with young plants, lay behind the buildings and absorbed her unfailing devotion and care. She just *had* to propagate all her favourite subjects, many of them rescued from near-extinction in cottage gardens, and to distribute them among those plant-lovers who cared for the old and simple things.

It is essential to describe the house, because there was no sharp division between it and the garden. Wistaria and roses meandered round the stone mullions of the casement windows and looked into our bedrooms, while sprays of lace-cap Hydrangeas peered outwards from jugs placed on the sills. Bowls of dried Acanthus, Teasel, Artichoke, Physalis and Eucalyptus were in every ground-floor room, and I was offered a posy of white Jasmine to take upstairs 'to sweeten', as the old herbalists put it.

When I woke next morning, mingled scents from farm and garden blew in, sharply fresh, while perching robin and cackling fowl made a cheerful descant to the sombre lowing of cows, from a herd which pattered along the road in single file on its way to be milked. The night before, as Mrs. Fish kindled logs and peat on the hearth below, she had told me that some of her friends were surprised to find her living in a house so close to a village street. To her mind this was very far from being the drawback they seemed to think it. 'I love being right in the village—part of the community—and would hate to be isolated from it,' she said in her forthright way. One felt that she would have been proud to be called 'a villager', in the best sense of the word. There was nothing pretentious about Margery Fish.

In her first book, *We Made a Garden*, she explained how she and her husband wanted it to be modest and simple—a cottage garden, with crooked paths and unexpected corners. They succeeded so well that, although by no means an ordinary garden, it keeps quietly in line with its environment and makes no attempt to step out of the frame. There is not a single touch of grandeur or sophistication of the kind that most Londoners who settle in the country after retirement seem unable to resist. It is a marvellous lesson in restraint and good manners, silently telling its tale to those who will pause to read the message.

The Manor House at Lambrook is an L-shaped building, constructed of that local stone which is so often described as 'honey-coloured'. Because run honey varies so much, I prefer to call it the colour of honey-*comb*; it is a stone that shades from the pale hue of beeswax to the deep tone of honey-filled cells, and in places it has the waxy texture, while in others it shows patches of old gold, bright as a polished cairngorm. No garden planner could wish for a better background for plants. This lovely material has been quarried ever since Englishmen outgrew wattle and daub. It comes from the Hamdon Hills, whose sharpest knoll—*Mons Acutus*—gave its name to the neighbouring great house of Montacute. Humbler dwellings, especially when they are long and low, look their best under thatch— a roof-style for which the Lambrook manor-house was obviously designed; but owing to fire risks and the expense of maintenance, Mrs. Fish had to be content with clay tiles.

Together with her husband, Walter Fish, she first saw the place on a warm September day in 1937. It had been in use as two cottages, and now stood empty and derelict, the roof crudely patched with corrugated iron. In the small front garden a jungle of overgrown laurels made an almost impenetrable barrier. At the main door Mr. Fish stopped, refusing to go any further. 'It smells of dry rot,' he said. 'I won't have it at any price.'

After two months of fruitless searching they drove along the Yeovil road on a different errand, and seeing on a signpost *East Lambrook 1 mile*, they decided to take another look at the house. It may be that Margery Fish had an intuition that this was to be their home; if so, she wisely kept quiet about it. This time the frontage had been cleared, the roofing tiles restored, and a smell of paint smothered that of decay. Mr. Fish allowed himself to enter, and before very long the purchase of house, outbuildings, garden and orchard—in all about 2 acres of land—had been accomplished.

After the formalities of purchase were completed, the builders took many months to make the house habitable. Every week-end the new owners came down from London to see it, and Margery Fish longed to get busy in the garden, but there was seldom time to do more than pull up some handfuls of annual weeds. When they finally moved in, there was so much to be done indoors that the ground had to take second place. Looking back afterwards she admitted that the delay, exasperating at the time, proved to be an advantage, for it gave them breathing-space to settle down and to get the 'feel' of the land before doing any serious work outdoors. The bones of a garden are lasting things, not easily altered, and they are of such importance that it is always worth while to allow ideas to develop and mature on the site, instead of plunging, as most of us do, into the making of paths and lawns with feverish haste because soon we must invite our friends to see it.

At Lambrook one thing was quickly settled. The layout as it stood was fussy and unpleasing, with a lot of small dividing walls and amateur rock-work (stones stuck in vertically like almonds in a trifle) and all this must be removed. There were piles of stone all over the place, and cartloads were offered freely to farmers for tipping in muddy hollows on their farmland. Afterwards this generosity was seen to be mistaken, and Mrs. Fish would tell people that by degrees they bought in far more stone than they had possessed at the beginning. Few beginners realize that gardens eat stone, and that, unless it is of an ugly colour or texture, it should never be given away.

Those gardeners who long for stone and have none may be surprised to hear that at first it provided Mrs. Fish with problems. She disliked the vertical row of 'cock-ups' set in traditional style on top of the garden walls, and one of her first jobs was to clothe those jagged stones with Alyssum, Aubrietia, Arabis and Valerian, which she raised from seed. At a later stage flat, horizontal stones replaced the cock-ups, and then climbing roses, Honeysuckle and Clematis were allowed to hang over the top of the wall, to the benefit of passers-by in the street outside.

To begin with this was an immaculately kept 'man's garden', for

Walter Fish liked to raise giant Delphiniums, Dahlias and the like, and everything had to be placed in orderly clumps or rows. Little by little his wife's unconventional ideas crept in, but not until after his death in 1947 was she able to give them free rein. She believed in setting her plants as closely as possible, so that scarcely a square inch of soil was visible in summertime. Certain visitors assumed, quite wrongly, that the intermingled and entwining growths were allowed to do as they liked. They could never have seen how constantly Margery Fish was at work, pinching, pruning, thinning and training her subjects to give a natural effect, while allowing to each one its due amount of essential light and air. To bring it to perfection this type of garden requires even greater skill and care than the more regimented arrangements preferred by Walter Fish.

The character of Mrs. Fish and her method of gardening were all of a piece: a combination of ruthlessness and compassion, controlled by a first-class brain. A little too much compassion would turn such a garden into a muddle, while too much ruthlessness can give excellent results so far as separate plants are concerned, but seldom produces a satisfying picture in the garden as a whole. The entirely ruthless gardener is usually motivated by ambition. At risk of being thought sentimental, I am certain that the greatest gardens are made by people whose love of plants overrides the wish for personal success, and transcends any desire to shine in the world of horticulture. If a blaze of glory comes, as it came to her, it is a by-product. Everyone knows how character creeps out over the radio, and cannot be disguised; but few of us are aware that gardens mirror their gardeners.

When one attempts to point out useful lessons to be gleaned from visiting East Lambrook Manor it soon becomes clear that it is above all a versatile place, all things to all men, the ideas varying for everyone according to his or her needs. The comments of one admirer make a useful summing-up; but this is eminently a garden to be visited for yourself. The anonymous visitor told me that it was a *generous* garden. Most people, she said, who find groups of self-sown Hellebores, Fennels, Spurges and the like will heedlessly uproot them along with the weeds, because there are enough in the garden already. Margery Fish would leave all such seedlings, even when they established themselves in path or drive, for she said that someone would be sure to want them. She abhorred carelessness and waste, but solely in order to have the means to be generous.

Time and again I have seen a visitor arrive, express a longing for this or that plant, and immediately Mrs. Fish, trowel and trug in hand, has dived beneath the parent plant for a handful of its progeny. She knew where the least plant was, too. I have worked on the herb garden in shocking November weather, smothered in mud, and when wheeling away a barrowful of dead top-hamper and weeds, have been questioned as to the whereabouts of two or three tiny specimens of *Helleborus foetidus* which had been growing beside the Elecampane. Even if one had not understood the motive, and seen her open-handedness at work, the spirit of the place gave out a generous warmth which only the least sensitive person could have failed to notice.

Like Gertrude Jekyll, here was a gardener who developed green fingers and very well-informed plantsmanship at a late stage in her career. In response to considerable probing, she admitted that in earlier life there had been no interest whatever in gardening. Her parents were keen and accomplished, but she resented being used as a garden help with no say in what should be sown or planted, and no experimental plot of her own. Apparently her father and mother had not been influenced by Gertrude Jekyll's book *Children and Gardens*, issued during the early childhood of their family. 'You can't really be keen on gardening until you have one of your own. Doing as you are told in other people's gardens is a *bore*,' said Margery Fish, and it was easy to imagine Miss Jekyll's grunt of approval in the background.

Once the garden at East Lambrook had become her own, she kept up an intense enthusiasm for garden-making for the last 22 years of her life, not only with hard labour and watchfulness in her demesne, but by designing new gardens and re-designing older ones for people all over the southern part of England. Her own nursery garden supplied for these schemes plants difficult or impossible to obtain elsewhere: in particular many Spurges and Hellebores; old-fashioned kinds of Polyanthus and Primrose; Astrantias; variegated subjects; Pulmonarias; the Green Rose Plantain; and silver Artemisias ranging from the 5-foot tall Chinese Mugwort to cushions of *A. lanata pedemontana*, most of which have become so firmly associated with her name that they are sometimes called 'Fish plants'.

I was in regular contact with her for the last four years, going down to Lambrook for a week or two in summer and autumn to help with pruning and training of climbers, and with the herb garden and other chores which sometimes overwhelmed her, taken in conjunction with the demands on her time made by writing, lecturing and advising people on the plants best suited to their gardens and their tastes. Being let loose with secateurs and saw in what she described as '*My* garden'—to distinguish it from the nursery—was at first an alarming experience. The soil was crammed with treasures and I feared to overlook and wreck some small unidentified object which she might value. While removing dead wood from a Skimmia I ripped a thumb on a concealed thorny twiner, and was about to dig it out when a sudden thought stayed my hand. I called to Mrs. Fish to ask what it was. 'That,' she said, towering above my stooping form, '*that* is a common bramble.' Replying that I had thought so, but feared lest it turned out to be a rarity from Outer Mongolia, I smiled up at her—without response. Presently, as I weeded cracks between paving stones, I found a patch of withered foliage and called out again. 'Are these things common Plantains, or not?' She became instantly alert, saying 'Oh no, don't touch them—those are my Green Rose Plantains, mentioned in Gerard's *Herbal*.' 'Ah yes; but in any other garden they *would* have been weeds.' This time she smiled down at me, and we were truly friends from that moment. Afterwards I was trusted with almost anything in her own garden.

She died on 24th March 1969 at the age of 77, after a sudden collapse which she had been warned might occur if she persisted in gardening and exerting herself without pause. She elected to carry on, hoping to 'drop dead in the garden', as she put it. When the news came it seemed as though a storm had uprooted a splendid tree overnight, leaving a gaping hole in the garden world. At the memorial service in the packed village church (to which she had given freely of her time and thought, as well as money), the Bishop of Bath and Wells spoke of her great integrity and her genius for friendship. Fred Whitsey read the Lesson, the congregation sang *All Things Bright and Beautiful*, and we went away in a cold April wind to revisit her garden. It was sad to see it in spring glory without its presiding genius; yet there was a measure of comfort in the news that her nephew will do his best to maintain garden and nursery as Margery Fish would have liked, while her out-of-print books are to be re-issued. That saves me from the impossible task of trying to summarize her work, for every keen gardener may be sure of getting her own words on the printed page.

2 Moyles Cottage, Quenington

Enid Money chose to settle in the Cotswold village of Quenington after the death of her first husband and the sale, in the early 1950s, of their Georgian house in Berkshire. I can remember her present home as it was before she bought it: a little box of a cottage, smothered in unkempt creepers, with adjacent hen and pig houses, rather smelly, and at the back a neglected orchard in which a score of good old apple trees struggled for survival amidst rank growths of ivy and nettle. The whole property amounted to rather less than one and a half acres.

Within a couple of years it had been so transformed as to be unrecognizable. The cottage, lovingly restored, re-roofed with stone slats, and enlarged, now looked inviting; but it was the garden that took my eye. Gone were the sparrow-riddled creepers, the pig and hen squalor, the ivy and nettles, together with a layer of broken bedsteads, old boots, wire-netting and an aged earth-closet, and in their place a garden—which, even at that stage, was obviously to be one of some distinction—had begun to take shape. A trail of newly planted Wistaria, pale and indecisive, clung to the otherwise bare west wall of the cottage, which was constructed of that Cotswold stone, in the leached colour of sun-dried grass, which makes so admirable a foil to every kind of climbing plant. The Wistaria seemed to point downwards into a small enclosure fronting the village street, and visible through a wrought-iron gate.

Here, in a space about 30 feet long, bounded by Moyles Cottage, its stable buildings, a neighbouring cottage and the front wall, lay a paved court, raised some 2 feet above the entrance path, with a circular pond in the middle surmounted by a well-head and hanging bucket. All around in cracks between the stones little Thymes, Sedums, Campanulas, Marjorams, and the Pasque-flower with silky seed-heads seemed already well established, while four little domes of clipped Box gave stability to the design. Against the stable wall I saw the russet stems of *Hydrangea petiolaris*, with Santolina below it, and Lavender. A great stone trough, once the sink of the cottage, stood against the stable, and in it some sturdy plants of *Lilium auratum*. A *Mahonia bealei* grew beside the entrance gate, and the wall had Honeysuckle and roses planted against it, which would soon be visible from the road. Although so new, this little garden seemed to know just what it was intended to be. I had to see more.

It was not difficult, for the owner welcomed anyone with a real keenness for gardening, and I was soon through her great cedar door and standing on the terrace behind the house. She had designed her garden to suit the restored cottage and its village environment, and with an eye to reducing the work of maintenance so far as was compatible with the result she had in mind. First a firm structure was achieved by means of a broad paved terrace right across the back of the house, laid in a wide curve opposite the French windows of the new drawing-room, and leading to a generous flight of stone steps which rose to the higher level of the old orchard. Here the best of the trees, cleared of ivy and dead wood, were bearing good fruit. A few of the poorer specimens had been retained as hosts for Clematis and Jasmine, and in the grass spring bulbs were broadcast freely.

A mown walk cleaved straight through the centre of the orchard, leading to a stone summerhouse at the far end. With this simple, established background, as Mrs. Money explained, she had instantly seen an opportunity for making a new garden that would not look 'raw'. In fact, that old orchard had induced her to buy the place: for the making of gardens was her chief joy in life.

At either hand beside the top step leading to the orchard she had planted little fastigiate Irish Yews, and I was told how those would have to be kept pruned and tied in to maintain the slender shape of the 'exclamation marks' which were needed there. She had a keen and experienced outlook, having already made gardens in many parts of the world during the military career of her late husband. Also she came of a long line of artistic and plant-loving ancestors, and had practised painting and embroidery with considerable success, I gauged, though modestly describing herself as an amateur without training. My excitement at seeing the courtyard garden had clearly been stirred by the fact that here was someone with a talent for designing, both indoors and out.

The adjective most suitable for this whole conception would be 'elegant'. The shapes of the layout, the proportions of tree to grass and grass to paving, the gradual transition from the more sophisticated plantings near the house, all have elegance. The *Hydrangea paniculata*; the 'Smoke Tree', *Cotinus coggygria foliis purpureis*; the gold-splashed Elaeagnus; *Clematis recta*; the lovely Peony with the terrible name—*P. mlokosewitchii*; then a border of clipped *Lonicera nitida*; then some Japanese Cherries of the least banal sort; and finally the sturdy old country apples and plums—all fit together as though they had been made for their parts in this picture. Even the Golden Privet, used here in clipped specimens at focal points, has lost all trace of urban style and is perfectly integrated with the Cotswold landscape and its stone walls.

This is not Rose country, but the Old Roses do reasonably well, and fragrant 'Albertine' and 'Phyllis Bide'; the latter has been planted against the house on a north-facing wall. Green Hellebores, both *H. foetidus* and *H. corsicus* (*argutifolius*) seed themselves everywhere and are much liked by the owner, who takes an interest in rarer subjects but has no use for plant snobbery.

A beloved elder sister, who used to garden with conspicuous success in Ireland, had provided a number of special plants from Old Connor, including a particularly large and well-marked 'Marbled Arum'; a fine and brilliantly coloured version of the 'Vatican Sage'; a laurel-leaved Ribes with greenish-yellow flowers in February (an excellent evergreen, shallow-rooting, which sometimes layers itself); the scarce gilded Rosemary; and a handsome silver-variegated Acanthus not seen before by Margery Fish, to whom a root was given. After I had grown to know Enid Money better, I brought her a cutting of an Euonymus, taken from the wall of an old Wiltshire manor-house, which I thought unusual. It still seems to be exciting—and possibly confounding—the experts. It looks very like the well-known *E. radicans* 'Silver Queen', but nobody can explain why this one should climb right up the stable wall to the roofline, putting on 6 to 8 feet of growth annually, and bearing quantities of blossom and the attractive pink 'Spindleberries' usually seen only on the deciduous species.

Margery Fish and Christopher Lloyd thought it must be a specimen of 'Silver Queen' feeling particularly happy in that garden, yet Enid says her other specimens of the same plant behave at Quenington as we are all accustomed to see them: slow to move, staying small and neat for many years, and seldom showing sign of bloom or berry. The plant growing on her stable wall makes admirable wall cover, its foliage withstanding the hardest knocks given by severe winter weather and invariably looking fresh and well. One hesitates to recommend it, because those who buy 'Silver Queen' from a nursery in hopes that it will climb for them may be very disappointed. If any authority can explain the behaviour of this Euonymus, we shall be glad to hear from him or her.

To the east of Moyles Cottage there is a fair-sized lawn, with one curving edge made into a rocky slope for Thymes, Bugles, variegated Dead-nettle, small perennial Geraniums, Dryas, and the like. Two gnarled apple trees, outliers from the orchard proper, lean above lawn and flower beds to bridge over the meeting of new and old plantings. The south-eastern angle of the boundary walls, which are about 4 feet in height and fashioned of drystone in the local manner, proved to be a draughty corner when winds swept across these wolds, so the Scotch Briar was planted to form a thick, suckering barrier that effectively screens the beds.

Most of the plantings are mixed, consisting of golden and glaucous conifers; prostrate Juniper and the columnar *J. communis hibernica*; *Thuya ericoides*, delicately feathered in coppery green tones; various Viburnums; 'Snowy Mespilus'; Ceanothus, Chaenomeles, Spiraea, Jerusalem Sage, Elaeagnus, Leycesteria and Cotoneasters—the grey-leaved *C. franchetti* is lovely, but needs drastic pruning. Between these are shrubby Potentillas, and Bronze Fennel, Vatican Sage, Delphiniums and Lilies, placed casually in drifts. Around them are Ericas, Hostas, Hellebores, Bergenias and Santolinas, with edgings of Golden Marjoram, Silver Thyme, Nepeta, Variegated Applemint, Sedums and the smaller Artemisias, such as *A. canescens*. The humble Marigold is permitted to self-sow; the paler gold single flowers with dark centres are perfect in association with Lavender and the other herb plants.

Perhaps the Dahlia is a surprising plant to see employed in so natural a garden, yet it is used here with very pleasing effect. Only the quieter colours—cream, pale yellow and peach-pink are grown, of the cactus type, and they are placed in drifts between shrubs. The varied and attractive foliage shrubs disguise the lumpish green of the Dahlias, and when the flowering season of the former is coming to an end the latter begin to show up, many shrubs having been thinned or pruned by that time. This is the best use for the rather stiff and artificial bedding Dahlias that I have ever seen. The Tobacco Plant (fragrant, tall white, or dwarfer and scentless lime-green) also features in the late summer plantings, but this completes the story of bedding-out: a very small amount for a garden of this size. That old country favourite, Love-in-a-mist, self-sows every year, and Flax.

Although the plants are fairly close-set, their number is limited, and they are not encouraged to grow into and through one another as they were at East Lambrook Manor. The whole effect is of great simplicity and restfulness, with a deep-seated feeling for the surrounding country, of which this garden is very much a part, in harmony with landscape and vegetation. I always feel that people trained in the art of flower-arranging could use it as a model for extending their designs to the living picture outside.

When she heard that I intended to write about her work in a book on the design of modest gardens, Enid sent me a characteristic letter. 'You can of course make any use of my bit of garden, which has had so many suggestions and much help from you. What a strange subject it is—design. One tries to create a picture, changing in its mood of seasons and sun and shadow. To me it can't be finally designed, except some of the tone-work, perhaps. It grows with one and changes with the years.

'As to my basic ideas and plan for the layout, as you call it, much seemed really to happen by chance. When the furniture van arrived and the men wanted to know where to put the well-head, I told them to dump it there, in the little courtyard on the west of the house. But it looked right where it stood, so it never got moved, except to have a low circle of wall built for it to stand on, enclosing the water-lily pool below.

'When the old cellar became an entrance hall, a small courtyard had to be excavated and paved on this side of the house, allowing access to my new front door at that lower level. The builders were going to remove all the surplus soil, but I saw that it was good soil, so I told them to throw it up there. 'Up there' then turned into a raised bed and lawn, with a retaining wall built at right-angles to the wrought-iron gates which open on the pavement outside. The width of that little courtyard was, of course, fixed by the size of my gates, which had been brought from Winkfield.

'The summerhouse at the end of the orchard walk was an existing pig-sty, and I had the walls raised and the old roofing tiles put back. It happened to be in the right place, at the far end of the main vista from the doors of the drawing-room, across the terrace and through the orchard, where I had the original track widened and made straight.'

All this sounds casual, even haphazard; yet the quick eye of the artist, accustomed to grasp and set down on paper fleeting impressions of landscape, had been at work all through the initial purchase and the development of the garden, so that the intermediate donkey-work with measurements on paper was side-stepped without doing any harm to the result. This garden may be described as a spontaneous and inspired sketch, made with soil and growing plants. Moyles Cottage garden has been open to the public on two days each year for the past 11 years, under the National Gardens Scheme, Gloucestershire.

3 GREYFRIARS

Greyfriars is a splendid example of a fifteenth-century town house, half-timbered with that lavish use of oak which, in 1480, had not yet been restricted by law. It is but two minutes' walk from the cathedral, and fronts the only street of that period in Worcester where the machinations of property developers have so far left intact whole groups of buildings which saw (and in one case sheltered) King Charles the Second after the disastrous Battle of Worcester.

The house is said to have been built by the Franciscans as a hospice for travellers, the care of guests being an obligation on the friars of those days. At the Dissolution of the Monasteries the freehold was acquired by the Corporation of Worcester and the building let on lease to various citizens, ending with a family named Street for the exceptional term of 400 years. By the beginning of the twentieth century it had been degraded into a number of poor tenements and shops, and at the end of World War II the local Authority put it on their list of properties to be demolished. After considerable trouble it was saved, and vested in the Worcester Archaeological Society. A very large amount was then spent on restoration, provided by Mr. and Miss Matley Moore, who were in return given a lease of the house for their lifetime.

These members of an old Cheshire family are a brother and sister who have lived in Worcestershire for most of their lives. Their combined zeal in unearthing and preserving the lovely old treasures of the neighbourhood has been matched by antiquarian knowledge and taste of the highest order. Greyfriars received at their hands skilled and sympathetic restoration, in which general effect and minute detail have been watched over with equal precision and success. Antiquarians are not often skilled in horticulture and garden design, but in this case the garden is worthy of the house and well worth a visit for its own sake.

On a warm day in early September it made a cool sanctuary from streets crowded with visitors to the Three Choirs Festival, its high walls of mellow brick clothed in draperies of Fig, Rose, Clematis and Vine. The walls of the house support a *Viburnum fragrans* which grows like a beanstalk right up to the bedroom windows; those open casements must receive innumerable benefits of fragrance in the winter and early spring flowering season of this plant. The late Reginald Farrer, who discovered it, says that it was cultivated all over northern China. Old specimens were to be seen in almost every palace or temple yard, and its loveliness carried it to Peking, where it was highly prized in the Imperial Gardens and reserved for that purpose until the death of the Dowager Empress of China. Only after the fall of the Dynasty was it allowed out at last into the eager hands of the common people.

SMALLER GARDENS IN TOWN AND COUNTRY

Seeing this apparently old-established oasis of a garden, I imagined that it must be an ancient monkish pleasance whose remains had been unearthed from the deep litter of neglectful generations. But this idea was entirely mistaken, and immediately shattered by Miss Matley Moore in one breath. The garden is a modern creation, made in some 12 years out of a heap of rubble, with no traces of earlier horticultural usage. When she and her brother took over the property, the site of their garden was cluttered with a row of poor decaying cottages built against the north boundary wall. The Matley Moores were obliged to live overlooking these eyesores for eight years, until they were evacuated and demolished. During this waiting period they employed the time in planning the layout of their future garden, and were able to evaluate the material in the condemned dwellings, subsequently paying the contractors to salvage and stack such stone, brick, tiles and paving setts as they desired to make use of in their design. That long wait must have been trying, but they put it to good use, and it paid dividends in the result.

All this required vision. In such unpromising conditions few of us would have had the imagination to picture a charming garden, and fewer still could have carried the plan through to such a splendid conclusion. With Mr. Moore as designer for the structural 'bones' of the layout, and his sister to plan the planting, the partnership managed to evolve a most satisfying little work of art, although neither of them had had any training in garden craft, and their previous experience had been negligible. In about a quarter of an acre they have produced an effect of spaciousness and peace right in the heart of a busy city. It was no parlour game on paper for them. They employed labour for the heaviest manual work—levelling, paving, making raised beds and lawn; but brother and sister supervised it all, and subsequently laid more paving and did all the planting themselves. They were not young people, and when looking back must sometimes wonder how they managed to do it. As the years pass they are enjoying their reward in this delightful retreat, which is attractive at all seasons and not too demanding or expensive to maintain.

Each morning the great oak gates fronting the street are thrown open so that passers-by may step aside from shopping and wander in underneath the gallery, which links the two wings of the house at first-floor level, as far as some wrought-iron gates opening on to the main paved terrace. From this point it is possible to see through to the green sanctuary beyond, and very enticing it looks. The terrace has been made of a generous width, and runs the whole length of the building. The cost of paving such a large area with stone proved to be too high, so clever use has been made of cheaper concrete slabs, set in alternate rectangles with chequer-work composed of blue midland brick and cobblestones. It makes a satisfying pattern, and redeems the concrete from monotony. By laying the bricks lengthways across the terrace the designer has contrived to lead the eye forward into his garden picture. Little touches of that nature, while not always immediately apparent to the casual observer, combine to give distinction to the effect as a whole.

On the far side of the terrace there is a low wall with widely spaced brick pillars supporting wooden cross-beams, used as a pergola for climbing roses. In the central opening a semi-circular flight of shallow steps leads down to the lawn. This is nearly 20 feet shorter than a standard tennis court, but by juggling with the shape, which is full court width (36 feet) at the front, narrowing to 29 feet at the far end, the natural perspective is enhanced to give an illusion of greater length. Such cunning, known to earlier generations of garden planners as 'false perspective', was delighted in by Alexander Pope at his Twickenham garden.

For the end of the greensward Miss Moore has herself built from rough-hewn stone a massive raised circular bed, some 15 feet in diameter, forming a focal point. In spring it is full of blossoming bulbs, and later in the year Hypericum makes the rondel into a golden pool. The first-floor gallery, which is in constant use as a bridge between the north and south wings of the house, looks down on the plants in this bed, and it gives constant pleasure to those who pass to and fro. For background there is a mixed plantation of trees and shrubs—pear, quince, birch, sumach, broom and syringa—

grown thickly and thus able to give an air of mystery and shadow, to prevent the feeling of constriction that may develop from too clear a view of enclosing high walls. This method of avoiding claustrophobia may be compared with the device suggested in Figure 5, where a walled garden behind a Georgian house has been re-designed with a central paved feature to take the eye away from the encircling brick.

A narrow border for roses and other climbers runs below the southern wall, facing north, and on the opposite side of the grass there is a wider one with clipped bushes and climbing plants trained on poles. A way leads through to a paved walk of generous width, near the northern boundary wall, which faces south and is able to accommodate some of the more tender subjects. Along this paving is a splendid procession of great terracotta vases, and these are not set in a straight line, but given far greater interest because the edge where they stand has been made in a subtle curve, which is echoed by the vases. The curve is so slight as to be almost unnoticeable at first glance, yet the fluid liveliness it gives to the picture is immensely worth while.

The northern boundary wall is buttressed by brick pillars, wide at the base and narrowing towards the top, and some are edged with clipped golden privet, rather like gold braiding on a naval uniform; a most attractive device where too much brick might become overpowering (Plate III a). Miss Moore revels in the screen provided by the buttresses, for her high walls seem to funnel the wind along, to the detriment of clingers. Raised beds in between the buttresses meet the paved terrace in a series of semi-circular bays, housing garden seats. The design of this terrace repays study, for again salvaged material from the demolitions has been cleverly used to produce pattern and texture in the paving.

At the west end near the house a small semi-circular surround of finely carved Ligurian marble, made originally for a window, has been set into a brick structure, with a tiled recess adapted from an old fireplace. This forms a niche for a basin where tiny jets of water play with soothing sounds. A submerged electric pump creates the illusion of running water by circulating a limited supply, which is contained in the basin and has no outlet. Anyone could have the illusion of running water by using this economical device, and it may be a more pleasing way of employing water in the garden than the more common, often rather stagnant, lily pool (Plate XV b).

If Mr. Moore has an obsession, it is for the value of spacious effect in human environment, and by spacious effect he does not mean a large area—few today can have that luxury. He demonstrates here how a small space may give the impression of greater size, by careful planning and clever limitation of plants and ornaments. Lawns should always be laid out in a simple sweep, uninterrupted by cut out beds for flowers; vases and tubs should be placed where they make a real contribution to the design, and not dotted around in every possible place in order to cram in more flowering plants. His sister restricts her planting to a limited number of subjects, and chooses only those which are at home in her soil and suited to a town garden. *Clematis tangutica* does very well here, and smothers the northern wall in a tangle of yellow lantern flowers and silky seed-heads. There is a Fig, which sometimes ripens its fruit; the charming Rose 'Phyllis Bide', peaches-and-cream and fragrant; *Crataegus lavallei*, whose yellow berries, being disliked by birds, last the winter through; and of course the tall *Viburnum fragrans* on the house.

Greyfriars has in recent years been endowed and given to the National Trust, but the Moores continue to live there and to show visitors round house and garden on the first Wednesday of each month, in summertime. One more of our national treasures has been saved from the bulldozers, which are leaving greater trails of destruction than the bombers of 25 years ago.

4 A Garden in Kensington

Mrs. Cecily Mure decided, early in the 1960s, to convert her fairly commonplace town garden, then a mixture of herbaceous plants and bulbs, followed by summer annuals and a winter blankness, into a permanent picture with plants—chosen largely for their foliage—which would stand the winter. She quotes Gertrude Jekyll: 'People forget that green is a colour.' Together with purple, silver, variegated and glaucous leaved subjects, she has been able to create with greenery an enchanting composition of closely packed plants, full of contrast and variety.

Wisely, she began with the soil. It is possible to commission a nursery to remove exhausted soil and replace it with good loam—an operation many a town garden would appreciate, but it costs in the region of £3 a square yard. This garden in Kensington consists of two separate plots, one behind the house and one in front, each measuring nearly 100 square yards. Mrs. Mure decided that most of the soil in her beds must be renewed, but fortunately a considerable part of both sections was already paved, so that the amount of soil required was limited. All that consigned to the back garden had to be carried through the house in polythene sacks, and presumably the waste was removed by the same route. The intensive cultivation employed to keep an all-the-year garden going uses up the vital humus, which needs constant replenishment. Here the easily handled peat and hop manure are added, also some composted farmyard stuff, all obtained from garden suppliers in the useful polythene bag.

It was desired to extend the range of plants by growing climbers, and to exclude draughts, for Mrs. Mure knew that many plants could endure wind on open sites but not funnelled currents such as are man-made in built-up areas. The erection of higher walls and fences entails consultation with neighbours, with whom the gardener must be on friendly terms. Walls are expensive to build, but overlapping panels of cedar wood are efficient and reasonably priced, while hurdles of wattle filter the wind and look pleasing. Lattice to hold the trained plants must be fixed on to whatever wall or fence has been chosen. Mrs. Mure has an intense dislike of anything obtrusive in the way of colour, and in so small a garden this point is naturally of particular importance. The usual creosoted trellis is finished in a sticky dark brown which seems to push forward through all but the thickest growths. Here Solignum has been used instead, obtainable in several colours and easily mixed to whatever subtlety the gardener wants as a cool and unobtrusive background for his plants. We shared a horror of glutinous greens produced by makers of the otherwise admirable plastic-coated wire trellising.

The principle on which the fences have been clothed is that of training flowering shrubs flat against them, with the Clematis (Mrs. Mure has 40 kinds) arranged so as to climb through the shrubs. Pruning the latter to a thin flatness involves some loss of bloom, but the entwined Clematis makes up for that. By clever combination of early shrub and later Clematis, the flowering season can be made to last over a long period. Where borders are narrow it is of course essential to keep the shrubs very flat against the wall or fence, otherwise there is no room for plants in front.

While I like to grow Chaenomeles ('Japonica') as a kind of weeping tree, Mrs. Mure trains hers very neatly close against the fence, which suits it admirably. Then she has the useful and attractive *Hydrangea petiolaris*, a natural climber which is at home on a north-facing wall, and *H. villosa*, a fine mauve Lace-cap, beside it. Another Lace-cap, known as 'Grayswood', does well in London, and the silky-leaved Moroccan Broom, *Cytisus battandieri* with its yellow pineapple-scented flowers. *Garrya elliptica*, the male form with long catkins of pale green, looks well, and there is the unfailing Winter Jasmine to light up the worst corner. I have yet to visit a garden where this plant will not grow, and flower for over two months. As at Lambrook, the versatile large-leaved Dead-nettle with that awful name—*Lamium galeobdolon variegatum*, which looks and sounds like a witch's incantation—serves as both ground-cover and climber. In Kensington it goes up the low front wall and hangs over outside along the street.

Tougher shrubs are here used to protect the weaker, and the indestructible Laurustinus leans over the brilliant silver *Senecio leocostachys*. Other, artificial, kinds of winter protection used include branches of Fir or Broom, Bracken, and sheet plastic, all of which must be applied and removed at the right moment, neither put in position too soon nor removed too early. In our British climate such decisions require a mixture of horticultural knowledge and prescience about the weather, and some of us who are not so gifted prefer to grow only those subjects which are able to take care of themselves.

I have seldom seen a better plant of *Clematis armandii*—that leathery evergreen with a quantity of white blossom in spring. It spans a 12-foot width of wall, and has risen to 8 feet. Next to it there was a *Clematis montana*, but competition became too fierce, so Mrs. Mure killed the latter, then pruned away the fuzz of smaller branches, retaining the hoary stems as a host for other, less invasive species. It is impossible to list all the varieties of Clematis here; they range through the species and the small-flowered hybrids to the herbaceous *C. davidiana*, which has flowers that look and smell like Hyacinths: unexpected reminders of spring in late summer.

In the front garden a fine pair of that useful shrub *Viburnum davidii* produce the valuable blue berries, a male and female plant in association being necessary. The apricot-flowered Alstroemerias (Ligtu hybrids) grow up through the Viburnums in summer and associate well with the dark blue-green foliage of the latter. Then there is *Senecio laxifolius*, and various Hebes, all kept small and shapely by constant skilful pinching. Distasteful though the duty can be, the successful gardener in a small space must become an expert and regular pincher.

The arrangement of paving and raised beds in these two small plots could not be bettered, it being most imaginatively designed to give variety of height and shape. In one corner of the back garden the highest level is reached by a flight of three stone steps. Above these a splendid plant of Corsican Hellebore (now called *Helleborus argutifolius*) is enthroned; its trusses of pale green flowers look their best when seen from below. A stout pole, cut from a sapling, with bark left on, is firmly fixed near it in the bed. The owner admitted that this was not intended to support a plant, but to assist her on her many trips up to the bed, where Clematis on the fence required constant attention. 'The training of all these nearly kills me!' she said. Senior gardeners may care to adopt this aid to the rather less agile human frame.

Much of this garden is paved, and in the centre rectangle at the back of the house there is a large raised bed, 14 inches high, with more paving on top in which spaces for plants have been made of differing size and in an irregular formation, with a still higher raised part, L-shaped, at one end. In the top pockets are tall shrubs to emphasize the height; it is interesting to see the New Zealand Flax (*Phormium tenax purpureum*) established here, with *Senecio laxifolius* and other subjects. In the lower section of the bed are flatter plants, including Bugles, *Euphorbia myrsinites*, and *Helichrysum petiolaris*, kept low. A dark fastigiate Yew is just right as a little monument in the corner.

There are many original ideas in this small London garden. The coal-hole beside the front door is disguised by a rather handsome old iron incinerator on legs. Lined now with zinc, holes being cut through it to allow plants to hang down outside, it is pretty with the silver and white Ivy (*Hedera helix* 'Glacier'), together with Campanulas and Silver Thymes. On top rock plants grow among pieces of tufa. This device is attractive, and practical in that it may be removed when necessary. On the opposite side of the garden a manhole, originally at a slightly lower level, has been given the look of a real sunk garden by the expedient of building up a low wall round it, with little plants set there, and *Cotoneaster dammeri* trailing across the cover of the manhole. Its long branches may be pushed aside to allow access.

Then there is an old zinc water tank, holed for drainage, placed in a cool spot, half-filled with rubble, with 6 inches of John Innes compost and topping of sharp sand. In this Mrs. Mure raises her cuttings successfully; the outside has been covered with *Cotoneaster horizontalis* and the popular *Euonymus radicans* 'Silver Queen'. A recent acquisition, an old London chimney-pot of rectangular shape and pale buff colour, will make a 'planter' of unusual type and provide yet another level. After some precious Spanish pots had been stolen from the front garden, Mrs. Mure substituted heavy stone troughs, and when that supply ran out she covered a white glazed sink with the material known as Hypatufa (see Chapter 9).

I had not known that one of my own favourite shrubs, Rosemary, refused to survive in London, even in a smokeless zone. In its place the *Helichrysum rosmarinifolium* is grown, and the foliage is indeed very like its namesake, except for the absence of that delicious resinous smell. This garden could suggest ideas to almost any gardener, however experienced and whatever size his garden happens to be. Mrs. Mure insists on the value of cool root-runs for most of her subjects, and provides not only large areas of paving at different levels for that purpose, but places loose pieces of stone round many plants in the borders. Peat blocks will serve for this, but they harbour more pests. Even stones must be turned frequently to eliminate lurking slugs. The care taken here to create a harmonious picture is minute and unflagging. It extends to the choice of colour in the twine used to tie up plants unobtrusively. It was no surprise to hear that Mrs. Mure shares with Enid Money a flair for embroidery, in particular *petit-point* and *gros-point*, stitchery done on canvas and erroneously described in needlework shops as 'tapestry'. Both women design and work their gardens with similar finesse, and may truly be said to embroider with plants.

5 Herbers

About ten years ago I was faced with the task of making a garden on a small plot in a country town, a hill slope of poor, dusty soil where summer showers disappeared in a matter of minutes, like bath water going down a drain. When first seen in winter the place was a dismal muddy patch full of rotting cabbage stumps. It was sheltered on the north, west and east by stone walls of varying heights, and at the lower, southern, end an iron railing guarded a 12-foot drop to the neighbours' garden below. This unsightly but necessary barrier was quickly planted with a row of small plants of the 'fishbone' Cotoneaster, *C. horizontalis*, an attractive screen and invaluable where space is severely limited.

Having removed several sackfuls of broken crockery, drain-pipes, door-handles, stay-bones, locks and hinges, clinker and pieces of barbed wire, I decided to make a couple of terraces. Even a gradual slope can be tiresome to work on; without a level place to put your feet standing soon becomes unpleasant, and the smaller tools and balls of twine slide or roll away incessantly unless fastened to the person. All that gave me a feeling of restlessness which I was determined to eliminate. But it is one thing to plan terraces and quite another to find sufficient material to construct retaining walls, steps, paving and edging. All the available stone, some excavated from the ground, other chunks salvaged from waste land, and old stone roofing slats from a derelict coal-house, proved to be insufficient, even on this tiny piece of land measuring about 130 square yards in all. The garden was accessible only from a footpath, and the work of barrowing stone up from a lorry on the road added nearly 50 per cent to the cost. Such imports were beyond my means, so another solution had to be found.

In a mood of desperation I formed a shallow bank, from which in dry spring weather the soil had been running down like sand through an hour-glass, by making mats from wire-netting doubled over with thick wads of newspaper between. These were pegged down with outsize 'hairpins' made from galvanized wire. Friends offered pieces of many small ground-cover plants, such as Bugle, variegated Deadnettle, Arabis, Aubrieta, Campanula, Sedum, and the lesser Periwinkle in blue, white and purple. These were poked through the large mesh of the wire, holes being cut through the newsprint with a dibber, and the improvised mats not only retained the soil but kept the little plants moist, acting as a mulch until they were established. By the time my wire-and-paper sandwiches had fallen apart the plants had taken over the work of binding the soil.

Plants will do almost anything for you if you ask them. The next bit of alteration in levels involved the scooping out of a sort of bowl, to be grassed and used for sun-bathing. It suggests an outsize Victorian hip-bath, with three wattle hurdles taking the place of the raised back seen on the best of those bygone domestic treasures. I happened to have a row of earthenware seed-pans which had become thoroughly pot-bound with that heartiest of sedums, *Sedum spurium*. Most people will know this plant, although its name is seldom used and it does not appear to have a vernacular one. It has occasional pink tufts of flower, and runs with little snake-like stems all over the ground. It came out of the pans in tight rectangular blocks which were easily laid in the same way as turves, with wooden pegs hammered in to support them until they took root on the semi-circular bank around my grass bowl. After rain they made a firm green edge which might have been there for years. This useful substitute for stone happened to be available by chance, but it would be a simple matter to grow such 'turves' purposefully for use in retaining a bank of loose soil.

The patch of *Sedum spurium* is kept clipped with shears, thus losing most of its bloom, but ensuring solid ground-cover and fresh foliage; when young, this has an attractive pink tinge. The summer was unusually hot, reminding me of countries bordering the Mediterranean, and the sunbaked dusty soil seemed hopeless for anything which required a cool root-run: that was available only for such plants as were placed in crevices between my stone-slat paving blocks. Yet the land behind Nice and Mentone is clothed most acceptably with fragrant Rosemary, Lavender, Cistus and other herbs. Here was clearly the sort of planting that my garden required. It would have to be a herb garden.

So a hedge of Rosemary and Lavender was set against the wattle hurdles, on the southern side behind the little lawn, with Bronze Fennel, Red Sage, and the everlasting Pearl Flowers, *Anaphalis margaritacea* and *A. triplinervis*. By this time my grass hip-bath had become so secluded that from the gate many visitors were unaware of its existence, proving that even a mini-garden may have an element of surprise. The fruit-scented Chamomile was put in as ground cover beneath the taller subjects, and cushions of Thyme. The different scents of all these herbs mingled into a delicious pot-pourri and greatly added to the pleasure of sun-bathing. Many people think of herbs entirely for their practical uses in cooking, but to my mind their fragrances outdoors in the garden are even more to be prized. They do need to be enclosed in some measure, in order to concentrate the scent, and this is not always remembered by designers of herb gardens.

Gradually I collected a large number of Thymes, from *Thymus vulgaris* and *T. citriodorus* (the latter, lemon flavoured, being favourite for most culinary purposes), to little creeping ones like 'Pink Chintz' and *T. herba barona*, with a caraway taste, once chosen to flavour the baron of beef. Then there are the Marjorams—*Origanum onites*, the best for cooking, and the golden form of *O. vulgare* in large clumps, with the somewhat shyer form, *O. aureum*, a deeper gold with pink flower heads that do not clash. Chives forms an edging to the lowest bed. It is cut for salads from alternate roots, leaving those between to flower with decorative effect. Near the sitting-out places, where onion smells might be disliked, Thrift takes its place.

Under the west wall, which is overhung by a pear tree from next door, are the moisture-loving herb plants; the Mints, from culinary Spearmint to cream-splashed variegated Applemint, and the strong growing Eau-de-Cologne Mint, lovely in pot-pourri and sweet-bags; the brightly gilded Ginger Mint, and the tall grey Buddleia Mint with its tassels of mauve blossom like miniature flowers of the 'Butterfly Bush'. The Bergamots like this bed too, and various Hellebores, and the great *Euphorbia wulfenii* with its beehive hair-do, also the smaller *E. griffithii* with red and gold colouring—a spreader.

Myrtle and Lemon Verbena grow under the top wall, facing south, together with Jackman's Blue Rue, Gold-variegated Sage, Winter Savory and more Thymes, particularly the gold-edged one and 'Silver Queen', a silver-striped variety of *T. citriodorus* which bears delightful pink buds and young foliage in the early part of the year. It is less hardy than T. 'Silver Posie', so it is as well to grow both. Tarragon and Hyssop are here, and the Curry Plants, *Helichrysum siculum* and *H. angustifolium*, to add silver foliage, the former standing well throughout the winter, both providing a hot smell of curry when the sun is on them.

I have chosen the Hidcote Lavender, for it has a neat habit, not too dwarf, with flowers of a rich purple, and it seems to be long-lived, not vulnerable to wind as are so many lavenders. Shrub roses are best in such a garden, and here we have pink 'Grootendorst' with its delicately fringed petals, the pale 'Moonlight', and 'Queen of Denmark', grown between the tall glaucous Meadow Rue and some recently planted species of Eucalyptus. If these are kept low they will continue to produce attractive juvenile foliage (the prunings are valued for indoor decoration) and do not swamp a small garden. Some of the glaucous ones are mauve at certain stages, and with my golden Elder the effect is striking. My favourite Eucalyptus (*E. viminalis*) is different from all the others, producing foliage which is golden and foxy red at all seasons, without a trace of the blue-grey colouring commonly associated with the gum tree. Around its roots I have planted gold-variegated Lemon Balm from Lambrook, and the ferny Sweet Cicely.

In summer the gentian-blue stars of Borage, which self-sows, lavender whorls of Upright Pennyroyal, deep purple of Honesty—this is a plant that haunts me wherever I go, which I hope is a good omen—and the deep plushy red of Clove Carnations bring far richer colour into the picture than most people expect of a herb garden. Then there is the majestic Elecampane, a medicinal herb plant with an architectural sweep of leaf and woody pillar of a stem, crowned in late summer with golden 'sun' flowers. The white Florentine Iris below it was the source of the Orris Root used in perfumery for centuries.

The glaucous foliage of Woad and its yellow flowers I would not be without, although most people are chiefly interested in the pendant seed-pods, black when ripe, which go so well in flower arrangements for the winter. This plant is a biennial, but seeds itself freely. The magnificent great Sage known as the 'Vatican'—*Salvia turkestanica*—is also biennial, but it is unreliable as a self-sower, and I find it advisable to collect seed and raise a few plants each year. The glory of this Sage is in the bracts, which are almost the colour of that hospital paint known as Gentian Violet. Cooled down by greyish foliage and the lavender-blue blossom, this makes a large bush of great value in the herb garden, or indeed in any garden where it will grow to full stature. Near it I have the curled Tansy which Gertrude Jekyll loved, *Tanacetum vulgare* var. crispum.

Alchemilla mollis, the lime-flowered Lady's Mantle, seeds itself all over the place, and pink spires of Bistort appear in the least expected spots. One of the few plants in this garden not associated with herbal medicine, cookery, dyeing or pot-pourri is the shrubby Potentilla, which is chosen in the paler yellow—primrose colour—because that accords well with everything else. I have lately introduced a cream coloured Tree Lupin, and found that it is valuable as a companion for the Potentilla. The greenery of the Lupin stood up well to a trying winter, and by growing it close by the Potentilla one can achieve the effect of evergreen foliage on the latter. It has puzzled several casual onlookers.

In spring there are Snowdrops, Winter Aconites, species Crocus and Tulip, with some of the smaller Narcissi. I am never tired of the Hellebores—whether these are the white or pink Christmas and Lenten Roses or the green-flowered *H. corsicus* and *H. foetidus*. I have a greenish-yellow Japanese Cherry 'Ukon', which blooms just as the Wormwood underneath shows its fresh silver foliage, and the fragrant Southernwood too. One shady corner houses a patch of Lily-of-the-Valley, which is also a herb. It is truly astonishing to see how many varieties of foliage can be produced in this confined space, ranging from vivid spring green and gold, through smoky blue, jade, maroon and plum-purple in summer, with silver-grey at all times, and in autumn a score of different russets and reds. A tiny garden, even on the poorest soil, need never be dull to look at.

BOOK LIST

Anderson, E. B. *Rock Gardens* Penguin
Balfour, Lady Eve *The Living Soil* Faber & Faber
Bean, W. J. *Ornamental Trees for Amateurs* Country Life
Bloom, Alan *Alpine Plants of Distinction* Collingridge
Brett, W. S. *Planning Your Garden* Ward, Lock
Bruce, M. E. *Commonsense Compost Making* Faber & Faber
Concrete in Garden-making Cement & Concrete Association
Crowe, Sylvia *Garden Design* Country Life
Fish, Margery *We Made a Garden* Collingridge
Fish, Margery *Cottage Garden Flowers* Collingridge
Fish, Margery *Gardening in the Shade* Collingridge
Fish, Margery *Ground-cover Plants* Collingridge
Fish, Margery *An All-the-year Garden* Collingridge
Fish, Margery *A Flower for Every Day* Collingridge
Fish, Margery *Carefree Gardening* Collingridge
Hellyer, A. G. L. *Your New Garden* Collingridge
Hyams, Edward *The Gardener's Bedside Book* Faber & Faber
Jekyll, Gertrude *Home and Garden* Longmans
Jekyll, Gertrude *Wood and Garden* Longmans
Jekyll, Gertrude *Children and Gardens* Country Life
Lilley, S. E. *A Handbook of Rock Gardening* Alpine Garden Society
Lloyd, Christopher *Gardening on Chalk and Lime* Pan Piper
Lloyd, Christopher *Shrubs and Trees for Small Gardens* Pan Piper
Lloyd, Christopher *Clematis* Country Life
Perry, Frances *Water Gardens* Penguin
Phillips, C. E. Lucas *The Small Garden* Pan Piper
Phillips, C. E. Lucas *Roses for Small Gardens* Pan Piper
Roper, Lanning *Hardy Herbaceous Plants* Penguin
Shewell-Cooper, W. E. *The A.B.C. of Soils* English Universities Press
Snook, Leslie *Gardening for the Elderly and Handicapped* Pan Piper
S-W., V. *V. Sackville-West's Garden Book* Michael Joseph

SOME USEFUL ADDRESSES

Alpine Plants
Jack Drake, Inshriach, Aviemore, Inverness-shire, Scotland.
Joe Elliott, Moreton-in-the-Marsh, Gloucestershire.
W. T. Ingwersen, Birch Farm Nurseries, Gravetye, E. Grinstead, Sussex.

Clematis, etc.
Treasures of Tenbury Ltd., Tenbury, Worcestershire.

Conifers (dwarf and slow-growing)
The Wansdyke Nursery, Hillworth, Devizes, Wiltshire.

Cottage Garden and Foliage Plants
H. Boyd-Carpenter, East Lambrook Manor, S. Petherton, Somerset.
John V. Panton, Coombe House, Exbridge, Dulverton, Somerset.
Mrs. Desmond Underwood, Colchester, Essex.

Eucalyptus (hardy)
Sandhurst Nurseries, Sandhurst, Camberley, Surrey.

Herb Plants
E. and A. Evetts, Ashfields Herb Nursery, Hinstock, Market Drayton, Shropshire.
Mrs. A. E. Keen, Valeswood Herb Farm, Little Ness, Shrewsbury, Shropshire.

Peonies
Kelway & Son, Langport, Somerset.

Roses
Edwin Murrell, Portland Nurseries, Shrewsbury, Shropshire. (Including shrub roses.)
S. McGredy & Son, Portadown, N. Ireland.

Conifers, Climbers, Foliage Plants, Roses and Shrubs
Hillier & Sons, Winchester, Hants.
G. Jackman & Sons, Woking Nurseries, Woking, Surrey.
John Scott & Co., The Royal Nurseries, Merriott, Somerset.
Slieve Donard Nursery, Newcastle, Co. Down, N. Ireland.
Sunningdale Nurseries, Windlesham, Surrey.

Water Plants
Perry's Hardy Plant Farm, Enfield, Middlesex.

Garden Pottery
Brannam Potteries, Barnstaple, N. Devon.

Fibre-glass Planters, etc.
Verine Products & Co., Folly Faunts House, Goldhanger, Maldon, Essex.

Non-slip Garden Paving
Noelite Ltd., Borough Green, Kent.

INDEX

A
Acacia—see Robinia
Acanthus 166, 185, 194
Accents 31, 37, 136, 193
Acer 75, 182
Aconite, Winter 8, 212
Acorus calamus (Sweet Flag) 60
Actinidia kolomikta 95
Aesculus (Chestnut) 164, 182
Agapanthus 152
Akebia 95
Alchemilla mollis (Lady's Mantle) 39, 100, 212
Alkanet 101
Aloysia triphylla (Lemon Verbena) 29, 56, 100, 210
Alpine (or Rock) gardens 17, 52, 64, 110–114, 213
Alstroemeria 205
American garden design 40, 118, 141, 147
American Museum in Britain 126, 147 (Plates VII a, X a)
Ampelopsis veitchii—see *Vitis inconstans*
Anaphalis 39, 209
Anderson, E. B. 110, 112, 213
Anemone, Japanese 4, 152–153
Anemone pulsatilla (Pasque Flower) 57, 192
Angelica 55, 101 (Plate XV a), 103
Anthemis nobilis (Chamomile) 44, 209
Applemint, Variegated—see *Mentha*
Applemint, Woolly—see *Mentha*
Arboretum, Westonbirt 68, 74, 146
Arrowhead 59
Art in garden design 7–8, 26, 40, 42, 141, 155, 160–161, 166, 167, 172–174, 193, 197, 200–201, 203, 207

Artemisia 26, 44 (Plate II b), 100, 102, 152, 190, 195
Artichoke, Globe 55, 185
Ash, Weeping 18–19, 73
Aspect 46–47
Astrantia 32, 190
Atriplex halimus 62, 122
Atriplex hortensis (Orach) 103
Azalea 42–43, 70, 78, 150, 179
Azara microphylla 79

B
Background 127, 167 (Plate XIII), 200–201, 204
Balfour, Lady Eve 118, 136, 213
Barnstaple Pottery 131, 214
Basil 63
Bay 90
Bean, Indian—see Catalpa
Bean, Scarlet Runner 32, 55
Bed, flower 11, 13, 77–78, 149
Bed, 'jam tart' 106
Bed, mixed 37, 78, 152
Bed, raised 20, 37, 192, 196, 199, 200, 205, 206
Bed, Rose 11, 106, 201
Beech (see also Hedge) 10, 32, 41, 43, 57, 61, 70, 73, 74, 120–121, 141, 144, 163, 164, 175, 182
Berberis 31, 77
Bergamot 51, 55, 100, 103, 210
Bergenia 32, 152, 195
Billardiera longiflora (Tasmanian Apple Berry) 166
Birch 7–8, 10, 61, 67–8, 163, 200
Bird bath, table 136
Bistort—see *Polygonum bistorta*
Bladder Senna—see Colutea

[215]

INDEX

Bleeding Heart 7, 51
Bloodroot—see Sanguinaria
Bog plants 60
Bonfire, site of 118
Borage 39, 103, 211
Botanical garden 172
Botanical terms, some 82
Botanist 62, 148, 172, 183
Bottle Brush—see Callistemon
Box 22, 57, 99, 121, 145, 150, 153
Box edging—see *Buxus suffruticosa*
Bramble, ornamental—see Rubus
Brazil, garden design in 40, 41
Bristol Evening Post 19
Broom, 60–61, 77, 93, 200, 204
Broom, Butcher's—see *Ruscus aculeatus*
Broom, Moroccan—see Cytisus
Buckthorn, Sea—see Hippophae
Buddleia 77, 120, 122, 167
Buddleia Mint—see *Mentha*
Buffalo Currant—see *Ribes aureum*
Bugle 39, 44, 78, 206, 208
Butterfly Bush—see *Buddleia*
Buttresses, Privet 32, 201 (Plate III a)
Buxus suffruticosa (Box edging) 11, 22, 31, 119, 134

C

Calamintha (Calamint) 162
Calico Bush—see *Kalmia latifolia*
Callistemon citrinus (Bottle Brush) 166
Calluna (Scottish Ling) 46, 79
Caltha (Kingcup) 60
Camellia 78, 96–97, 168
Camphor Plant 162
Campsis grandiflora (Tecoma) 94
Caragana arborescens 81
Cardiocrinum (Himalayan Lily) 168, 178
Carnation 55, 100, 211
Caryopteris 31, 60
Catalpa (Indian Bean) 73
Ceanothus 10, 85, 195

Cedar 70, 73, 84, 141 (Plate XI), 148, 149, 150, 182
Celastrus orbiculatus 88–89
Cement and Concrete Association, The 40, 109, 213
Cement in 'Hypatufa' 124, 132
Cement 'joggles' 123–124
Cercidiphyllum japonicum (Katsura Tree) 74
Chaenomeles 86, 195, 204
Chamaerops excelsa (Chusan Palm) 96 (Plate VI)
Chamomile—see *Anthemis nobilis*
Cherry, Flowering 15, 71, 73, 75, 76, 152, 179, 182, 193, 212
Chestnut—see Aesculus
Children 52, 128–130, 189
Children and Gardens by Gertrude Jekyll 189, 213
Chimonanthus fragrans (Wintersweet) 77
Chives 99, 101, 210
Choisya ternata 31
Chrysanthemum, dwarf, for foliage 44
Chusan Palm—see *Chamaerops excelsa*
Cineraria maritima 26
Cladastris sinensis (Chinese Yellow Wood) 179
Clay soil—see Soil
Clematis 27 (Plate IIIb), 59 (siting), 75 (Bush), 87, 89–90, 94, 144, 178, 187, 192, 193 (Bush), 198, 202, 204–205 (in London)
Clematis by Christopher Lloyd 89, 213
Clianthus puniceus (Lobster Claw) 166
Climate 51, 59, 111, 204, 205
Climbers 10 (training), 43, 46–47 (placing), 57, 83–97, 144, 177 (shelter for), 182 (training), 192 (hosts for), 102 (shelter for), 204–205
Cobaea scandens 93
Cockspur Thorn—see *Crataegus crus-galli*

[216]

INDEX

Colour 14, 26, 42, 71–72, 99, 134–135, 152, 153, 161, 167, 174, 203–204, 207, 212
Colour, autumnal 74–77, 91, 146, 179
Colutea arborescens (Bladder Senna) 80
Comfrey—see Symphytum
Commonsense Compost Making by M. E. Bruce 135–136, 213
Compass points 27, 50
Compost 28, 118, 135–136
Compost, John Innes 128, 206
Concrete in Garden Making 40, 109, 213
Concrete 8, 9, 10–11, 35, 40, 112, 124–125, 130, 131–132
Concrete for pools 108–109
Conifers 10, 22, 31, 43, 68–71, 73, 122, 137, 149, 152, 182, 193, 195, 206
Contrasts 58, 142, 152, 153, 203
Coral Tree—see Erythrina
Cornus (Dogwood) 60, 75, 76–77, 79
Corylopsis 79
Corylus contorta (Corkscrew Hazel) 60
Cotinus coggygria (Smoke Tree) 75, 193
Cotoneaster 43, 77, 93, 122, 195, 207
Cotoneaster dammeri (prostrate) 46, 206
Cottage garden and gardener 22, 55, 142, 159, 185–186, 191–197, 213
Cotton Lavender—see Santolina
Crab, Flowering—see *Malus sargentii*
Cranesbill 78
Crataegus crus-galli (Cockspur Thorn) 75
Crataegus lavallei 202
Creeping Thyme—see Thyme
Creeping Wintergreen—see Gaultheria
Crinodendron hookerianum (Chilean Lantern Tree) 79, 96
Crowe, Sylvia 121, 122, 141–142, 152, 154, 213
Crown Imperial 55

Culinery herbs 99–103, 209–210
Cupressus and Chamaecyparis 10, 22, 31, 43, 61, 62, 68–71, 122, 195
Currant, Buffalo—see *Ribes aureum*
Current, 'Flowering'—see *Ribes sanguineum*
Currant, Laurel-leaved—see *Ribes laurifolium*
Curry Plant—see *Helichrysum*
Cytisus battandieri (Moroccan Broom) 93, 204

D

Daboecia (Irish Heath) 46, 79
Dahlia 78, 195
Daphne 31, 80
Davidia involucrata (Handkerchief Tree) 179
Day Lily—see Hemerocallis
Dead-nettle—see Lamium
Desfontainea spinosa 79, 180
Design garden 3–4, 5–8, 30–34, 70–71, 110, 112–113, 129–130, 136–137, 141–145, 150–154, 159, 172–173, 180–181, 189, 196, 198, 200–203, 207, 213
Design, effect of landscape on 180
Dog 53–54, 118
Dogwood—see Cornus
Drainage 13 (path), 81 (for trees), 105 (sunk garden), 109—110 (pool), 113 (for alpines), 117 (lawn), 123 (drive)
Draughts, exclusion of 111, 195, 201, 203
Drifts 76–78, 195
Drimys colorata 177
Drimys winterii 166, 180
Drive 10–11, 123, 168
Dye-plants 100–101, 109, 162, 178, 211–212

E

East Lambrook Manor 22–23, 35, 89, 117, 125, 184–191, 196 (Plates II a, XV a)

[217]

INDEX

Eggshell garden 128–129
Elaeagnus 31, 32, 62, 78, 193, 195
Elder 15, 63, 102–103, 211
Elecampane 100, 189, 211
Elliott, Joe 132
Elm, golden Cornish 76
Embothrium lanceolatum (Chilean Fire-bush) 179
Embroiderer 103, 193, 207
Enclosure for herbs 161, 210
Enkianthus 78, 179
Ericaceae 19, 20, 46, 58, 78, 195
Erythrina christa-galli (Coral Tree) 161
Escallonia 62, 77, 122, 169
Etceteras 127–137
Eucalyptus (Gum) 61, 76, 81, 164, 168, 185, 211
Eucryphia 179, 182
Euonymus (Spindle) 57, 194, 206
Euphorbia (Spurge) 44, 78, 188, 216, 210
Everlasting Pea—see Lathyrus

F

Fabbrica Mennella, Ischia 131
False Nutmeg—see Leycesteria
Farrer Reginald 198
Fastigiate Beech 68, 182
Fastigiate conifer 68, 137, 152 (Plate X b), 193, 195, 206
Fence 5, 7, 10, 14, 42–43, 46, 70, 113, 120, 126, 203–204
Fennel 44, 55, 78, 100, 188, 195, 209
Fertosan herbal activator 135
Fig 63, 149, 158, 198, 202
Fir, Douglas 61, 164
Firethorn—see Pyracantha
Fish, Margery 22, 35, 117, 123, 125, 149, 184–191, 194, 213
Fish, Walter 123, 186, 188
Flag, Sweet—see *Acorus calamus*
Flame Flower—see *Tropaeolum speciosum*

Flat land 15, 17, 30
Flax 7, 195
Flax, New Zealand—see *Phormium tenax*
Flower arrangement 26, 55, 101, 104, 196, 211
Focal point 7–8, 31, 42, 57, 137, 193, 200
Foliage, autumn 57, 74–77, 91, 93, 146, 179
Foliage, charm of 31, 32, 77, 90, 203
Foliage, Dahlia 78
Foliage, Euonymus 194
Foliage, gold—see Golden
Foliage, Holly 74
Foliage, Rhododendron 167
Foliage, Rose 88, 104
Foliage, silver 44, 59, 153, 190, 204, 210
Foliage, unusual 29, 55, 178, 211, 212
Foliage, Vitis 7, 91, 158
Forget-me-not, Chatham Island—see *Myosotidium hortensia*
Forsythia 77, 81, 84
Fothergilla 179
Fountain 42, 148, 150, 153, 201–202
France—garden design in 142
France—Marjoram 102
France—plant breeder 108, 147
France—Rose garden, Bagatelle 161
Fraxinus mariesii 146
Fruit 30, 34, 47, 52, 56, 57, 69, 83, 127, 153, 166, 168, 191–194, 202

G

Garden Design by Sylvia Crowe 121, 141, 213
Garden lay-out and construction 5–8, 13, 15–17, 23–25, 30–37, 39–51, 105–106, 107–108, 109–114, 117, 123, 125, 141–142, 154, 163–166, 176, 180–181, 187, 193, 196–197, 199–202, 207–209, 213
Gardeners, some well-known—see Anderson, E. B.; Elliott, Joe; Fish,

INDEX

Margery; Hellyer, A. G.; Nyams, Edward; Jekyll, Gertrude; Johnston, Major L.; Lloyd, Christopher; Loads, Fred; Mackenzie, Osgood; Moore, Armytage; Murrell, Hilda; Perry, Frances; Reiss, Phyllis; Roper, Lanning; Sackville-West, V. (see also Nicolson); Sawyer, Mairi (see also Mackenzie); Thomas, Graham S.; Whitsey, Fred.
Gardener's Bedside Book, The, by Edward Hyams 95, 173, 213
Garden Centre 77, 98, 124, 135
Garden frame, greenhouse 134
Garden pot, trough, urn—see Ornament
Garden room, loggia 44, 53, 152
Gardening on Chalk and Lime by Christopher Lloyd 107, 213
Gardens, alpine—see Alpine (or Rock) gardens
Gardens, Brazilian—see Brazil
Gardens, Cotswold—see Hidcote and Moyles Cottage
Gardens, cottage-style—see Cottage garden
Gardens, French—see France
Gardens, front 10-12, 118, 136-137
Gardens, George Washington's—see American Museum
Gardens, Hanover 21-22
Gardens, herb—see Herb garden
Gardens, kitchen—see Kitchen garden
Gardens, labour-saving 9-10
Gardens, National Trust—see National Trust
Gardens, pool 24 (Plates VII b and VIII); 107-110, 113, 147, 150-153 (Plate X b), 165 (Plate IV)
Gardens, 'room' 24-25, 58, 141-144, 147, 148, 150, 153-154, 159
Gardens, rose—see Rose garden
Gardens, Scandinavian 22, 40, 171

Gardens, specialized 98-114
Gardens, sunk 17, 24, 105, 107, 110, 113-114, 121 (Plate VII b)
Gardens, Swiss 40
Gardens, town 197-212 (Plates III a, XV b, XVI)
Gardens, water 107-110, 113, 213, (Plates IV, VII b, VIII, X b)
Garrya elliptica 32, 85-86
Gaultheria procumbens (Wintergreen) 79
Gevuina avellana (Chilean Hazel) 182
Globe Artichoke 55, 185
Golden Acacia—see Robinia
Golden Alder 60
Golden conifer 41, 43, 72, 195
Golden Cornish Elm 76
Golden Dogwood 77
Golden Elaeagnus 32, 193
Golden Elder 102, 211
Golden Holly 74, 128
Golden Marjoram 44, 102, 195, 210
Golden plants 44, 59 (conditions for)
Golden Poplar 15, 69
Golden Privet 32, 193, 201 (Plate III a)
Golden Rosemary (gilded) 194
Golden Sage 210
Golden Saxifrage 44
Golden Thyme 102, 210
Golden Yew 71
Gravel 7, 113 (for Alpines), 123, 126
Greenhouse—see Garden frame, greenhouse
Greyfriars 32, 133, 197-202 (Plates III a, XV b)
Great Dixter 24 (Plate VII b), 89
Griselinia 62, 122, 169
Ground cover 9, 39, 43-44, 46, 63, 78, 79, 91 106, 162, 188, 208-209, 213
Guincho 86
Gulf Stream 166
Gunnera manicata 60

[219]

INDEX

H

Hamamelis mollis (Wych Hazel) 29, 77, 180
Handkerchief Tree—see Davidia
Hanvey, John 176–177, 179–180, 182
Hazel Chilean—see Gevuina
Hazel, Corkscrew—see Corylus
Hazel, Wych—see Hamamelis
Hebe (Veronica) 31, 61, 62, 77, 122, 205
Hedge 118–121
Hedge for Alpines 111
Hedge, Beech 10, 32, 41, 43, 57, 70, 74, 120–121
Hedge, Box 11, 31, 99, 119, 145
Hedge, edging 11, 22, 31, 44, 101, 119, 145
Hedge, mixed 74, 120, 121
Hedge, Rhododendron 169
Hedge, Rose 105, 120
Hedge, Yew 70, 119, 145, 149, 152, 154, 155–156
Helichrysum (Curry Plant) 44, 72, 210
Helichrysum *rosmarinifolium* 207
Hellebore 32, 37, 44, 78, 188–189, 195, 205, 212
Hellyer, A. G. 117, 118, 213
Hemerocallis (Day Lily) 60
Herbal, Herbalist 63, 103, 178, 182, 185, 190
Herb garden 55, 99–103 (Plate VII a) 161–162, 207–212
Hidcote 24, 96, 121, 141–147, 176 (Plate XI)
Hidcote Hypericum 144
Hidcote Lavender 146, 210–211
Hidcote Rose 147
Hippophae rhamnoides (Sea Buckthorn) 62, 122
Hoheria 178
Holly 43, 51, 63, 74, 121, 128, 146
Honeysuckle (flowering) 5, 10, 90–91, 120, 136, 187, 192 (see also Lonicera)
Hornbeam 121, 144

Horticultural Adviser 20, 28, 29
Horticultural School (Waterperry) 159
Horticultural student 63
Hospital patients, gardens for 129
Hosta 32, 44, 46, 60, 78, 195
Hurdles, wattle—see Wattle
Hyams, Edward 95–96, 173, 213
Hydrangea 32, 168, 179, 185, 204
Hydrangea Bush 193
Hydrangea, climbing 57, 90, 94, 192, 204
Hypatufa, 124, 132, 207
Hypericum calycinum (St. John's Wort) 60, 200
Hypericum patulum 31, 60
Hypericum hybrids, see Hidcote and Rowallane
Hyssop 11, 55, 101, 119, 210

I

Incense Cedar—see *Libocedrus decurrens*
Indian Bean—see Catalpa
Indigofera tinctoria (Indigo) 101, 146
Inverewe Gardens 59–62, 81, 90, 95–96, 122, 124–125, 157, 163–174 (Plates IV, VI, XIII), 178, 179
Ipomoea (Morning Glory) 14
Iris 59–60, 101, 156, 162, 211
Isatis tinctoria (Woad) 101, 211
Ivy, Variegated 27, 91, 206

J

Jackman, G. (*Planter's Handbook*) 48, 88
'Japonica'—see Chaenomeles
Jasmine 31, 86–88, 185, 192
Jekyll, Gertrude 62–63, 76, 92, 98–99, 100, 121, 189, 213
Jenkinson, R. C. 183
Jerusalem Sage—see *Phlomis fruticosa*
John Innes compost 128, 206
Johnston, Major L. 141, 146–147, 148
Juniper 31, 78, 102, 137, 152, 195

[220]

INDEX

K
Kaffir Lily—see Schizostylis
Kale, Variegated 55
Kalmia latifolia 79
Katsura Tree—see Cercidiphyllum
Kells, Book of 180
Kensington 202–207 (Plate XVI)
Kerria japonica 32, 77, 92–93
Kingcup—see Caltha
Kitchen garden 5, 52, 54, 57, 127, 144, 148, 153, 166, 168
Knole—see National Trust
Kolkwitzia amabilis 31
Kreutzberger, Sybille 159

L
Lady's Mantle—see Alchemilla
Lambrook Silver (Wormwood) 44 (Plate II b), 100
Lamb's Ear—see *Stachys lanata*
Lamium (Dead-nettle) 78, 204, 208
Land, drainage—see Drainage
Land, flat—see Flat land
Landscape Architects 3, 121, 141–142, 154
Lantern Tree, Chilean—see Crinodendron
Lathyrus latifolius (Everlasting Pea) 5, 152
Laurel 62–63
Laurustinus 204
Lavender 11, 31, 44, 56, 61, 90, 101, 119, 134, 136, 146, 192, 195, 210–211
Lawn 33, 46, 51, 52–53, 71, 73, 136, 142–144, 149–151, 154, 159, 173, 187, 195, 196, 199–200, 202, 208, 209
Lawn, division of 106, 110, 114
Lawn edging 7
Lawn making 115–117
Lawn of Thyme 162
Lawn, stepping-stones in 11, 32, 43, 44
Lees-Milne, Alvilde 158

Lemon Balm—see *Melissa officinalis*
Lemon Verbena—see *Aloysia triphylla*
Levelling 5, 116, 117, 199
Leycesteria formosa (False Nutmeg) 80, 195
Libocedrus decurrens (Incense Cedar) 68
Lilium auratum 57, 192
Lilium regale 26
Lilley, S. E. 132, 213
Lily, 'Bugle'—see Watsonia
Lily, Day—see Hemerocallis
Lily, Himalayan—see Cardiocrinum
Lily, Kaffir—see Schizostylis
Lily-of-the-Valley 51, 63, 212
Lily pond 57, 108–110, 192, 196, 202
Lily, Water—see Nymphaea
Lime trees—see Tilia
Lime trees pleached—see Pleached
Lippia citriodora—see *Aloysia triphylla*
Liquidambar styraciflua (Sweet Gum) 74, 146
Living Soil, The by Lady Eve Balfour 118, 213
Lloyd, Christopher 86, 89, 107, 194, 213
Lloyd, Nathaniel 121
Loads, Fred 129
Lobster Claw—see Clianthus
Loggia—see Garden room
Lombardy Poplar—see Poplar
London 17, 71, 202–207
London Pride 4–5, 7
Lonicera (hedging) 22, 119, 134, 145, 193
Lonicera (variegated) 90 (see also Honeysuckle, flowering)
Lovage 55, 101
Lucas, Phillips, C. E. 107, 213
Lungwort—see Pulmonaria
Lutyens, Sir Edwin 121
Lutyens/Jekyll garden 121

INDEX

M

Mackenzie, Lady Mary of Gairloch 163–164
Mackenzie, Mairi (Mrs. Sawyer) 61, 166, 169–170, 172, 173–174
Mackenzie, Osgood 61, 163–166, 168
Magnolia 93, 95, 144, 149, 177, 179, 182
Mahonia japonica (bealei) 192
Malus sargentii 73
Manure (see also Compost) 28, 43, 108, 116, 135, 158, 203
Maple 75, 76, 146
Marjoram 44, 51, 55, 102, 103, 192, 195, 210
Markers, for planting 29–30
Marliac, Monsieur 108
Marx, Burle 40–41
Matley Moore, Mr. and Miss 133, 198–202
Measuring ground 47–50
Melissa officinalis (Lemon Balm) 100
Mentha (Mint) culinary 51, 103, 210
Mentha (Mint) creeping 44, 100
Mentha (Mint) decorative 55, 78, 100, 210
Mentha (Mint) Pennyroyal 51, 55, 100, 103
Metrosideros 166
Mint—see Mentha
Mitraria 166
Money, Enid 57, 191–197, 207
Montacute 21, 148, 186
Moore, Armytage 176, 180, 183
Morning Glory—see Ipomoea
Moroccan Broom—see *Cytisus*
Mosaic—see Pattern
Mount or Mound 17–19, 133
Moyles Cottage 34–37, 56–58 (Plate V b), 69, 89 (Plate III b), 91, 126, 191–197
Mullein 102
Mure, Cecily 202–207
Murrell, Hilda 104
Myosotidium hortensia 169
Myrtle 28, 90, 210

N

Names, plant, charm of 157, 158, 178
National Gardens Scheme, The 58, 197
National Trust, The, gardens—see Greyfriars, Hidcote, Knole, Montacute, Sissinghurst Castle, Tintinhull
National Trust in Northern Ireland—see Rowallane
National Trust for Scotland—see Inverewe
Nettle, Dead—see Lamium
New Zealand Flax—see *Phormium tenax*
Nicolson, Sir Harold 23, 24, 47, 64, 155–157
Nicolson, Lady (Vita Sackville-West) 23, 24, 26, 47, 64, 79, 95, 115, 120, 121, 142, 146, 155–162, 167, 213
Nicolson, Nigel 156
Nicotiana (Tobacco Plant) 34, 107, 195
Noelite—see Paving
Nurserymen 46, 48, 70, 88, 89, 98–99, 104, 116–117, 120, 128, 156, 189–190, 194, 214
Nymphaea 107–109

O

Oak—see Quercus
Old-fashioned & cottage plants 44, 185, 190, 213
Olearia hastii 62, 122
O'Neill, the Hon. Mrs. Terence 177, 183
Orach—see *Atriplex hortensis*
Orchard 34–35, 56, 127, 186, 191–197
Ornaments, garden 54, 57, 127–133, 136, 137, 149, 152, 154, 160–161, 192, 196, 201–202, 206, 214
Orris Root 101, 162, 211
Osmarea burkwoodii 120
Otter submersible pump 42, 201–202
Oxalis floribunda 44

INDEX

P

Parrotia persica (Persian Ironwood) 74
Parrot's Bill—see Clianthus
Parterre 21, 142
Pasque Flower—see *Anemone pulsatilla*
Path—concrete 8, 11, 106, 124–125
Path—grass 32, 37, 52, 110, 154, 179
Path—gravel 7, 13–14, 126
Path—stepping-stone 11, 32, 43, 44, 137, 158
Path—width of 125, 144
Path—winding 124, 170, 179–180
Path—woodland 124, 171
Pattern 21, 39, 42, 43, 44, 70, 129, 153–154, 180–181, 200, 201
Paving—concrete block 35, 39, 124, 200
Paving—formal 31, 105, 201
Paving—grass verges 7, 9
Paving—Noelite 40, 42, 124, 201, 214
Paving—stone and pebble 39, 123
Paving—terrace, 200, 201, 208
Pea, Everlasting—see *Lathyrus latifolius*
Pear, grey-leaved—see *Pyrus salicifolia*
Pearl Flower—see Anaphalis
Pennyroyal—see Mentha
Pergola 15–17, 83, 95, 200
Pernet-Ducher, Monsieur 147
Pernettya mucronata 62, 79
Perry, Frances 108–109, 213
Persian Ironwood—see Parrotia
Perspective, false 133, 200
Pets—in gardens 53–54
Philesia buxifolia 96, 179
Phlomis fruticosa (Jerusalem Sage) 31, 61, 75, 195
Phormium tenax (New Zealand Flax) 60, 206, pH scale 20, 78
Pieris japonica 78
Pinus montana (Mountain Pine) 61
Pinus nigra austriaca (Austrian Pine) 62, 164

Pinus nigra var. *calabrica* (Corsican Pine) 61, 163
Pinus radiata syn. *insignis* (Monterey Pine) 62
Pinus sylvestris (Scots Pine) 59, 61, 164, 182
Planning and planting 5–19, 23–37, 39, 42–51, 61–62, 69–71, 98–99, 142, 154, 155, 164–166, 172, 173, 176, 187, 192–193, 194–196, 199, 205–207, 208–209
Plantain, Green Rose 190
Planter's Handbook—see Jackman
Plants, alpine—see Rock plants
Plants, choice of 98–99, 190
Plants, companionship 63
Plants, cottage—see Old-fashioned plants
Plants, foliage—see Foliage plants
Plants, herb—see Herb garden
Plants, limitation of 152, 195, 202, 203
Plants, water 59–60, 107–109
Plants, weed-suppressant—see Ground cover
Plants, woodland 63–64, 77, 78, 79 (Plate XIII)
Plantsmen and plantswomen 108, 111, 142, 146, 166, 172, 176, 189, 198
Pleached Hornbeam (Hidcote) 144
Pleached Lime (Sissinghurst) 68, 155, 159
Pokeroot 101
Polygonum baldschuanicum (Russian Vine) 92
Polygonum bistorta (Bistort) 60, 101, 212
Polygonum campanulatum (shrubby) 80
Polythene—bags and sheets 135, 203
Pool or pond 17, 24 (Plate VIII) 41, 42, 44, 52, 57, 59, 73, 108–110, 113, 147, 150 153 (Plate X b), 192, 196, 202 (Plate XV b)

INDEX

Pope, Alexander 132–134, 200
Poplar 15, 67, 68, 69
Portland Nurseries 105, 214
Pot or Vase—see Ornaments, garden
Pot plants outdoors 103, 161
Potentilla, shrubby 31, 75, 78, 195, 212
Price, Dr. J. S. M. 148
Price, Uvedale 173
Prickly Heath—see Pernettya
Primrose 63–64, 190
Primrose, Evening 147
Primula 178
Primula Bog 60
Primula 'Rowallane Rose' 178
Privet 10, 32, 84, 118–119, 134, 193, 201 (Plate III a).
Proportion 5, 72, 142, 154, 193
Pruning and pinching 28, 30, 77, 188, 190, 195, 204, 205
Prunus avium (Wild Cherry) 15
Prunus cerasifera (Myrobolan) 121
Prunus cerasifera nigra 71
Prunus sargentii 76, 179
Prunus serrula tibetica 182
Pulmonaria (Lungwort) 32, 103, 190
Pump, submersible—see Otter
Pyracantha (Firethorn) 43, 92
Pyrus salicifolia pendula 32, 161 (Plate XII)

Q

Quenington, Glos. 34–38, 69, 89, 91, 126, 191–197
Quercus (Oak) 61, 76, 150

R

Rabbit 53–54, 164
Raised beds—see Beds, raised
Reiss, Captain and Mrs. F. E. 148, 150
Reiss, Phyllis 149, 152, 154
Reseda luteola (Weld) 101
Rheum (Rhubarb) 58, 178
Rhododendron 19, 42, 43, 59, 61, 70, 78, 79, 122, 164, 167, 169, 177, 179

Rhododendron hybrid 42, 78, 167, 177, 179
Rhododendron natural species 59, 78, 167, 169, 177, 179 (Plate XIV a), 180
Rhododendron wild 59, 61, 122, 164, 169
Rhubarb—see *Rheum*
Rhus cotinus (Smoke Tree) 74–75, 76
Rhus typhina (Stag's Horn Sumach) 74 (see also *Cotinus coggygria*)
Ribes aureum (Buffalo Currant) 81
Ribes laurifolium (Laurel-leaved currant) 194
Ribes sanguineum ('Flowering' Currant) 81
River, artificial 37–38
Robinia friesia aurea (Golden Acacia) 76
Rock garden, gardener—see Alpine
Rock or alpine plants 17, 52, 59, 110–114, 213, 214
Rock Gardening, A Handbook of, by S. E. Lilley 132
Rocky anchorages 59, 80, 113, 207, 209
Rodgersia 60
Rohde, Eleanour Sinclair 17
Rondel 157, 200
'Room' garden—see Gardens, 'room'
Room, garden—see Garden room, loggia
Roper, Lanning 147, 213
Rosa anemonoides 158
Rosa filipes 26
Rosa gallica officinalis (Apothecary's Rose) 100
Rosa genus 104
Rosa rubiginosa 120
Rosa Tour de Maures 23
Rose, briar 119, 120, 195
Rose, climbing 7, 26, 88, 156, 158, 193, 202
Rose, Floribunda 103, 105, 106, 107
Rose garden 99, 103–107, 157–158, 159, 161

INDEX

Rose, Hybrid Tea 103, 104
Rose, miniature 105
Rose, 'old', shrub 23, 88, 100, 104, 105, 106, 107, 157–158, 211
Rosemary 31, 61, 102, 103, 119, 134, 209
Roses for Small Gardens by C. E. Lucas Phillips 107, 213
Rowallane 95, 96, 171, 175–183 (Plate XIV)
Rowallane Chaenomeles 86
Rowallane Hypericum 179
Rowallane 'Rose'—see Primula
Rowallane Viburnum 178
Rowan—see *Sorbus aucuparia*
Royal Gardens, Hanover—see Gardens
Royal Horticultural Society, The 108, 176
Royal Horticultural Society, The *Journal* 132, 156, 183
Rubus (Ornamental Bramble) 94
Rue, Goat's 7, 100
Rue, Jackman's Blue 72, 92, 100, 119, 162, 210
Rue, Meadow 211
Ruscus aculeatus (Butcher's Broom) 31
Russian Vine—see Polygonum

S
Sackville-West, V.—see Nicolson
Sage 44, 56, 99, 100, 102, 103, 194, 195, 209, 210, 211
Sage, Jerusalem—see Phlomis
St. John's Wort—see Hypericum
Salix gracilistyla 180
Salix purpurea pendula (Weeping Willow) 73
Sanguinaria canadensis (Bloodroot) 178
Santolina (Cotton Lavender) 44, 101, 119, 192, 195
Sarcococca (Sweet Box) 79–80
Satureia montana (Winter Savory) 11, 44, 55, 101, 119

Sawyer, Mairi—see Mackenzie
Saxifrage 44, 64 (see also London Pride)
Scale 49, 142
Scale pH (soil) 20
Scarlet Runner—see Bean
Schizandra 95
Schizophragma integrifolia 90
Schizostylis coccinea (Kaffir Lily) 166
Schwerdt, Pam 159
Screens 51, 74, 103, 111, 113, 119, 120–122, 134, 136, 195, 201, 203–204, 207, 208, 209
Sculpture 125, 130, 133, 160–161, 174
Sea Buckthorn—see Hippophae
Seats 134, 136, 153, 161, 201
Sedum 32, 57, 78, 192, 195, 208–209
Seed 14, 53, 58, 116–117, 128–129
Seed beds, protection of 53
Senecio 31, 61, 62, 72, 152, 204, 205
Shelter-belts 122, 164, 166, 169
Shrubs 27–29, 48, 62, 76–82, 83–86, 92–93, 102, 144, 177–180, 200, 204–205
Shrubs, choosing 98—99
Shrubs, dimensions of 48
(see also Pruning and pinching)
Silver Birch—see Birch
Silver foliage—see Foliage
Silver Thyme—see Thyme
Silver variegated Acanthus 194
Sink 57, 124, 132, 207
Siphonosmanthus delavayi 78
Sissinghurst Castle 23–26 (Plate I), 47, 64, 67, 68, 91, 115 (Plate IX), 125 (Plate XII), 155–162 (Plate V a), 167, 176
Siting garden ornaments 136
Skimmia 31, 77, 190
Smoke Tree—see Cotinus and Rhus
Snowball Tree—see Viburnum
Soapwort 101
Soil Association, The 118, 136

INDEX

Soil 13–14, 19–20, 28, 32–34, 58–59, 60, 62, 75, 77, 78, 96, 98, 112–113, 117, 122, 164, 166, 175, 188, 196, 203
Soil mixture for cuttings 206
Soil mixture for lilies 57
Soil mixture for rhododendrons 43
Solanum crispum 94, 144
Sorbus 75, 146, 182
Sorbus aucuparia (Rowan) 75
Southernwood 61, 102, 212
Space—effect of 202
Spindleberry, climbing—see Euonymus
Spurge—see Euphorbia
Stachys lanata (Lamb's Ear) 26, 78, 125 (Plate XII)
Statue—see Sculpture
Stauntonia hexaphylla 93
Stepping-stones—see Path
Steps 124–126, 131, 144, 154, 192, 208
Stewartia 182
Sumach, Stag's Horn—see Rhus
Summerhouse 30, 31, 32, 37, 53, 83, 126, 183, 193, 196
Sunk garden—see Gardens, sunk
Sussex garden 13–17, 48–50
Sweet bags and pot-pourri 101, 210, 212
Sweet Box—see Sarcococca
Sweet Briar—see Rose
Sweet Chestnut—see Aesculus
Sweet Cicely 55, 101, 103, 162, 211
Sweet Flag—see *Acorus calamus*
Sweet Gum—see Liquidambar
Sweet Marjoram—see Marjoram
Symphytum grandiflora (Comfrey) 44

T
Tansy, Miss Jekyll's 100, 212
Tarragon 210
Taste 52–64
Taxus (Yew) 22, 31, 37, 43, 70, 71, 73, 92, 119, 121, 145, 149, 152, 154, 155–156, 193, 206

Terrace—see Paving
Texture 5, 71, 124, 125, 201
Thomas, Graham S. 147, 158
Thorn, Cockspur—see Crataegus
Thyme 44, 55, 56, 99, 101–102, 103, 162, 192, 194, 195, 209, 210
Thyme, creeping 162, 210
Thyme, silver 44, 102, 195, 210
Tilia (Lime) 68, 155, 159
Tintinhull 24, 147–154, 176 (Plates VIII, X b)
Topiary 22, 119, 128, 147, 149
Trachelospermum jasminoides 178
Trees 15, 26–27, 28, 29, 31, 32, 67–82, 141–142, 163–164, 175, 176, 182, 200
Trees, coniferous—see Conifers
Trees, development of 48, 68–69
Trees, flowering 15, 67, 71, 73, 75, 76, 115, 152, 179, 182, 193, 212
Trees for autumn colour—see Foliage
Trees, fruit 30, 34, 56, 69, 115, 127, 191, 192
(See also Shelter-belts)
Trellis 5, 31, 134, 135, 203–204
Trochodendron aralioides 182
Tropaeolum speciosum (Flame Flower) 59, 95–96
Trough, tub—see Ornaments, garden

U
Ulex (Gorse) 119–120
Urn—see Ornaments, garden

V
Vase—see Ornaments, garden
Verbena, Lemon—see Aloysia
Veronica—see Hebe
Verticals 15, 67, 73, 83
Viburnum 32, 51, 84, 94, 144, 178, 195, 198, 202, 205
Viburnum *opulus sterile* (Snowball Tree) 92
Vine—see Vitis
Vine, Russian—see Polygonum

[226]

INDEX

Virginia Creeper—see Vitis
Vista 15, 24, 27, 83, 133, 144, 150, 153, 170
Vitis henryana ⎫
Vitis inconstans ⎬ Virginia Creepers 91
Vitis quinquefolia ⎭
Vitis coignetiae ⎫
Vitis vinifera brandt ⎬ Ornamental Vines 91, 92
Vitis vinifera purpurea ⎭

W

Walls 30–32, 113, 121–122, 195, 198, 201
Walls, climbers for 83–85, 88, 90, 91–96, 198
Wansdyke Nursery, Devizes 70, 214
Water Gardens by Frances Perry 108, 213
Water gardens—see Gardens
Water plants—see Plants
Water lilies—see Nymphaea
Water in gardens 42, 107–110, 147, 150–153, 201–202
Waterperry Horticultural School 159
Watsonia (Bugle Lily) 178
Wattle hurdles 5, 7, 10, 51, 103, 111, 136, 203, 208, 209
Weather-vane 127
We Made a Garden by Margery Fish 123, 117, 185, 213
Westonbirt Arboretum 68, 74, 77, 146
Whitsey, Fred 191
Willow—see Salix
Wintergreen—see Gaultheria
Winter Savory—see Satureia
Winter's Bark—see *Drimys winterii*
Wintersweet—see Chimonanthus
Wisteria 94–95
Woad—see Isatis
Woodland plants—see Plants
Woodruff 63
Wormwood 44, 90, 100, 212
Wych Hazel—see Hamamelis

Y

Yew—see Taxus
Your New Garden by A. G. L. Hellyer 117, 213